KS3 Maths Progress

Confidence • Fluency • Problem-solving • Progression

π TWO

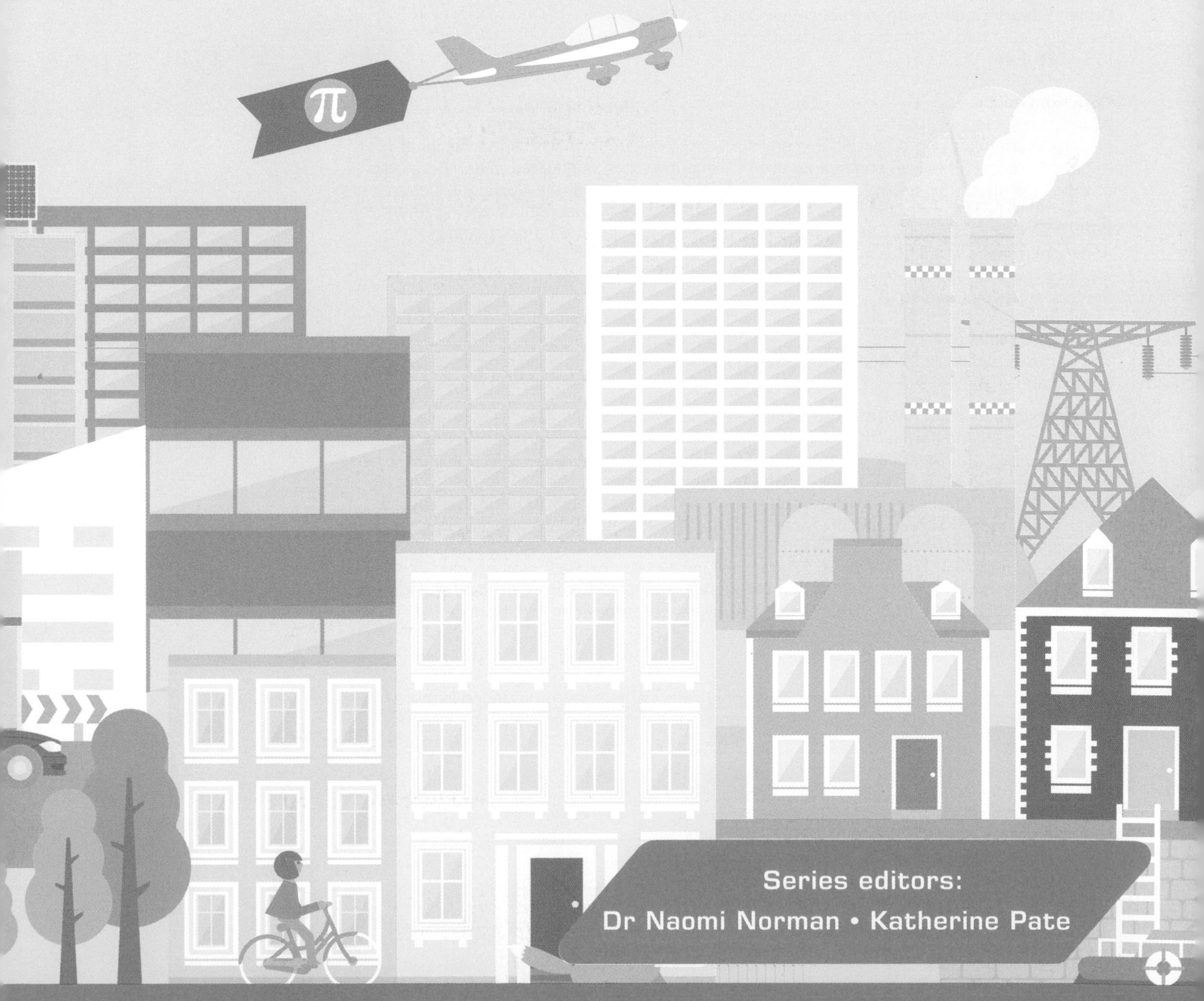

Series editors:
Dr Naomi Norman • Katherine Pate

ALWAYS LEARNING

PEARSON

Published by Pearson Education Limited, Edinburgh Gate, Harlow, Essex, CM20 2JE.

www.pearsonschoolsandfecolleges.co.uk

Text © Pearson Education Limited 2014
Typeset by Tech-Set Ltd, Gateshead
Original illustrations © Pearson Education Limited 2014
Cover illustration by Robert Samuel Hanson
Index by Wendy Simpson

The rights of Nick Asker, Sharon Bolger, Lynn Byrd, Andrew Edmondson, Bobbie Johns, Catherine Murphy, and Harry Smith to be identified as authors of this work have been asserted by them in accordance with the Copyright, Designs and Patents Act 1988.

First published 2014

17 16 15 14
10 9 8 7 6 5 4 3 2 1

British Library Cataloguing in Publication Data
A catalogue record for this book is available from the British Library
ISBN 978 1 447 96233 5

Printed in Italy by Lego S.p.A

Acknowledgements
The publisher would like to thank the following for their kind permission to reproduce their photographs:

Alamy Images: Cultura RM 169, 187, Dmitriy Podlipayev 129, Steven May 143; **Fotolia.com:** Steve Mann 146; **Masterfile UK Ltd:** Blend Images 165; **PhotoDisc:** Photolink 75; **Rex Features:** Nils Jorgensen 213; **Science Photo Library Ltd:** Cultura / Monty Rakusen 219, David Hay Jones 6, Eye of Science 33, Richard Kail 222; **Shutterstock.com:** alexskopje 225, Andrea Danti 151, bikeriderlondon 1, Bork 13, David Crockett 199, Ferenc Szelepcsenyi 196, hfng 57, JaySi 51, Leszek Glasner 30, marekuliasz 60, Mark III Photonics 54, Mauro Pezzotta 119, Milkos 35, Vadim Sadovski 81; **Veer / Corbis:** andreus 171, c 105, Dmytro Tolokonov 7, 148, EpicStockMedia 37, Henryk Sadura 124, 127, John Takai 27, michaeljung 173, Michal Bednarek 97, mik122 189, Monkey Business Images 100, 216, Olena Mykhaylova 192, stockarch 167, T.Baibakova 11, twixx 4, Vladyslav Starozhylov 103, wildcat78 122; **www.imagesource.com:** Dirk Lindner 194

All other images © Pearson Education

Every effort has been made to contact copyright holders of material reproduced in this book. Any omissions will be rectified in subsequent printings if notice is given to the publishers.

CONTENTS

Unit 8 Sequences

Unit 9 Fractions and percentages

Unit 10 Probability

KS3 Maths Progress

Confidence • Fluency • Problem-solving • Progression

Pedagogy at the heart – This new course is built around a unique pedagogy that's been created by leading mathematics educational researchers and Key Stage 3 teachers. The result is an innovative learning structure based around 10 key principles designed to nurture confidence and raise achievement.

Pedagogy – our 10 key principles

- Fluency
- Mathematical Reasoning
- Multiplicative Reasoning
- Problem Solving
- Progression

- Concrete-Pictorial - Abstract (CPA)
- Relevance
- Modelling
- Reflection (metacognition)
- Linking

Progression to Key Stage 4 – In line with the 2014 National Curriculum, there is a strong focus on fluency, problem-solving and progression to help prepare your students' progress through their studies.

Stretch, challenge and support – Catering for students of all abilities, these Student Books are structured to deliver engaging and accessible content across three differentiated tiers, each offering a wealth of worked examples and questions, supported by key points, literacy and strategy hints, and clearly defined objectives.

Within each unit:

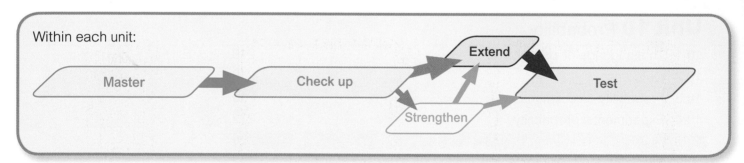

Master → Check up → Strengthen → Extend → Test

Differentiated for students of all abilities:

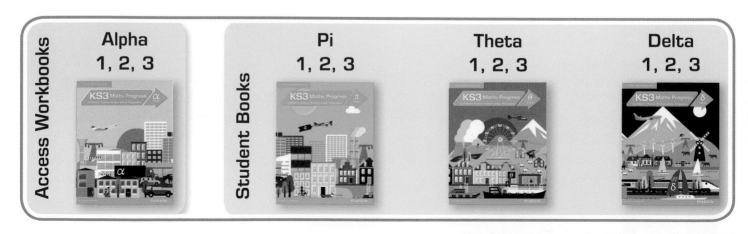

Access Workbooks: **Alpha** 1, 2, 3

Student Books: **Pi** 1, 2, 3 · **Theta** 1, 2, 3 · **Delta** 1, 2, 3

Progress with confidence!

This innovative Key Stage 3 Maths course embeds a modern pedagogical approach around our trusted suite of digital and print resources, to create confident and numerate students ready to progress further.

Help at the front-of-class – ActiveTeach Presentation is our tried and tested service that makes all of the Student Books available for display on a whiteboard. The books are supplemented with a range of videos and animations that present mathematical concepts along a concrete - pictorial - abstract pathway, allowing your class to progress their conceptual understanding at the right speed.

Learning beyond the classroom – Focussing on online homework, **ActiveCourse** offers students unprecedented extra practice (with automarking) and a chance to reflect on their learning with the confidence-checker. Powerful reporting tools can be used to track student progression and confidence levels.

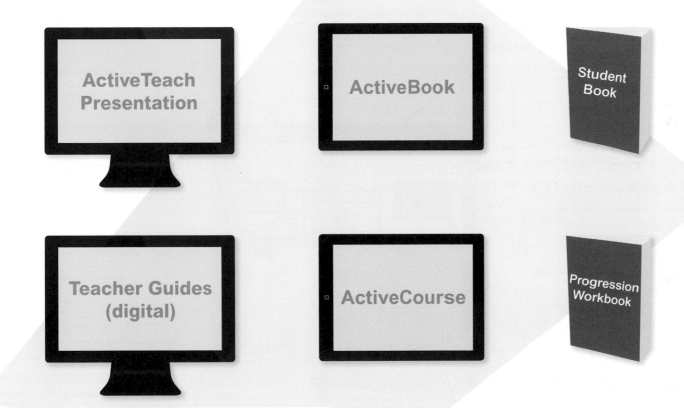

Easy to plan, teach and assess – Downloadable **Teacher Guides** provide assistance with planning through the Schemes of Work. Lesson plans link both front-of-class **ActiveTeach Presentation** and **ActiveCourse** and provide help with reporting, functionality and progression. Both **Teacher Guides** and **ActiveTeach Presentation** contain the **answers** to the Student Book exercises.

Teacher Guides include **Class Progression Charts** and **Student Progression Charts** to support formative and summative assessment through the course.

Practice to progress – KS3 Maths Progress has an extensive range of practice across a range of topics and abilities. From the **Student Books** to write-in **Progression Workbooks** through to **ActiveCourse**, there is plenty of practice available in a variety of formats whether for in the classroom or for learning at home independently.

> **For more information, visit www.pearsonschools.co.uk/ks3mathsprogress**

Welcome to KS3 Maths Progress student books!

Confidence • Fluency • Problem-solving • Progression

Starting a new course is exciting! We believe you will have fun with maths, at the same time nurturing your confidence and raising your achievement.

Here's how:

At the end of the *Master* lessons, take a *Check up* test to help you decide to *Strengthen*, or *Extend* your learning. You may be able to mark this test yourself.

Choose only the topics in *Strengthen* that you need a bit more practice with. You'll find more hints here to lead you through specific questions. Then move on to *Extend*.

Extend helps you to apply the maths you know to some different situations. *Strengthen* and *Extend* both include *Enrichment* or *Investigations*.

When you have finished the whole unit, a *Unit test* helps you see how much progress you are making.

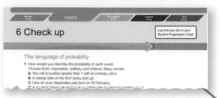

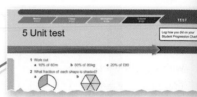

Clear *Objectives*, showing what you will cover in each lesson, are followed by a *Confidence* panel to boost your understanding and engage your interest.

Have a look at *Why Learn This?* This shows you how maths is useful in everyday life.

Improve your *Fluency* – practise answering questions using maths you already know.

The first questions are *Warm up*. Here you can show what you already know about this topic or related ones…

…before moving on to further questions, with *Worked examples* and *Hints* for help when you need it.

Your teacher has access to Answers in either ActiveTeach Presentation or the Teacher Guides.

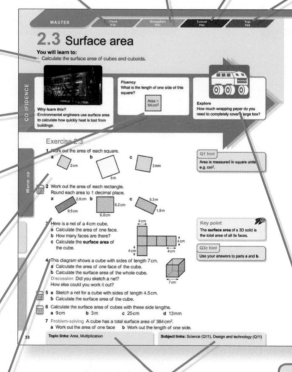

Topic links show you how the maths in a lesson is connected to other mathematical topics. Use the *Subject links* to find out where you might use the maths you have learned here in your other lessons, such as science, geography and computing .

Explore a real-life problem by discussing and having a go. By the end of the lesson you'll have gained the skills you need to start finding a solution to the question using maths.

You can find out how charities use maths in their fundraising, how scientists display data about moon rocks, and how engineers use maths when designing gear wheels (among other things!)

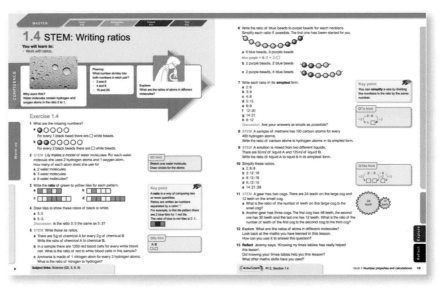

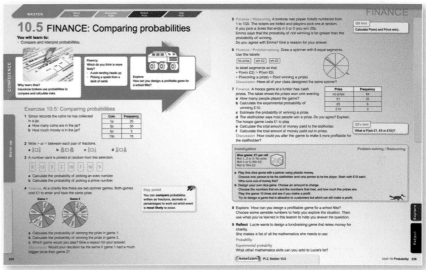

As well as hints that help you with specific questions, you'll find *Literacy hints* (to explain some unfamiliar terms) and *Strategy hints* (to help with working out).

You can improve your ability to use maths in everyday situations by tackling *Modelling, Reasoning, Problem-solving* and *Real* questions. *Discussions* prompt you to explain your reasoning or explore new ideas with a partner.

Some questions are tagged as *Finance* or *STEM*. These questions show how the real world relies on maths. Follow these up with whole lessons that focus on how maths is used in the fields of finance, science and technology.

At the end of each lesson, you get a chance to *Reflect* on how confident you feel about the topic.

Your teacher may give you a Student Progression Chart to help you see your progression through the units.

Further support

You can easily access extra resources that tie in to each lesson – look for the ActiveLearn icon on the lesson pages for ActiveCourse online homework links. These are clearly mapped to lessons and provide fun, interactive exercises linked to helpful worked examples and videos.

The Progression Workbooks, full of extra practice for key questions will help you reinforce your learning and track your own progress.

Enjoy!

1.1 Adding and subtracting with larger numbers

You will learn to:

- Add and subtract larger numbers.

Why learn this?
Adding and subtracting is important for working out results in science.

Fluency
Round each number to the nearest 10.
- 46
- 81
- 128

Explore
How many people are there in your school building?

Exercise 1.1

1 Work out

a 27
+ 42
————

b 126
+ 237
————

c 298
− 126
————

d 362
− 139
————

e 700
− 192
————

f 36.1
+ 11.3
————

g 17.4
− 12.8
————

2 Round each number to the nearest 100.
  a 251
  b 249
  c 1489
  d 5237

3 Round to the nearest 100 to estimate
  a 277 + 406
  b 4173 + 5869

4 Use the column method to find the answers to the calculations in Q3.
Discussion How do your estimates in Q3 help you with Q4?

Q4 hint
```
  277
+ 406
─────
```

5 For each addition
  i estimate the answer
  ii work out the total.
  a 3757 + 505
  b 43 049 + 371
  c 691 + 2380
  d 367 + 52 + 89
  e 609 + 38 + 267
  f 190 + 3009 + 436

Q5a hint
Make sure that you line the columns up correctly.
```
  3757
+  505
─────
```

6 Karen's grandmother gave her £24.
She won £250 in a competition and has £54 in the bank.
How much money has Karen got altogether?

7 Patrick, Majid, Serena and Dominic collect money for charity.
Patrick collects £312, Majid collects £90, Serena collects £120 and
Dominic collects £284. How much money do they collect altogether?

8 Work out
  a £3.37 + £10.52
  b £15.99 + £7.99
  c £2.70 + £25 + £15.20

Q8a hint
Make sure that you line the columns up correctly.

9 **Problem-solving / Reasoning** José has a newspaper delivery round.
On a Sunday he needs to deliver these newspapers.

Sunday News	News on Sunday	World Sport	Weekly Review	Sunday Special
20	54	38	24	80

He has room in his bag for 200 newspapers.
Will he be able to carry them all in one go?
Explain how you worked it out.

10 Work out these subtractions.
  a 8463 − 3252
  b 7456 − 627
  c 4737 − 365 − 262
  d 2090 − 576 − 448
  Check your answers using estimates.

Q10c hint
Work out 4737 − 365 = ☐
Then ☐ − 262 = ☐

Q10 hint
Round the numbers to the nearest 100 to make the estimates.

11 An elephant weighs 6150 kg. He should weigh 5865 kg.
How much weight does he need to lose?

12 Work out
  a £8.47 − £6.35
  b £17.25 − £5.99
  c £20 − £3.75

Q12c hint
```
 20.00
− 3.75
─────
```

13 Sharon is painting strips of skirting board.
She has to paint 542 m altogether on a large job.
She painted 97 m on Monday and 122 m on Tuesday.
How much more does she have to paint?

14 On a skiing holiday, Tomislav has to pay €115 for a lift pass,
   €75 to hire his skis and €255 for his skiing lessons.
   He starts the week with €500.
   How much does he have left at the end of his holiday?

15 Jacob buys a yearly train ticket that costs £3100.
   The cost increases by £400 the next year.
   How much will Jacob pay for his ticket next year?

16 **Problem-solving** Nora raises £825 for charity.
   Peter raises £285 less than that.
   How much money do Nora and Peter raise in total?

17 Work out
   a 35 + 427 − 115
   b 800 − 270 − 137

Q17 hint

For a mix of + and −, work from left to right.

18 Choose two numbers from the box that have:
   a a sum of 10 000
   b a difference of 350
   c a sum of 3930
   d a difference of 1415

   6530   1015   2080   2915   2430   7920

19 **Explore** How many people are there in your school building?
   What have you learned in this lesson to help you answer this
   question? What other information do you need?

20 **Reflect** Look back at Q13. Andrea uses this bar model to help solve
   the problem.

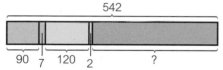

542

90   7   120   2   ?

   Did you use the same method as Andrea?
   If not, describe the method you used.
   Compare your method with others in your class.
   What are the advantages of your method?
   What are the advantages of Andrea's method?

MASTER

Check
P15

Strengthen
P17

Extend
P21

Test
P25

1.2 More calculations

You will learn to:
- Multiply larger numbers
- Use brackets.

Why learn this?
Builders, scientists and engineers need to be able to do calculations to work out the materials they need.

Fluency
Work out
- 20×6
- 500×7
- 40×8

Explore
How many hours are there in a month? What about a year?

Exercise 1.2

1 Work out
   a 24×3 b 52×4 c 65×8

2 Write down the inverse operation for
   a $\times 45$ b $- 128$ c $\div 702$
   d $+ 59$ e doubling

3 Work out
   a $3 \times 11 + 6$ b $3 \times (11 + 6)$ c $22 - (10 - 7)$
   d $18 \div (4 + 2)$ e $(8 + 17) \div 5$

Q2a hint

Which operation will do the opposite to $\times 45$?

Q3b hint

Work out the calculation in the brackets first.

Warm up

Investigation   Problem-solving

Put brackets in different places in the calculation $3 + 7 \times 4 - 1$.
1 How many different answers can you get?
2 Will three numbers inside the brackets give you more answers?

Strategy hint

Work in order, starting with $(3 + 7)$.

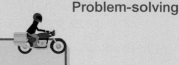

Worked example

Work out 46×28.

Estimate: $46 \times 28 \approx 50 \times 30 = 1500$

$$
\begin{array}{r}
46 \\
\times\ 28 \\
\hline
920 \\
368 \\
\hline
1288 \\
\end{array}
$$

First work out 46×20.

Now work out 46×8.

Add to give the final answer.

Check: 1288 is close to 1500 —— Check the answer against the estimate.

Literacy hint

$\approx$ means 'approximately equal to'.

4 Work out
   a 26 × 15   **b** 35 × 23   **c** 53 × 43
   d 67 × 32   **e** 78 × 48   **f** 94 × 62

5 Misha has 57 £20 notes. How much money has she got?

6 Zack needs to buy grass seed for his new lawn.
   His lawn is a rectangle 23 m by 45 m.
   What is the area of his new lawn?

Q6 hint

area of rectangle = length × width

7 Calculate
   a 124 × 23   **b** 366 × 37   **c** 634 × 74

Q7a hint

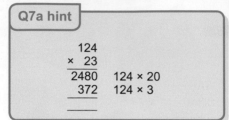

8 **Real / Finance** Karl earns £246 a week.
   How much does he earn in a year?

9 a 45 × 21 = 945
      i What is 945 ÷ 45?
      ii Write down the other division that you could work out from
         this fact.
   b 1380 − 456 = 924
      i What is 924 + 456?
      ii Write down the other calculation that you could work out from
         this fact.

Q8 hint

There are 52 weeks in a year.

10 A shop has cut its prices in half for a sale.
   What must the shop do to prices to return them to the original
   amounts after the sale?

11 A cinema has seats arranged in rows with 17 seats to the left of the
   aisle and 15 seats to the right.
   There are 24 rows of seats in the cinema. How many seats are there
   altogether?

12 Eggs are packed in boxes of dozens (12 eggs) and half-dozens
   (6 eggs).
   A shop has 14 dozen boxes and 23 half-dozen boxes.
   How many eggs does the shop have altogether?

13 **Problem-solving** A garden centre sells bedding plants in boxes
   of 6 and 10.
   At the start of the day there are 24 boxes of 6 and 36 boxes of 10.
   During the day 7 boxes of 6 and 13 boxes of 10 are sold.
   How many plants are left unsold at the end of the day?

14 **Explore** How many hours are there in a month? What about a year?
   Is it easier to explore this question now you have completed
   the lesson? What further information do you need to be able to
   answer this?

15 **Reflect** Shanaz says, 'Multiplying big numbers is just like multiplying
   small numbers, because you just split up the big number into small
   numbers first.'
   Do you agree with Shanaz?
   If so, give an example to show what she means.
   If not, explain why not.

1.3 Negative numbers

You will learn to:

- Add and subtract with negative numbers
- Multiply and divide negative numbers.

Why learn this?
Climate scientists subtract positive and negative numbers to work out temperature differences.

Fluency
Work out
- $9 + 6$
- $9 - 5$
- 3×4
- $8 \div 4$

Explore
How much warmer is it in summer than in winter?

Warm up

Exercise 1.3

1 Find the new temperatures.
  a The temperature is −3°C. It increases by 7°C.
  b The temperature is −8°C. It rises by 13°C.
  c The temperature is 4°C. It falls by 9°C.
  d The temperature is 7°C. It decreases by 11°C.

Worked example

Work out
a $-5 + 12$

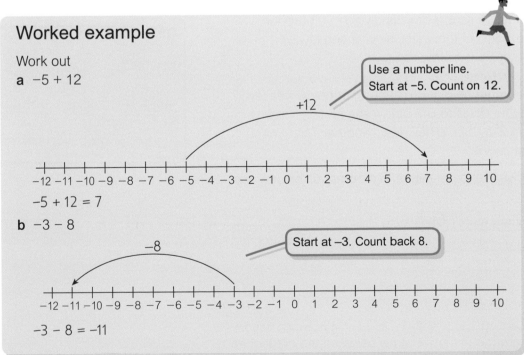

Use a number line.
Start at −5. Count on 12.

$-5 + 12 = 7$

b $-3 - 8$

Start at −3. Count back 8.

$-3 - 8 = -11$

2 Work out
  a $-8 + 10$ **b** $-4 + 13$
  c $-18 + 19$ **d** $-25 + 14$

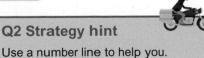

Q2 Strategy hint
Use a number line to help you.

3 Work out

  a −4 − 5   **b** −6 − 15

  c −14 − 21   **d** −7 − 13

4 a Copy the tables and work out the answers to the blue calculations.

Calculation	Answer
3 + 3	6
3 + 2	
3 + 1	
3 + 0	
3 + −1	
3 + −2	
3 + −3	
3 + −4	
3 + −5	

Calculation	Answer
3 − 3	
3 − 2	
3 − 1	
3 − 0	
3 − −1	
3 − −2	
3 − −3	
3 − −4	
3 − −5	

  b Continue the sequences to work out the rest of the answers.

  c Fill in the missing signs.

    i 3 + −5 is the same as 3 ☐ 5

    ii 3 − −5 is the same as 3 ☐ 5

  d Copy and complete the rules.

    + − is the same as ☐

    − − is the same as ☐

5 Work out

  a 9 + −5   **b** 6 − −7

  c −4 − −9   **d** −11 + −5

  e −18 + −21   **f** 8 + −12

  g −39 − −23   **h** 10 − −41

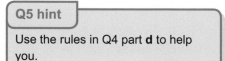

Q5 hint

Use the rules in Q4 part **d** to help you.

6 **Problem-solving / Real** A scuba diver is diving in a harbour.
When he is on the surface of the water he is at sea level.
When he is underwater he is below sea level.

  a The diver is 4 m below sea level.
How much deeper must he dive to reach 13 m below sea level?

  b On a different day he dives to 6 m below sea level.
Then he comes up 2 m, then dives down another 7 m.
What level is he at now?

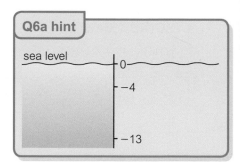

Q6a hint

sea level

7 The table below shows the temperature in different cities one day in January.

City	Temperature (°C)
Anchorage	−11
Baltimore	−4
Detroit	−7
Kansas City	−5
Las Vegas	4

  a What was the difference in temperature between the coldest and warmest cities?

  b How much warmer was Baltimore than Anchorage?

  c How much colder was Detroit than Kansas City?

Subject links: Geography (Q7)

Investigation

1 Start with the calculation 5 × 2.

Copy and complete each sequence by following the pattern.

5 × 2 = 10   6 × 3 = ☐
4 × 2 = ☐   6 × 2 = ☐
3 × 2 = ☐   6 × 1 = ☐
2 × 2 = ☐   6 × 0 = ☐
1 × 2 = ☐   6 × −1 = ☐
0 × 2 = ☐   6 × −2 = ☐
−1 × 2 = ☐
−2 × 2 = ☐

> **Investigation hint**
>
> Look carefully at the pattern in the answers.

2 Copy and complete the rules.
 • any number × 0 = ☐
 • positive × positive = positive
 • negative × positive = ☐
 • positive × negative = ☐

8 Work out
 a 35 × 0   **b** 67 × 0
 c 0 × 89   **d** 2456 × 0

> **Q8, 9 hint**
>
> Use the rules in the investigation to help you.

Discussion Why is it always easy to multiply by zero?

9 Work out
 a 8 × −5   **b** 9 × −3
 c −4 × 6   **d** −7 × 5

10 Richard draws number cards from a pack and adds them together to find their total.
 He draws these cards.

 What is the total score?

11 What are the missing numbers in these number facts?
 a 3 × −4 = −12 so −12 ÷ 3 = ☐
 b 6 × −4 = −24 so −24 ÷ 6 = ☐
 c −11 × 4 = −44 so −44 ÷ 11 = ☐
 d −8 × 5 = −40 so −40 ÷ 5 = ☐
 e Copy and complete the rules.
   positive ÷ positive = _____
   negative ÷ negative = _____

12 A diver's depth is −48 m.
 She comes to the surface in four equal stages.
 Write a calculation to work out how far she rises in each stage.

13 **Explore** How much warmer is it in summer than in winter?
 Look back at the maths you have learned in this lesson.
 How can you use it to answer this question?

14 **Reflect** Look back at the work you have done this lesson.
 Write down one thing that is the same and one thing that is different
 about calculating with positive numbers and with negative numbers.

Explore   Reflect

1.4 STEM: Writing ratios

You will learn to:
- Work with ratios.

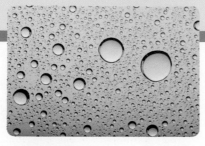

Why learn this?
Water molecules contain hydrogen and oxygen atoms in the ratio 2 to 1.

Fluency
What numbers divide into both numbers in each pair?
- 3 and 9
- 4 and 8
- 15 and 25

Explore
What are the ratios of atoms in different molecules?

Exercise 1.4: Ratios in science

1 What are the missing numbers?

  a

    For every 1 black bead there are ☐ white beads.

  b

    For every 2 black beads there are ☐ white beads.

2 STEM Lily makes a model of water molecules. For each water molecule she uses 2 hydrogen atoms and 1 oxygen atom.
How many of each atom does she use for
  a 2 water molecules
  b 3 water molecules
  c 6 water molecules?

> **Q2 hint**
>
> Sketch one water molecule.
> Draw circles for the atoms.

3 Write the **ratio** of green to yellow tiles for each pattern.

  a [tiles]   **b** [tiles]

  c [tiles]   **d** [tiles]

4 Draw tiles to show these ratios of black to white.
  a 3:5
  b 5:3
  Discussion Is the ratio 3:5 the same as 5:3?

> **Key point**
>
> A **ratio** is a way of comparing two or more quantities.
> Ratios are written as numbers separated by a colon ':'
> For example, in this tile pattern there are 2 blue tiles for 1 red tile.
>
>
>
> The ratio of blue to red tiles is 2:1.

5 STEM Write these as ratios.

  a There are 5 g of chemical A for every 2 g of chemical B. Write the ratio of chemical A to chemical B.

  b In a sample there are 1250 red blood cells for every white blood cell. What is the ratio of red to white blood cells in this sample?

  c Ammonia is made of 1 nitrogen atom for every 3 hydrogen atoms. What is the ratio of nitrogen to hydrogen?

> **Q5a hint**
>
> A:B
> ☐:☐

Subject links: Science (Q2, 5, 8, 9)

6 Write the ratio of blue beads to purple beads for each necklace.
Simplify each ratio if possible. The first one has been started for you.

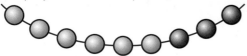

   a 6 blue beads, 3 purple beads

blue:purple = 6:3 = 2:☐

   b 2 purple beads, 2 blue beads

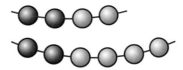

   c 2 purple beads, 4 blue beads

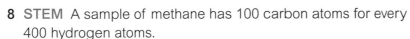

7 Write each ratio in its **simplest** form.
   a 2:6
   b 3:9
   c 4:8
   d 5:15
   e 6:9
   f 12:20
   g 14:21
   h 8:12
   Discussion Are your answers as simple as possible?

> **Key point**
>
> You can **simplify** a ratio by dividing the numbers in the ratio by the same number.

> **Q7a hint**
>
>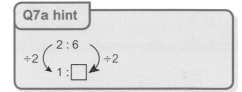

8 **STEM** A sample of methane has 100 carbon atoms for every 400 hydrogen atoms.
Write the ratio of carbon atoms to hydrogen atoms in its simplest form.

9 **STEM** A solution is mixed from two different liquids.
There are 50 ml of liquid A and 125 ml of liquid B.
Write the ratio of liquid A to liquid B in its simplest form.

10 Simplify these ratios.
   a 2:6:8
   b 3:12:18
   c 8:12:16
   d 6:12:15
   e 14:21:28

> **Q10a hint**
>
>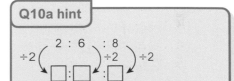

11 **STEM** A gear has two cogs. There are 24 teeth on the large cog and 12 teeth on the small cog.
   a What is the ratio of the number of teeth on the large cog to the small cog?
   b Another gear has three cogs. The first cog has 48 teeth, the second one has 30 teeth and the last one has 12 teeth. What is the ratio of the number of teeth of the first cog to the second cog to the third cog?

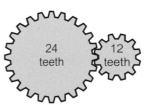

12 **Explore** What are the ratios of atoms in different molecules?
Look back at the maths you have learned in this lesson.
How can you use it to answer this question?

13 **Reflect** Jeremy says, 'Knowing my times tables has really helped this lesson.'
Did knowing your times tables help you this lesson?
What other maths skills have you used?

Explore

Reflect

CONFIDENCE

1.5 Using ratios to solve problems

You will learn to:

- Find equivalent ratios
- Solve simple word problems involving ratio
- Understand the relationship between ratio and proportion.

Why learn this?
When making curry you need to use spices in the correct ratio.

Fluency
What is
- 24 ÷ 6
- 28 ÷ 7
- 32 ÷ 4
- 54 ÷ 6?
What fraction of this rectangle is red?

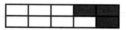

Explore
How much of different spices would you need to make a curry for your class?

Exercise 1.5

Warm up

1 A box contains 10 milk chocolates and 3 white chocolates.
Write the ratio of milk chocolates to white chocolates.

2 Simplify these ratios.

  a 6 : 3   **b** 15 : 20   **c** 8 : 24

3 Write an **equivalent ratio** of white to green beads for each necklace.

  a

  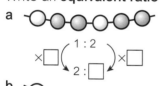

$$\times\square \overset{1:2}{\underset{2:\square}{(\quad)}} \times\square$$

  b

  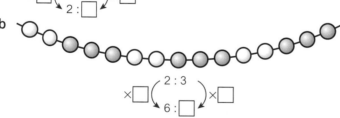

$$\times\square \overset{2:3}{\underset{6:\square}{(\quad)}} \times\square$$

> **Key point**
>
> Multiplying all the numbers in a ratio by the same number gives an **equivalent ratio**.

4 Copy and complete these equivalent ratios.

  a 5 : 2 = □ : 4   **b** 6 : 1 = □ : 3   **c** 7 : 3 = 14 : □

> **Q4a hint**
>
> $$\times\square \overset{5:2}{\underset{\square:4}{(\quad)}} \times\square$$

Worked example

The ratio of cumin to paprika in a recipe is 1 : 2.
Nimah uses 3 teaspoons of cumin.
How many teaspoons of paprika does she use?

$$\overset{C:P}{\times3\overset{1:2}{\underset{3:6}{(\quad)}}\times3}$$

> Multiply each part by the same number to get an equivalent ratio.

Nimah uses 6 teaspoons of paprika.

Subject links: Cookery (Q6, 9, 13, 15)

5 Real A scarf is made from balls of purple wool and pink wool in the ratio 1:3.
How many balls of pink wool are needed for 4 balls of purple wool?

6 Real A recipe for Bolognese sauce uses tomato puree and fresh basil in the ratio 2:1. Neil uses 6 tablespoons of tomato puree.
How much basil does he use?

7 Problem-solving Write four ratios that are equivalent to 2:3.

8 Real Three packs of tent pegs cost £15.
How many packs can you buy for £30?

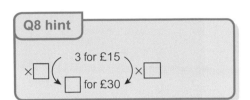

Q8 hint

9 Real A recipe for 6 cakes uses 100 g of flour.
a How much flour do you need for 18 cakes?
b How many cakes can you make with 500 g of flour?

10 a Write the ratio of blue tiles to white tiles.
b What fraction of the tiles are
  i blue   ii white?

11 a Copy the diagram. Colour $\frac{3}{8}$ of the tiles black.
b What is the ratio of
  i black to white tiles
  ii white to black tiles?

12 Real Bell metal is made from copper and tin in the ratio 4:1.
What fraction of bell metal is
a copper   b tin?

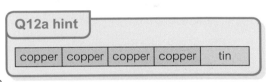

Q12a hint

| copper | copper | copper | copper | tin |

13 Real The sauce for a Thai dish uses Thai sauce and oyster sauce in the ratio 5:3.
a What fraction of the sauce is
  i Thai sauce   ii oyster sauce?
b Show how to check your answers to part **a**.

14 Real Joshua makes green paint by mixing blue paint and yellow paint in the ratio 4:7.
a What fraction of the green paint is
  i blue paint   ii yellow paint?
b Show how to check your answers to part **a**.
c **Problem-solving** Joshua needs 22 litres of green paint.
How many litres of each colour does he need?

15 Explore How much of different spices would you need to make a curry for your class?
Is it easier to explore this question now you have completed the lesson?
What further information do you need to be able to answer this?

16 Reflect Julio looks back at Q5 and says, '$\frac{1}{4}$ of the scarf is pink.'
Fabian says, '$\frac{1}{3}$ of the scarf is pink'.
Who is right and who is wrong? Explain the mistake that has been made.
Did you make the same mistake in this lesson?
If so, write yourself a hint to help avoid the mistake in future.

1.6 Multiplicative reasoning

You will learn to:

* Use proportion to solve simple problems.

Why learn this?
Chefs change recipes in proportion to the number of people they are cooking for.

Fluency
What is double 27?
What is double 56 g?
What is half of 16?
What is half of £36?

Explore
How much milk would you need to make pancakes for your class?

Exercise 1.6

1 Simplify these ratios.
   a 4:6
   b 21:35
   c 6:42

2 Copy and complete these equivalent ratios.
   a 2:5 = 6:☐
   b 3:2 = ☐:10

3 Work out
   a 4)¯160¯
   b 9)¯630¯

4 One dozen eggs cost £1.50.
   How much will two dozen eggs cost?

5 2 apples cost 50p. How much will 4 apples cost?

6 6 packets of sweets contain 42 sweets.
   How many sweets in 18 packets?

7 3 packs of gift tags contain 18 tags.
   How many tags in 6 packs?

8 A recipe for 4 people needs 100 g of sugar.
   How many grams of sugar are needed for 16 people?

9 A recipe for 12 people uses 150 g of flour.
   How many grams of flour are needed for 4 people?

10 On holiday Charlie exchanges £40 for €48.
   How many euros would he get for
   a £80
   b £20
   c £10?

Q4 hint

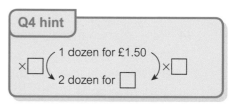

×☐ (1 dozen for £1.50 ↘ 2 dozen for ☐) ×☐

Topic links: Graphs

Subject links: Cookery (Q8, 9, 12)

Worked example

Six memory sticks cost £48.
How much do 11 cost?

£48 ÷ 6 = £8

£8 × 11 = £88

> Find the cost of one memory stick by dividing the total cost by the number of items.

> Multiply the price of one item by the number of items.

11 3 tickets cost £12. How much do 5 tickets cost?

12 A recipe for 4 people needs 100 g of sugar.
How many grams of sugar are needed for
  a 1 person   **b** 13 people?

13 Ben buys 7 football stickers for 56p. How much would he pay for
  a 12 stickers   **b** 18 stickers   **c** 20 stickers?

 14 5 equal sized coaches can carry a total of 215 people.
How many people can be carried by
  a 9 coaches   **b** 15 coaches   **c** 21 coaches?

 15 Mike can make 3 bird tables from 4.5 m of wood.
How many metres of wood will he need to make
  a 11 bird tables   **b** 17 bird tables   **c** 28 bird tables?

16 **Reasoning** On a particular day the exchange rate is £4 = €5.
Copy and complete this table.

£	€
4	5
20	
10	
25	
55	
75	
	125

Discussion How did finding £20 help you to find £10?

17 A 300 g pot of yoghurt contains 75 g of fat.
How much fat is there in a 700 g pot?

18 **Explore** How much milk would you need to make pancakes for your class?
Look back at the maths you have learned in this lesson.
How can you use it to answer this question?

19 **Reflect** Look back at Q15. April starts to work out the answer to
part **a** this way.

She isn't sure what to do next.
How did you work out the answer to Q15 **a**?
Describe a quicker method for April to use.

1 Check up

Log how you did on your Student Progression Chart.

Calculations

1 Work out

  a $5 \times (2 + 6)$ **b** $15 \div (2 + 3)$

2 Work out

  a $4320 + 5347$ **b** $7323 + 876$ **c** $435 + 63 + 47$

3 Work out

  a $6956 - 4134$ **b** $7073 - 836$ **c** $548 - 215 - 31$

4 Work out

  a £4.89 + £12.37   **b** £9.37 − £2.68

5 Work out

  a 67×21 **b** 324×56

6 $34 \times 41 = 1394$
What is $1394 \div 34$?

Negative numbers

7 Work out 325×0

8 Work out

  a $5 - 9$ **b** $-12 + 8$
  c $-18 - 13$ **d** $11 + -3$
  e $5 - -2$ **f** $-16 - -12$

9 Work out

  a -3×6 **b** 7×-4 **c** $-48 \div 8$

Ratio and multiplicative reasoning

10 Write the ratio of black to white.

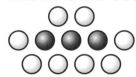

11 **a** In a box of sweets, there are 3 green sweets for every 7 red
    sweets. What is the ratio of green sweets to red sweets?
  b What fraction of the sweets are red?

12 Write these ratios in their simplest form.

    a 9:6   **b** 3:15:27

13 Complete this equivalent ratio.

    2:5 = 6:☐

14 The ratio of orange to lemonade in a drink is 1:3.

    a How much lemonade do you need for 100 m*l* of orange?

    b How much drink can you make with 600 m*l* lemonade?

15 6 identical dog biscuits weigh 24 g. What is the mass of

    a 3 dog biscuits

    b 18 dog biscuits?

16 10 bananas cost £3.20. What is the cost of

    a 16 bananas

    b 4 bananas?

17 How sure are you of your answers? Were you mostly

    😟 **Just guessing**   😐 **Feeling doubtful**   😊 **Confident**

    What next? Use your results to decide whether to strengthen or extend your learning.

Reflect

Challenge

18 One number is subtracted from another number. The answer is –3. What could the two numbers be?

19 You can use any of the four operations with the numbers on these cards.

    a What is the largest number you can make using all 4 cards?

    b What is the smallest number you can make using all 4 cards?

    c What is the number closest to zero you can make using all 4 cards?

Master
P1

Check
P15

STRENGTHEN

Extend
P21

Test
P25

1 Strengthen

You will:

• Strengthen your understanding with practice.

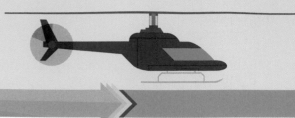

Calculations

1 Work out

    a 2564 + 273

    b 3942 + 909

    c 3 + 492 + 57

    d 389 + 48 + 5366

> **Q1a hint**
>
> 2564 =   2000 + 500 + 60 + 4
> 273 = +   200 + 70 + 3
>   ☐ + ☐ + ☐ + ☐ = ☐

2 Work out

    a 3783 − 656

    b 5403 − 875

    c 392 − 83 − 57

    d 4074 − 68 − 555

> **Q2a hint**
>
> Write the numbers in columns.
>   70   1
> 3783 =   3000 + 700 + 8̶0̶ + 3
> 656 = −   600 + 50 + 6
>   ☐ + ☐ + ☐ + ☐ = ☐

> **Q2c hint**
>
> First work out 392 − 83.
> Then subtract 57 from the answer.

3 Work out

    a £11.78 + £24.39

    b £207.91 + £32.83

> **Q3a hint**
>
> Add the £: £11 + £24 = £☐
> Add the p: 78p + 39p = ☐p = £☐
> Add the two together.

4 Work out

    a 64 × 23

    b 47 × 23

    c 75 × 31

    d 87 × 44

> **Q4a Strategy hint**
>
> Write 64 as 60 + 4.
> Write 23 as 20 + 3.
>
> | × | 60 | 4 | |
> |---|---|---|---|
> | 20 | 1200 | 80 | = 1280 (Add 1200 and 80) |
> | 3 | 180 | 12 | = 192 (Add 180 and 12) |
> | | | | 1472 (Add your two answers – don't forget |
> | | | | ₁ the 1 carried over) |

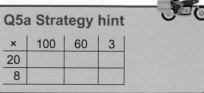

5 Work out

    a 163 × 28

    b 246 × 29

    c 472 × 48

    d 803 × 39

> **Q5a Strategy hint**
>
> | × | 100 | 60 | 3 |
> |---|---|---|---|
> | 20 | | | |
> | 8 | | | |

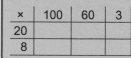

Subject links: Cookery (Ratio and multiplicative reasoning Q6, 11, 12)

6 Work out

  a 3 × (5 + 7)

    3 × ☐ = ☐

  b (18 − 7) × (4 + 2)

    ☐ × ☐ = ☐

  c (6 + 2) × 9

  d (16 − 7) ÷ (8 + 1)

7 Choose any number from the cloud.
Multiply the number by 0.
Repeat three times.
What do you notice?

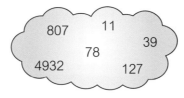

8 a Use the numbers 4, 3 and 12 to complete these calculations.

    i ☐ × ☐ = ☐

    ii ☐ ÷ ☐ = ☐

    iii ☐ ÷ ☐ = ☐

  b Write three calculations using 5, 7 and 35.

  c 15 × 6 = 90

    What is 90 ÷ 6?

> **Q8a hint**
>
> **ii** and **iii** must be different calculations.

Negative numbers

1 Work out

  a −2 + 5

  b −7 + 8

  c −8 + 11

  d −6 + 5

  e −4 + 4

  f −10 + 8

> **Q1a hint**
>
>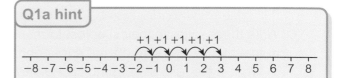

2 Work out

  a −1 − 3

  b 2 − 5

  c 5 − 7

  d −4 − 3

  e −6 − 2

  f −11 − 5

  g −23 − 14

> **Q2a hint**
>
>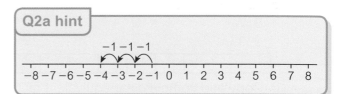

3 Work out

  a 4 + −2

  b 13 − −8

  c −7 − −5

  d −8 − −10

> **Q3 hint**
>
> Replace different signs with a minus (−).
> Replace same signs with a plus (+).

4 Calculate

  a 8 × −6

  b −7 × 11

  c −36 ÷ 6

  d −56 ÷ 7

> **Q4 hint**
>
> For multiplying and dividing, different signs give a negative answer.

Ratio and multiplicative reasoning

1 Copy the counters.

Shade them to show each ratio.

a B:W
  2:1

b B:W
  5:4

2 Write the ratio of blue circles to red circles for each pattern.

a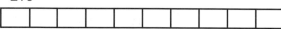

b

3 Write these as ratios.

a There are 7 girls in a group and 9 boys.
What is the ratio of girls to boys?

b On a website there are 11 sports pages and 17 news pages.
What is the ratio of sports pages to news pages?

4 Write the ratio 2:4 in its simplest form.

5 Write each ratio in its simplest form.

a 2:8
b 3:15
c 14:7
d 36:12
e 45:15

6 Write these ratios in their simplest form.

a In a recipe there are 40g of sugar and 15g of chocolate.
What is the ratio of sugar to chocolate?

b On a beach there are 25 adults and 30 children.
What is the ratio of adults to children?

7 a Shade a copy of this strip to show the ratio
B:W
2:3

b Copy and complete the equivalent ratio.

B : W
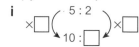

c Copy and complete these equivalent ratios.

i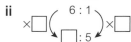

ii

iii 2:7
  1:☐

iv 3:8
  ☐:16

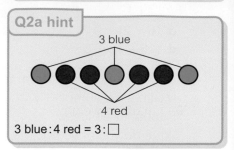

Q1a hint

B:W
2:1 means 2 black for every 1 white.

Q2a hint

3 blue

4 red

3 blue:4 red = 3:☐

Q3a hint

☐ girls:☐ boys
☐:☐

Q4 hint

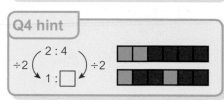

$÷2 \left(\begin{matrix} 2:4 \\ 1:☐ \end{matrix} \right) ÷2$

Q5 hint

Keep dividing until you can't divide any more.

Q5b hint

You cannot divide by 2.
Try dividing by 3.

Q6 hint

Write as a ratio, then simplify.

8 The ratio of boys to girls in a karate class is $5:4$.
There are 10 boys in the class.
   a How many girls are in the class?
   b What is the total number of children in the class?

Q8a hint
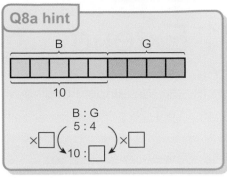

9 4 marbles weigh 60 g. How much do 12 marbles weigh?

Q9 hint

10 4 boxes of eggs contain 24 eggs.
How many eggs will there be in 20 boxes?

Q10 hint
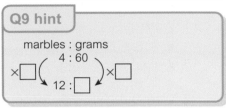

boxes : eggs
   4 : 24

11 A recipe for 20 people needs 5 litres of milk.
How much milk will be needed in the same recipe for 4 people?

Q11 hint
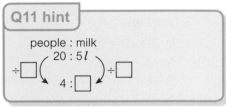

12 A recipe for 12 people needs 240 g of flour.
How much flour is needed for 4 people?

13 10 identical minibuses can carry a total of 130 people.
How many people can be carried by
   a 15 minibuses
   b 25 minibuses
   c 17 minibuses
   d 6 minibuses?

Q13a hint
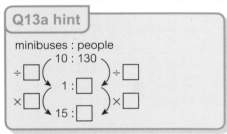

14 It costs 108p to send 9 picture messages.
What is the cost of
   a 12 picture messages
   b 24 picture messages
   c 3 picture messages
   d 34 picture messages?

Q14 hint
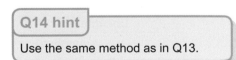

Use the same method as in Q13.

Enrichment

1 In a salsa dancing class $\frac{2}{3}$ of the group are girls and the rest are boys.
Amelia says, 'The ratio of girls to boys is $2:3$.'
Xabi says, 'The ratio of girls to boys is $2:1$.'
Who is correct? Explain your answer.

2 Reflect Look back at the different sections you have worked on in these strengthen lessons.
Now think back to your answers in the check up test.
Which section did you want to practise the most?
Do you feel more confident on that topic now?

Reflect

1 Extend

You will:

- Extend your understanding with problem solving.

1 Work out

   a 316 + 78 − 26   **b** 75 − 37 + 142

   c 564 − 231 + 35   **d** 789 + 3704 − 367 + 51

Q1 Strategy hint

Work from the left. Do the calculation with the first two numbers first.

2 Work out

   a $3 \times -4 \times 9$

   b $2 \times 4 \times -5$

   c $-8 \times 8 \div 4$

   d $20 \times -20 \div 25$

Q2 hint

For a mix of × and ÷, work from left to right.

3 Work out

   a $2 \times (5 - 7)$

   b $(4 + 7) \times -6$

   c $(11 - 2) \times (4 - 9)$

   d $(-3 - 5) \div 2$

4 **Problem-solving / Real** 40 000 children need an MMR vaccination.
Surgery A receives 16 879 MMR vaccines.
Surgery B receives 5896 more vaccines than Surgery A.
Can all the children be vaccinated?
Show working to explain your answer.

Q4 hint

Read the question carefully – Surgery B gets **more** vaccine than Surgery A.

5 The table gives the temperature at different locations in January 2014.

Location	Temperature (°C)
Scott Base (Antarctica)	−5
Auckland (New Zealand)	20
Chicago (USA)	−6
Montreal (Canada)	−9
Greenland	−21
Moscow (Russia)	−16
Melbourne (Australia)	25

   a What is the temperature difference (in °C) between the hottest and coldest places in the table?

   b How much warmer than Chicago is Auckland?

   c How much colder is Greenland than Scott Base?

   d How many degrees warmer is Montreal than Moscow?

   e The day after these figures were recorded, Scott Base suffered a temperature drop of 13°C. What was the temperature?

Topic links: Information in tables, Fractions, Converting metric units, Converting units (time)

Subject links: Geography (Q5, 6)

6 The heights of mountains are measured in metres above sea level.
The depths of ocean trenches are measured in metres below sea level.

Mountain	Height above sea level (m)	Ocean trench	Depth below sea level (m)
Everest	8848	Mariana	11 033
Elbrus	5642	Tonga	10 882
Mount McKinley	6194	Philippine	10 540
Aconcagua	6962	Kermadec	10 047
Kilimanjaro	5895	Puerto Rico	8 800

a What is the biggest difference between a mountain height and a trench depth?

b An explorer travels from the bottom of the Japan trench to the top of Mount McKinley. How many metres has she ascended?

c An explorer descends Aconcagua and goes to the bottom of the Tonga trench. How many metres has he descended?

7 **Problem-solving** Prakesh is a bus driver. He keeps track of how many people are on his bus by checking how many get on and off at each stop.

Q7 hint

Copy and complete the table.

Stop number	Number getting on	Number getting off	Total on the bus
1	45	0	45
2	23	17	
3	12	4	
4	19	13	
5	7	38	
6	28	2	

a What is the greatest number of people on his bus at any time?

b How many people are on the bus after bus stop 6?

c What is the smallest number of people on his bus at any time?

d There are 47 seats on the bus. When do people have to stand?

8 **Finance** Victoria's bank statement is shown below.

Q8 Literacy hint

Income is money paid in to an account.
Expenditure is money paid out.
Balance is the amount of money in the account.

Date	Income (£)	Expenditure (£)	Balance (£)
15 June	534	221	1095
17 June	8	172	931
20 June	b	250	740
21 June	376	c	1029
23 June	196	228	d
1 July	e	0	1001

a How much money was in the account before 15 June?

b How much is paid in on 20 June?

c How much is paid out on 21 June?

d What is the balance on 23 June?

e How much was paid in on 1 July?

9 **Problem-solving** Harif is a runner.
He is trying to improve his time to run 5 km.
On his first run he took 22 minutes 17 seconds.
His second run is 25 seconds quicker.
His third run is 12 seconds slower than his second run.
His fourth run is 27 seconds quicker than his second run.
a Which of Hanif's runs was the quickest?
b What was his quickest time?

Q9 hint

Write Hanif's times in a table.
Remember there are 60 seconds in a minute.

10 **Problem-solving** A machine in a factory makes components for a car engine.
It can make 230 components in an hour but some are rejected because they are faulty.
The table shows the numbers of faulty components in one shift.

Hour	Faulty components
1	27
2	45
3	15
4	36
5	14
6	9
7	27
8	17

a After how many hours will the machine have made 1000 good components?
b How many good components does the machine make in the shift?

11 Two of these calculations are wrong.
A $1775 \div 29 = 65$ B $1976 \div 52 = 38$
C $5852 \div 72 = 81$ D $3999 \div 93 = 43$
Use inverse calculations to find out which two.

Q11 hint

The inverse calculation for A is 29×65.

12 Write the measurements 60 cm and 90 cm as a ratio in its simplest form.
Is the ratio the same if the measurements are in mm?

Q12 hint

60 cm = ☐ mm
90 cm = ☐ mm

13 5 litres of a particular colour of paint is made using 45 ml of red dye, 40 ml of blue dye and 60 ml of green dye.
How much dye of each colour is needed for 12 litres of paint?

Q13 hint

Work out the amount of dye for 1 litre.

14 Blue paint and red paint are mixed in the ratio 1 : 3.
What fraction of the new mixture is red paint?

Q14 Strategy hint

How many parts are there altogether?
How many of them are red?

15 The ratio of boys to girls in a class is 5 : 7.
What fraction of the class are boys?

16 The ratio of cows to pigs on a farm is 16 : 19.
What fraction of the animals are pigs?

17 24 dishwashing tablets cost £4.60.
How much will 36 tablets cost?

18 The sides of this picture are in the ratio 3:4.

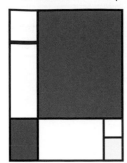

Q18 hint

$$\times\square \overset{3:4}{\underset{\square : 140}{\left(\right)} \times\square}$$

The longer side of a poster of the picture is 140 cm.
How long will the shorter side be?

19 Real / Reasoning Ian's scooter can travel 680 miles on 20 litres of fuel.
Ian has 3 litres left in his tank.
Does he have enough fuel to travel 120 miles?

Investigation   Modelling / Reasoning / STEM

Forensic scientists use the length of a footprint to estimate the height of a criminal.
For an adult, the usual ratio of foot length to height is 3:20.

1 Estimate the heights of the criminals who have left these footprints.
Give your answers in metres.

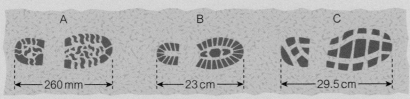

2 Measure your foot length and height.
See if this ratio works for you.

3 Is this a good model to use for young children?
Would it work for paw prints?
Explain your answer.

20 Reflect Look back at your work from these extend lessons.
Which question made you think the hardest?
What did you do to solve the problem?

1 Unit test

Log how you did on your
Student Progression Chart.

1 Work out
 a 4383 + 738
 b 485 + 7 + 1280

2 Work out
 a 7268 − 487
 b 383 − 149 − 77

3 Calculate
 a 36 × 17
 b 264 × 15

4 3304 ÷ 14 = 236
 What is 14 × 236?

5 You make orange paint by mixing 2 litres of red paint with 7 litres
 of yellow paint.
 What is the ratio of red paint to yellow paint?

6 4 new tyres cost £148.
 How much will 8 new tyres cost?

7 48 pens weigh 720 g.
 How much will 12 pens weigh?

8 A car costs £2400. It is reduced by £500.
 What is the new cost of the car?

9 Work out
 a −15 + 8
 b −19 − 24

10 Work out
 a −6 + −8
 b −8 − −6
 c 9 − −7

11 Work out
 a (4 + 7) × 8
 b (23 − 8) ÷ (12 − 7)
 c 3 × (4 − 10)
 d (−7 − 3) ÷ 5

12 Work out
 a −4 × 3
 b 8 × −7
 c −24 ÷ 6
 d 30 ÷ −5

13 Penny has £30.
She spends £14.99.
Her father gives her £7.50.
How much does she have?

14 Work out
   a $13 + 15 - 22$
   b $5 \times 3 + 2 \times 13$
   c $120 - 25 \times 4$

15 Write each ratio in its simplest form.
   a $3:15$
   b $63:27:45$

16 Copy and complete the equivalent ratio.
   $3:11$
   $\square:44$

17 A recipe for 4 people uses 50 g of chocolate.
How much chocolate is needed for the same recipe for 18 people?

18 There is a ratio of 2 left-handed students to 9 right-handed students
in a class.
What fraction of the class are right-handed?

19 The ratio of toffees to fudge in a sweet box is $4:5$.
A giant sweet box has 30 pieces of fudge.
How many toffees are there?

Challenge

20 Use as many 6s as you like to make the numbers in the grid.
You can use $+, -, \times, \div$ and ( ).

36	0	3
144	24	72
30	2	216

21 **Reflect** In this unit you have worked with
• calculations with big numbers
• calculations with negative numbers
• ratio
• multiplicative reasoning.
Which of these topics did you find the easiest?
Which of these topics did you find the most difficult?
Are your answers what you would have expected when you started
the unit?

MASTER

| Check P39 | Strengthen P41 | Extend P45 | Test P49 |

2.1 3D solids

You will learn to:
- Recognise and name 3D solids
- Count faces, edges and vertices
- Deduce properties of 3D solids from 2D representations.

CONFIDENCE

Why learn this?
Being able to visualise shapes in three dimensions can help you play 3D computer games.

Fluency
How many edges does this 2D shape have?
How many vertices?
Which sides are:
- perpendicular to AB
- parallel to DE?

Explore
Do different 3D solids look the same when drawn in 2D?

Exercise 2.1

Warm up

1 Draw these 2D shapes on triangular dotted paper.
  a rectangle   **b** isosceles triangle
  c right-angled triangle   **d** parallelogram
  e rhombus

2 Match the names to the 3D solids.

> square-based pyramid   cuboid   cube
> cylinder   triangular prism

A   **B**   **C**   **D**   **E**

3 Here is a sketch of a cuboid.
The hidden edges are shown with dotted lines.
Write down the number of
  a faces   **b** edges   **c** vertices.

4 Fill in the gaps using the words below.

> edge
>   vertex
>   face

  a A _____ is part of the surface of a 3D solid.
  b Two faces of a 3D solid meet at an _____.
  c The point on a 3D solid where edges meet is called a _____.

Key point

A 3D solid has **faces**, **edges** and **vertices**. Faces and edges can be flat or curved.

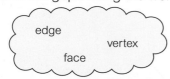

Faces   Vertex   Edges

Q4 Literacy hint

Vertices is the plural of **vertex**.

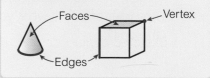

Topic links: 2D shapes   **Subject links:** Design and technology (Q5, Q10)

5 These 3D shapes have been made from straws and beads.

 A   B   C   D

For each shape, write down the number of
a straws used
b beads used
c edges
d vertices.
Discussion Describe a 3D shape that uses 7 beads.
How many straws does it use?

Q5c, d hint

Use your answers to parts **a** and **b**.

6 These solids have been constructed by joining two or more simple 3D solids together.

 A   B   C   D

1
A cylinder attached to a cone

2
A square-based pyramid joined to a cuboid

3
Three cubes joined together

a Match each solid to one of the descriptions.
b One of the solids does not have a description.
Write your own description for this solid.

Q6b Literacy hint

Use the correct mathematical names.

7 Here are some 3D solids drawn on **isometric paper**.

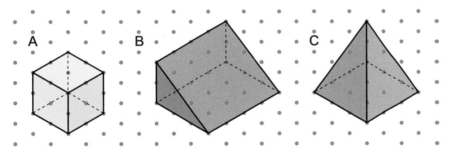
A B C

For each solid, write down
a its name
b the number of faces
c the number of edges
d the number of vertices.

Key point

3D solids can be drawn on **isometric paper**. This cuboid is 3 units wide, 5 units long and 2 units high.

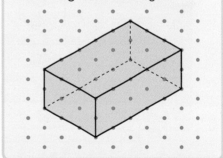

Key point

A **prism** is a solid shape that has the same **cross-section** throughout its length.

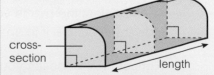

cross-section

length

The cross-section can be any flat shape. It is perpendicular to the length of the solid.

Worked example

Sketch a pentagonal prism.

    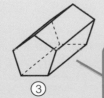
① ② ③

1 Draw the front face.
2 Draw the back face.
3 Join corresponding vertices.

8 On plain paper, sketch these 3D solids.

   a Cube

   b Triangular prism

   c Cylinder

   d Hexagonal prism

Q8c hint

The cross-section of a cylinder is a circle.

9 The vertices on this cube have been labelled with letters.

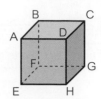

   Write down

   a three edges that meet at the same vertex

   b four edges that make one face

   c two edges that are parallel to each other

   d two edges that are perpendicular to each other.

10 Real This isometric drawing shows a design for a podium.
Each face of the podium needs to be painted, except
the bottom.

   a How many faces need to be painted?

Each vertex of the podium is reinforced with
a metal bracket.

   b How many metal brackets are needed in total?

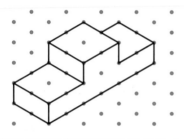

Investigation   **Reasoning**

1 Copy and complete this table showing the number of faces, edges and vertices for some solid shapes.
The first solid has been done for you.

	Cube	Triangle-based pyramid	Triangular prism	Square-based pyramid	Hexagonal prism
Faces	6				
Vertices	8				
Edges	12				

2 a Include a new row in the table to show 'Faces + Vertices'.

   b Compare your answer in the new row to the number of edges. What do you notice?

3 Write down a rule using words or algebra to describe the relationship between the number of faces,
edges and vertices in a 3D solid.

---

11 Explore Do different 3D solids look the same when drawn in 2D?
Look back at the maths you have learned in this lesson.
How can you use it to answer this question?

12 Reflect In this lesson you have used different 2D representations of
3D solids. Why do you think people use isometric paper to draw 3D
solids instead of plain or squared paper?

2.2 Nets of 3D solids

You will learn to:
- Identify nets of 3D solids including cubes and cuboids
- Draw nets of 3D solids using a ruler and protractor.

Why learn this?
Flat pack boxes make 3D solids.

Fluency
Describe the faces of these 3D solids.

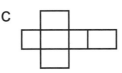

Explore
How many different ways can you draw the net of a cube?

Exercise 2.2

1 Use a ruler and pencil to accurately draw lines of length
  a 4.2 cm
  b 32 mm.

2 Draw each angle accurately.

  a
  7 cm
  50°
  5 cm

  b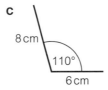
  6 cm
  30°
  3 cm

  c
  8 cm
  110°
  6 cm

3 **Reasoning** Which one of these shapes is the **net** of a cuboid?

  A   B   C

  Give a reason for your answer.

4 The diagram shows an **open cube**. Which of these nets shows the net of an open cube?

  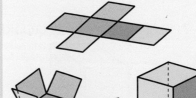

  A   B   C

  D   E   F

Warm up

The green squares are a net of a closed cube with one square missing.

1 Which of the other squares **A** to **I** could complete the net?

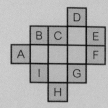

2 Is there more than one possible answer?

3 Using squared paper, find as many different nets of a closed cube as possible.
  Decide whether you are going to count reflections and rotations as different nets.

5 Match each net to the correct 3D solid.

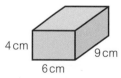

Discussion How did you decide which net matched each shape?

6 **Reasoning** Which pairs of edges meet when this net is folded to
  make a cuboid?

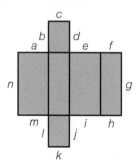

7 Sketch a net of this cuboid. Label each side with its length.

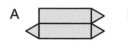

4 cm   9 cm
  6 cm

8 Here is a triangular prism.
  a Write down the number of faces
     on a triangular prism, and the
     shape of each face.

  b Which of these shapes shows the net of a triangular prism?

  A   B   C   D

 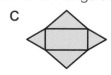 

  c Draw a different net for this triangular prism.

Topic links: Constructing lines and angles, 2D shapes   **Subject links:** Design and technology (Q11, Q13)

9 Match each net to the correct 3D solid.

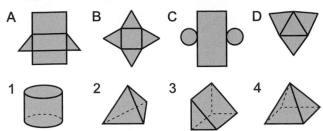

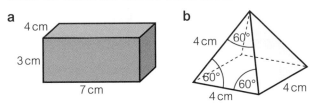

10 Draw an accurate net for each solid.

a

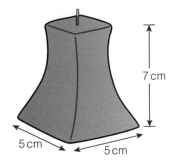

4 cm
3 cm
7 cm

b

4 cm 60°
60° 60° 4 cm
4 cm

Q10 hint

Use a protractor to draw angles.

Q10b hint

The base of the pyramid is a square.

11 **Real / Problem-solving** Alison sells candles at a craft fair. The base of each candle is a 5 cm square, and the candle is 7 cm tall.

7 cm

5 cm 5 cm

She puts each candle in a cuboid-shaped box.
a Sketch a cuboid box that will hold one candle.
b Draw the net of the box accurately.

Q11 hint

Label lengths on your sketch.
Sketch the net.

12 **Explore** How many different ways can you draw the net of a cube? Look back at the maths you have learned in this lesson and the nets you have made.
How can you use them to answer this question?

13 **Reflect** In this lesson you have learned about nets.
Sketch all the nets that a tea bag manufacturer might use.
Beside each one, explain
a what the net is for
b the advantages and disadvantages of using this shape.

Explore

Reflect

2.3 Surface area

You will learn to:
- Calculate the surface area of cubes and cuboids.

CONFIDENCE

Why learn this?
Environmental engineers use surface area to calculate how quickly heat is lost from buildings.

Fluency
What is the length of one side of this square?

Area = 64 cm²

Explore
How much wrapping paper do you need to completely cover a large box?

Exercise 2.3

Warm up

1 Work out the area of each square.

a
2 cm

b
5 m

c
3 mm

Q1 hint
Area is measured in square units e.g. cm².

2 Work out the area of each rectangle. Round each area to 1 decimal place.

a
2.8 cm
9.5 cm

b
6.2 cm
6.8 cm

c
5.3 m
1.9 m

3 Here is a net of a 4 cm cube.
  a Calculate the area of one face.
  b How many faces are there?
  c Calculate the **surface area** of the cube.

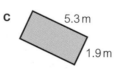

4 cm

4 cm

4 cm

4 cm

Key point
The **surface area** of a 3D solid is the total area of all its faces.

Q3c hint
Use your answers to parts **a** and **b**.

4 This diagram shows a cube with sides of length 7 cm.
  a Calculate the area of one face of the cube.
  b Calculate the surface area of the whole cube.
  Discussion Did you sketch a net?
  How else could you work it out?

7 cm

5 a Sketch a net for a cube with sides of length 4.5 cm.
  b Calculate the surface area of the cube.

6 Calculate the surface area of cubes with these side lengths.
  a 9 cm   **b** 3 m   **c** 25 cm   **d** 13 mm

7 Problem-solving A cube has a total surface area of 384 cm².
  a Work out the area of one face   **b** Work out the length of one side.

Topic links: Area, Multiplication   **Subject links:** Science (Q10), Design and technology (Q11)

Worked example

Work out the surface area of this cuboid.

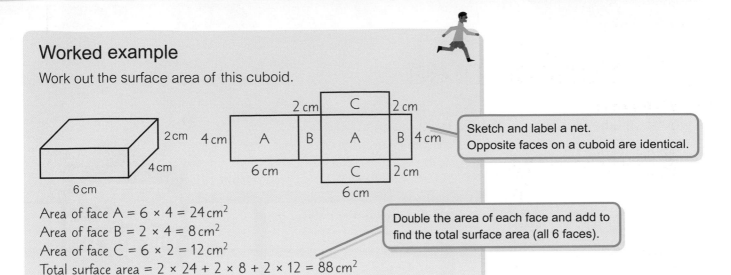

Sketch and label a net.
Opposite faces on a cuboid are identical.

Area of face A = 6 × 4 = 24 cm²
Area of face B = 2 × 4 = 8 cm²
Area of face C = 6 × 2 = 12 cm²
Total surface area = 2 × 24 + 2 × 8 + 2 × 12 = 88 cm²

Double the area of each face and add to find the total surface area (all 6 faces).

8 Here is the net of a cuboid.

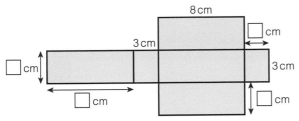

a Copy the net of this cuboid and write in the missing lengths.
b Calculate the surface area of the cuboid.

Q8b Strategy hint

There are 6 faces so add together 6 areas.

9 a Sketch a net of this cuboid.
   b Calculate the surface area of the cuboid. Round your answer to 1 decimal place.

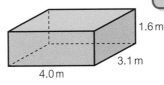

10 **STEM / Modelling** A factory is installing an air-conditioning system.
   a Model the factory as a cuboid. Calculate the total surface area of the factory walls and roof, not including the floor.
   The engineer calculates that he needs 5 watts of cooling power for each m² of surface area.
   b Calculate an estimate for the total number of watts of cooling power needed.
   Discussion Why is a cuboid a good model to use?
   Why isn't the factory an exact cuboid?

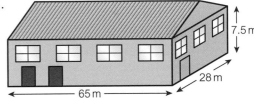

11 **Explore** How much wrapping paper do you need to completely cover a large box? Is it easier to explore this question now you have completed the lesson? What further information do you need to be able to answer this?

12 **Reflect** This lesson showed you two methods for finding the surface area of a cube or cuboid:
   Method 1: draw then add
   Draw a net, write the area of each face on the net, add them together (Q3).
   Method 2: visualise then calculate
   Visualise pairs of opposite faces, calculate 2 × area of face for each pair, add them together (Q10).
   Which method did you prefer? Why?

Q12 hint

What are the advantages and disadvantages of your method?

2.4 Volume

You will learn to:
* Find the volume of a cube or cuboid by counting cubes
* Know the formula for calculating the volume of a cube or cuboid.

CONFIDENCE

Why learn this?
Manufacturers advertise the volume of a fridge or oven. Understanding volume can help you choose the right appliance.

Fluency
Work out
* 50 × 7
* 4 × 4
* 6 × 6
* 2 × 2 × 2

Explore
Does bigger volume mean bigger surface area?

Exercise 2.4

Warm up

1 Work out
  a 30 × 4   **b** 5 × 6 × 2   **c** 7 × 2 × 5   **d** 4 × 5 × 8

2 $a = 7$, $b = 5$ and $c = 10$.
  Work out the value of
  a $a \times b$
  b $b \times c$
  c $a \times b \times c$

3 Here is a layer of centimetre cubes.
  a How many cubes are in this layer?
  Three identical layers make a cube with sides of length 3 cm.
  b Work out the **volume** of the cube.
  c Work out 3 × 3 × 3.
  Discussion What do you notice about your answers to parts **b** and **c**?

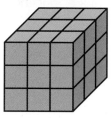
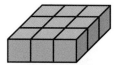

> **Key point**
> The **volume** of a 3D solid is the amount of space it takes up. You measure volume in **cubed units** such as mm³, cm³ and m³.
> A cube with sides of length 1 cm has a volume of 1 cm³.
>
> 1 cm, 1 cm, 1 cm

> **Q3 hint**
> How many cm³ are there?

4 These cubes are made from centimetre cubes.
  Work out the volume of each cube.

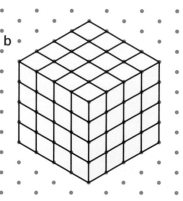

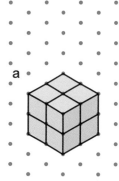

> **Key point**
> You can use this formula to calculate the volume of a cube:
> **volume of a cube** = side length × side length × side length
> $V = l \times l \times l$

Topic links: Multiplication, Substitution   **Subject links:** Science (Q10), Design and technology (Q10)

5 Work out the volume of each cube.

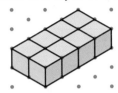

a 7 cm b 0.8 m c 32 mm

6 Here is a layer of centimetre cubes.

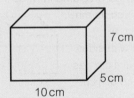

a How many cubes are in this layer?
3 identical layers make this cuboid.
b Work out the volume of this cuboid.
Discussion What is the rule for working
out the volume of a cuboid?

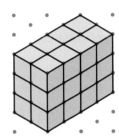

7 Work out the volume of each cuboid.

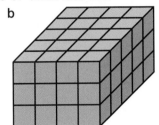

a b

> **Key point**
>
> You can use this formula to calculate the volume of a cuboid.
> **volume of a cuboid** = length × width × height
> $$V = l \times w \times h$$

Worked example

Work out the volume of this cuboid.

7 cm
5 cm
10 cm

Volume = $l \times w \times h$
= 10 × 5 × 7
= 50 × 7
= 350 cm³

> Write down the formula.
> Substitute the values for l, w and h.

> The units of length are cm so the
> units of volume will be cm³.

8 Work out the volume of each cuboid.

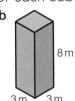 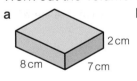 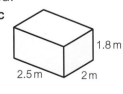 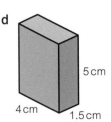

a 2 cm, 8 cm, 7 cm
b 8 m, 3 m, 3 m
c 1.8 m, 2.5 m, 2 m
d 5 cm, 4 cm, 1.5 cm

9 Explore Does bigger volume mean bigger surface area? Choose some
sensible numbers to help you explore this situation. Then use what
you've learned in this lesson to help you answer the question.

10 Reflect Maths is not the only subject where you use volume. You use it
in science too. Describe when you have used volume in science.
In what ways is volume the same or different in science and maths?
Do you think volume means the same in all subjects? Explain.

Explore

Reflect

2.5 Working with measures

You will learn to:
- Solve problems involving units of length, area and capacity
- Convert between cm^3 and litres.

Why learn this?
You need to be able to understand different units of length to read a map.

Fluency
Work out
- 4.6×100
- 0.35×1000
- $320 \div 10$
- $40 \div 1000$

Explore
How much fruit juice is needed to fill up a punch bowl?

Exercise 2.5

1 Convert each length into metres.
   a 2 km
   b 80 cm
   c 0.6 km
   d 250 cm

2 Convert each capacity into litres.
   a 500 m*l*
   b 2000 m*l*

3 Write >, < or = for each pair of quantities.
   a 400 ml ☐ 4 litres
   b 2 m ☐ 300 cm
   c 250 c*l* ☐ 3 litres
   d 0.6 km ☐ 600 m

Q1 hint

$\times 1000$ (

1 km	2 km	3 km	4 km	5 km
1000 m	☐ m	☐ m	☐ m	☐ m

) $\div 1000$

Q2 hint

$\div 1000$ (

200 m*l*	300 m*l*	400 m*l*	500 m*l*	600 m*l*
0.2 *l*	0.3 *l*	☐ *l*	☐ *l*	☐ *l*

) $\times 1000$

4 A triathlon event is a 1500 m run, a 600 m swim and a 10 km bike ride. Write the total length of the triathlon in km.

5 **Reasoning / Real** Nisha wants to mix together these ingredients for fruit punch:

   400 m*l* orange juice
   150 m*l* honey
   500 m*l* apple juice
   1.5 litres of lemonade

Nisha has a choice of punchbowls: 2.5 litres, 3 litres and 3.5 litres.
Which punchbowl should Nisha choose?
Give a reason for your answer.

Topic links: Measurement, Perimeter, Area, Volume   **Subject links:** Design and technology (Q10)

Worked example

Work out the area of this field. Give your answer in m².

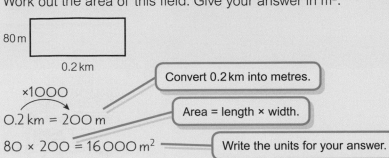

80 m

0.2 km

×1000

0.2 km = 200 m

80 × 200 = 16 000 m²

Convert 0.2 km into metres.

Area = length × width.

Write the units for your answer.

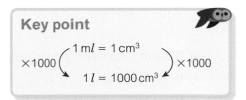

Key point

You need to convert lengths into the same units before calculating areas or volumes.

6 Work out the area of each rectangle.
Include the units with your answer.

a 300 m
2 km

b 60 cm
1.2 m

c 7 cm
90 mm

Discussion How did you decide which units to use?

7 Copy and complete.
a $4000 \text{ cm}^3 = \underline{\hspace{2cm}} \text{ m}l$
b $4000 \text{ cm}^3 = \underline{\hspace{2cm}} \text{ litres}$

Key point

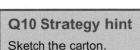

$1 \text{ m}l = 1 \text{ cm}^3$
×1000 ( ) ×1000
$1 l = 1000 \text{ cm}^3$

8 Work out each conversion.
a $5 \text{ litres} = \square \text{ cm}^3$
b $200 \text{ cm}^3 = \square \text{ litres}$
c $2.8 \text{ litres} = \square \text{ cm}^3$
d $1500 \text{ cm}^3 = \square \text{ litres}$

9 **Problem-solving / Real** A car's fuel tank has capacity $54\,000 \text{ cm}^3$.
A litre of petrol costs £1.30.
Work out the cost of completely filling the fuel tank.

10 **Modelling / Reasoning** A drinks company packages a smoothie
in a cube-shaped carton with sides of length 7 cm.
The company claims there is $325 \text{ m}l$ of smoothie in a carton.
Do you think their claim is reasonable? Explain.

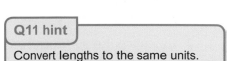

Q10 Strategy hint

Sketch the carton.

11 Work out the surface area
and volume of this cuboid.

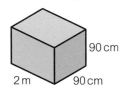

90 cm
2 m 90 cm

Q11 hint

Convert lengths to the same units.

12 **Explore** How much fruit juice is needed to fill up a punch bowl?
Is it easier to explore this question now you have completed
the lesson? What further information do you need to be able to
answer this?

13 **Reflect** Nastasia says, 'When I want to convert cm to mm
I need to multiply, because lots of mm fit into 1 cm.'
Write, in your own words, a way of remembering why you multiply
or divide to convert between different units.
Compare your answers with your classmates.

Explore

Reflect

2 Check up

Log how you did on your Student Progression Chart.

3D solids

1 Sketch the net of a cube.

2 Write down the number of faces, edges and vertices in this solid.

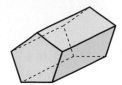

3 This is the net of a 3D solid.
Write down the name of the solid.

4 Sketch the net of a triangular prism.

5 This prism is drawn on isometric dotted paper.
Write down the number of faces, edges and vertices of this prism.

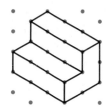

Surface area and volume

6 Write down whether each of these is a measurement of **length**, **area** or **volume**.
   a 38 cm^2 **b** 120 m^3 **c** 4.7 mm^2 **d** 300 cm

7 Calculate the surface area of this cube.

9 cm
9 cm
9 cm

8 This cuboid is made from centimetre cubes. Work out its volume.

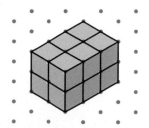

9 **a** Sketch a net of this cuboid.
  b Calculate the surface area of the cuboid.
  c Calculate the volume of the cuboid.

Measures

10 Here is a recipe for rice pudding.

200 g rice
100 g sugar
1.4 litres milk

Poppy has 750 ml of milk.
How much more milk does she need for the recipe?

11 Which of these containers holds
  a the most liquid
  b the least liquid?

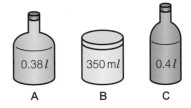

A   B   C

12 A medicine bottle contains 0.28 litres of medicine.
  Tim needs to take two 5 ml spoonfuls of medicine each morning
  and two 5 ml spoonfuls each evening.
  a How many 5 ml spoonfuls does the bottle contain?
  b How many days will the bottle last?

13 Convert 750 cm³ into litres.

14 The diagram shows a wooden planting box in the shape of a cuboid.

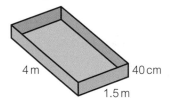

Calculate the volume of the planting box.

15 **How sure are you of your answers? Were you mostly**
  😟 **Just guessing**   😐 **Feeling doubtful**   🙂 **Confident**
  What next? Use your results to decide whether to strengthen or extend your learning.

Challenge

16 Sketch a net of this 3D solid.

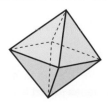

Q16 hint

How many faces does it have?
What shape are they?

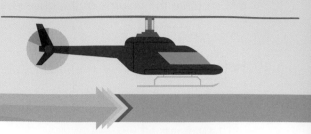

2 Strengthen

You will:
- Strengthen your understanding with practice.

3D solids

1 Copy this sketch and add three more squares to make the net of a cube.

Q1 hint

A cube has 6 square faces so its net must consist of 6 squares.

2 Which **two** of these could be the net of a cube?

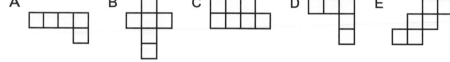

A   B   C   D   E

3 For each solid, write down the number of
  i faces
  ii edges
  iii vertices.

a   **b**

Q3 hint

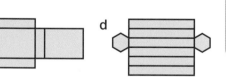
Vertex — Edge — Face

4 Write down the mathematical name of the solid that can be made from each net.

a   **b**   **c** 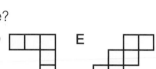   **d**

Q4 hint

Look at the shapes of the faces. Which solids have these shapes as faces?

5 Reasoning Here is a 3D solid made from simpler solids. Copy and complete this description of the solid:
This solid is made from a _____ and two _____.
It has _____ faces, _____ edges and _____ vertices.

Q6 hint

Start by drawing two identical rectangles like this:

Draw in the edges between pairs of vertices. Use dotted lines for hidden edges.

6 Draw a sketch of a cuboid.

7 Sketch a net for this triangular prism. Label the lengths.

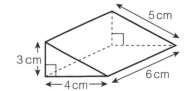
5 cm
3 cm
6 cm
4 cm

Q7 hint

Start with the bottom face. Draw the faces joined to it.

8 Copy the net for this cuboid. Label the lengths.

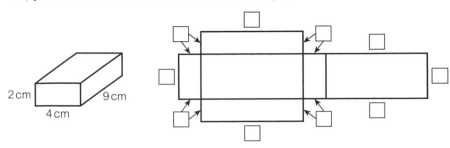

Q8 Strategy hint

Match each face on the cuboid to a face on the net.

9 For each solid
  i What shapes are the faces?
  ii Name the solid.

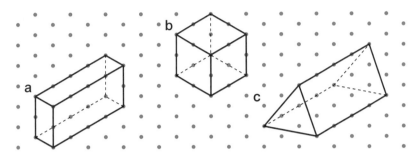

Surface area and volume

1 Here is the net of a cube with side length 8.2 cm.

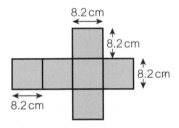

Copy and complete the table to work out the surface area.

Shape of face	Area of face	Number of faces	Total area
(square) 8.2 cm × 8.2 cm	8.2 × 8.2 = ☐ cm²	☐	☐ × ☐ = ☐ cm²

2 a Calculate the area of one face of this cube.
  b Calculate the surface area of the whole cube.

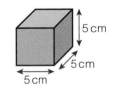

Q2 hint

Use the method in Q1.

3 Calculate the surface area of a cube with side length
  a 2.7 mm
  b 12 cm
  c 6.4 m.

4 Here is the net of a cuboid.

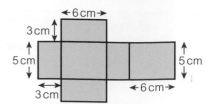

Copy and complete the table to work out the surface area.

Shape of face	Area of face	Number of faces	Total area
6 cm / 3 cm (rectangle)	6 × 3 = ☐ cm²	2	2 × ☐ = ☐
5 cm / 3 cm (rectangle)			
6 cm / 5 cm (rectangle)			

5 a Sketch a net of this cuboid.
   b Calculate the surface area of the cuboid.

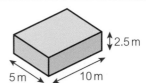

6 Work out the volume of a cube with side length 8.5 cm.

7 This cuboid is made of centimetre cubes.
   a Write down
     i the length
     ii the width
     iii the height of the cuboid.
   b Work out the volume of the cuboid.

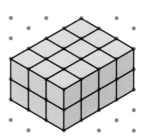

8 Calculate the volume of the cuboid in Q5.

9 Real This trunk is a cuboid. Work out the volume.

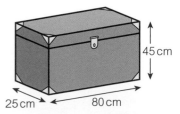

Measures

1 Calculate the area of each rectangle in the given units.

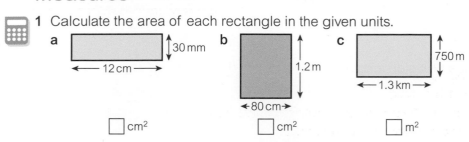

a 30 mm, 12 cm → ☐ cm²
b 1.2 m, 80 cm → ☐ cm²
c 750 m, 1.3 km → ☐ m²

> **Q6 hint**
>
> Volume of a cube
> = length × length × length
> = 8.5 × 8.5 × 8.5 = ☐ cm³

> **Q7b hint**
>
> This cuboid is made up of two identical layers. Here is one of the layers.
>
>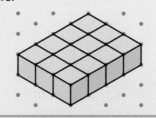

> **Q1a hint**
>
> For an area in cm², use lengths in cm.

2 A serving jug has a capacity of 2 litres. How many 250 ml cartons of orange juice are needed to fill the serving jug?

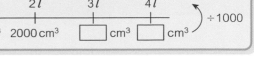
Q2 hint

1 litre = 1000 ml.
How many 250 ml cartons make 1 litre?

3 Copy and complete this calculation to convert 2.3 litres into cm³.
2.3 litres = ☐ ml
1 ml = 1 cm³
So 2.3 litres = ☐ cm³.

4 Work out these conversions.
  a 3 litres = ☐ cm³   **b** 4.5 litres = ☐ cm³
  c 8000 cm³ = ☐ litres   **d** 3200 cm³ = ☐ litres

Q4 hint

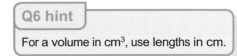

×1000 (1 *l*   2 *l*   3 *l*   4 *l*) ÷1000
1000 cm³ 2000 cm³ ☐ cm³ ☐ cm³

5 Copy and complete this sentence.
To convert from cm³ to litres you _____ by 1000.

6 Calculate the volume of this cuboid in cm³.

Q6 hint

For a volume in cm³, use lengths in cm.

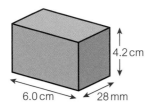

4.2 cm
6.0 cm   28 mm

Enrichment

1 Reasoning Work with a partner. Choose one of these solids.

cube   cuboid   triangular   cylinder   square-based   tetrahedron
                       prism   pyramid

Describe the solid to your partner without using its mathematical name.
You can use these words in your description:

  faces   edges   vertices   rectangle   triangle   square   circle

See how quickly your partner can identify which solid you are describing.

2 Problem-solving The diagram shows the same cube when looked at from three different directions.

Sketch a net of this cube. Draw the correct shapes in the correct positions on each face of your net.

3 Reflect In this unit you have had to do lots of different things to find the answers to questions.
Write these in order, from the one you found easiest to the one you found hardest:
• Working out the numbers of vertices, edges and faces of a shape.
• Working out what the net of a 3D solid will look like.
• Finding the surface area of a cuboid.
• Using the formula for the volume of a cuboid.
• Knowing when to multiply and when to divide when converting measures.
Write a hint, in your own words, for the one you found the hardest.

Q3 Strategy hint

Look back at some of the questions in this strengthen lesson to help you.

Reflect

2 Extend

You will:
• Extend your understanding with problem-solving.

1 **Problem-solving** One of the vertices has been cut off this tetrahedron.

   a How many faces, edges and vertices does it have?

   A second vertex is cut off at the red dotted lines.

   b How many faces, edges and vertices does the shape have now?

2 **Problem-solving** The diagram shows the net of a cube. Makarand wants to label the net with the numbers 1 to 6 to make a dice. Copy the net and label it so that when it is folded up to make a cube, numbers on opposite faces add up to 7.

3 **Reasoning** This block of wood is in the shape of a cube.

   The block is sawn in half and the red section is removed.

   Calculate the volume of wood remaining.

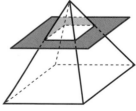

←5 cm→

4 This square-based pyramid has been sliced horizontally.

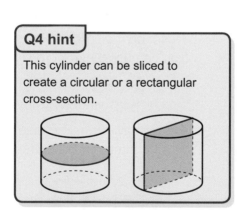

   a Describe the 2D cross-section produced by the slice.

   b Write down two other 2D shapes which could be produced by slicing the pyramid in two different ways.

> **Q4 hint**
>
> This cylinder can be sliced to create a circular or a rectangular cross-section.
>
>

5 Convert each capacity to litres.

   a $6\,cl$

   b $0.5\,cl$

> **Key point**
>
> $1\,cl = 10\,ml$

6 How many ml of drink are in

   a a $33\,cl$ can

   b a $70\,cl$ bottle?

   Jake has a 5 litre container.

   c How many cans can he fill?

   d How many bottles can he fill?

7 Put these capacities in order of size, smallest first.

   1.9 litres, $230\,cl$, 4 litres, $800\,ml$

8 Problem-solving / Modelling
This milk carton is in the shape of a cube.
Work out the length of one side of the carton.

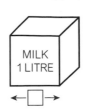

MILK
1 LITRE

Q8 hint

$1000 \, cm^3 = 1$ litre

9 Problem-solving Here is a net of a cuboid.

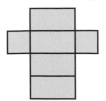

Freddie wants to fold the net up to make a solid shape.
Copy the net and add tabs for gluing so the cuboid will stay together.

Q9 Strategy hint

Make sure that there is one tab for every pair of edges that meet when the net is folded up.

10 Problem-solving This wooden planter is in the shape of an open cube, with sides of length 25 cm.

a Paul wants to varnish the whole planter on the inside and the outside. Work out the total area that Paul needs to varnish.

b Paul fills $\frac{1}{2}$ of the total volume of the planter with compost from a 15 litre bag. How much compost is left in the bag?

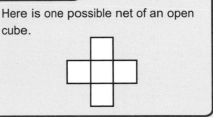

←25 cm→

Q10a hint

Here is one possible net of an open cube.

11 Problem-solving / Reasoning Jonah has some wooden blocks made from centimetre cubes.

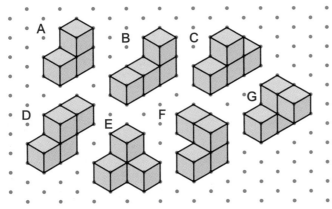

a He rearranges them all to make a cube.
Work out the side length of Jonah's cube.

b He removes block **A** and rearranges the remaining blocks to make a cuboid with length 3 cm and height 2 cm.
What is the width of Jonah's cuboid? Explain your answer.

Q11 Strategy hint

Start by counting the total number of centimetre cubes in Jonah's blocks.

12 Reasoning Sketch a net of a cone.

13 Sketch a net of this solid.

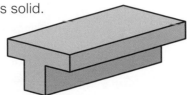

Q13 hint

This solid has 8 rectangular faces and 2 T-shaped faces.

14 a Sketch a net of this solid and label the different faces.

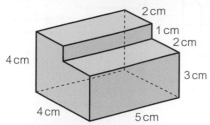

b Calculate the total surface area of this solid.

15 Use a ruler and protractor to draw an accurate net of this **regular tetrahedron**.

Q15 Literacy hint

A **regular tetrahedron** has four faces. Each face is an equilateral triangle.

16 Choose a value from the cloud that is closest to your estimate of the surface area of each object.
  a DVD case
  b matchbox
  c shoebox
  d wardrobe

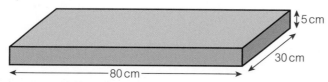

2100 cm²   60 cm²   0.8 m²   6.5 m²   600 cm²   10 cm²

 17 Problem-solving / Real The diagram shows a wooden shelf in the shape of a cuboid.

100 ml of wood stain covers an area of 4000 cm². How many identical shelves can be stained using one 500 ml tin of wood stain?

Q17 Strategy hint

Work out the surface area of the cuboid. Then work out what area can be covered using 500 ml of wood stain. Remember that your final answer must be a whole number.

18 Problem-solving Marius needs to cover the top and sides of this cake using packets of icing.

ICING
Covers 900 cm²

How many boxes of icing will he need?

19 Reasoning Without calculating, estimate which of these cuboids has the larger surface area. Give a reason for your estimate. Check your answers by calculating the actual surface area of each cuboid.

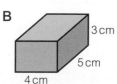

A   B

20 Problem-solving / Real The diagram shows a tank in an aquarium. The tank will be stocked with carp. Each carp requires 50 litres of water. Calculate the maximum number of fish that should be kept in the tank.

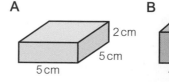

Q20 Strategy hint

Calculate the volume of the tank in cm³ first. Then use the conversion 1000 cm³ = 1 litre to find the capacity in litres. Your final answer needs to be a whole number.

Investigation

 You can make an open-topped box by cutting 4 small squares out of a larger square of card.
Copy and complete this table showing the volume of the box depending on the size of the squares removed.
Try some different sizes, and investigate how the volume of the box changes.

20 cm

Side length of removed square	Width of box	Height of box	Volume of box
1 cm	18 cm	1 cm	$18 \times 18 \times 1 = 324\ cm^3$
2 cm	16 cm	2 cm	$16 \times 16 \times 2 = \square\ cm^3$
3 cm			
4 cm			

21 **Real / Modelling** This coffee table is made from 5 cuboids.
The 4 legs are identical.
a Calculate the volume of one leg of the coffee table.
b Calculate the volume of the top of the coffee table.
c Calculate the total volume of the coffee table.

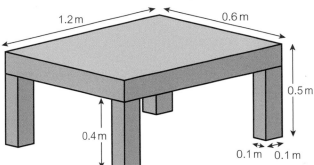

1.2 m   0.6 m   0.5 m   0.4 m   0.1 m   0.1 m

22 These solids are each made from two cuboids joined together.
Calculate the volume of each solid.

a
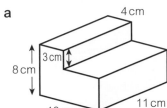
4 cm   3 cm   8 cm   10 cm   11 cm

b
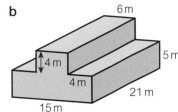
6 m   5 m   4 m   4 m   21 m   15 m

Q22a hint

This solid is constructed from two cuboids.

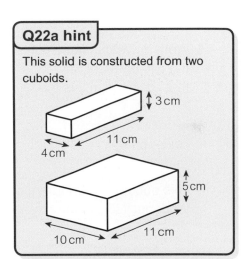
3 cm   11 cm   4 cm   5 cm   10 cm   11 cm

23 **Problem-solving** The diagram shows a triangular prism.
It has made by cutting a cuboid in half diagonally.

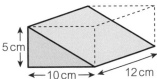
5 cm   10 cm   12 cm

Calculate the volume of the triangular prism.

24 The volume of this cuboid is 160 cm³.
Calculate the height of the cuboid.

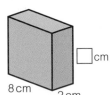
□ cm   8 cm   2 cm

25 **Reflect** In this unit you have learned lots of new vocabulary.
Look back at the work you have done and write a list of all the new words you have learned.
Write your own definition of what each word means.

Reflect

Master
P27

Check
P39

Strengthen
P41

Extend
P45

TEST

2 Unit test

Log how you did on your
Student Progression Chart.

1 Which of these is the net of a cube?

A 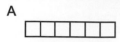   B   C   D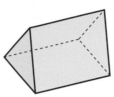

2 For this triangular prism, write down
  a the number of faces
  b the number of edges
  c the number of vertices.

3 A solid has 4 triangular faces, 6 edges and 4 vertices.
  What 3D solid is being described?

4 Copy this net of a cuboid.
  a Draw a tick next to two edges that meet
    when the net is folded up to make a cuboid.
  b Shade in two faces that are opposite when
    the net is folded up to make a cuboid.

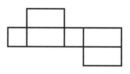

5 Write down the names of
  the two different 3D solids
  that are used in this model.

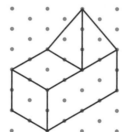

6 This cuboid is made from centimetre cubes.
  Work out its volume.

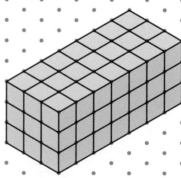

7 Work out these conversions.
  a $260\,\text{m}l = \square\,\text{cm}^3$ **b** $200\,\text{cm}^3 = \square\,\text{m}l$
  c $3.1\,\text{litres} = \square\,\text{cm}^3$ **d** $800\,\text{cm}^3 = \square\,\text{litres}$
  e $400\,\text{c}l = \square\,\text{m}l$ **f** $50\,\text{litres} = \square\,\text{c}l$

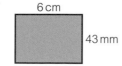 **8** Work out the area of this rectangle in mm^2.

6 cm

43 mm

9 Sketch a net of this prism.
Label the lengths.

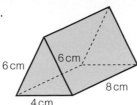

6 cm

6 cm

8 cm

4 cm

 10 A cube has side length 18 mm. Work out
  a the surface area
  b the volume.

11 Work out the volume of this solid.

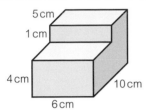

5 cm

1 cm

4 cm

10 cm

6 cm

 12 This diagram shows an accurate net
of a cuboid.
Measure the net to the nearest mm
and calculate
  a the surface area of the cuboid
  b the volume of the cuboid.

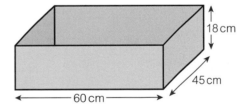

 13 A sandpit for a city beach is a cuboid
18 m long, 6 m wide and 15 cm deep.
  a Calculate the volume of sand needed to fill the sandpit.
Sand is sold for £80 per cubic metre.
  b Estimate the total cost of the sand needed to fill the sandpit.

 14 The diagram shows a sink in the shape of a cuboid.
  a Work out the capacity of the sink.
The sink is $\frac{1}{4}$ full of water.
  b Work out the amount of water in the sink in litres.

18 cm

45 cm

60 cm

Challenge

15 Here is a cube with sides of length 2 cm.
How many straight cuts would be needed
to divide this cube into 8 centimetre cubes?
Does your answer change if you are allowed
to rearrange the pieces after each cut?
Investigate this question for a cube with sides of length 3 cm.

16 **Reflect** Write a heading 'Five important things about 3D solids'.
Now look back at the work you have done in this unit, and list the five most
important things you think you have learned.
You may include:
  • formulae
  • conversions
  • methods for working things out
  • mistakes to avoid (with tips on how to avoid them in future).

Reflect

3.1 Data collection sheets

You will learn to:
- Design a data collection sheet
- Group data into equal class intervals.

CONFIDENCE

Why learn this?
Sports centres collect data to decide which activities to offer during the summer holidays.

Fluency
Continue each set of equal class intervals up to 30:
- 1–5, 6–10, 11–15, …
- 1–10, 11–20, …
- 0–4, 5–9, …

Explore
What data is collected in the National Census? How is the data grouped?

Exercise 3.1

Warm up

1 a Copy and complete this tally chart.

Favourite sport	Tally	Frequency
football		14
tennis		9
basketball	⃀ ll	
netball	⃀	
golf		12
badminton		4

b Which sport is the mode?

2 Safia's button box contains buttons with these sizes (in mm).
6, 1, 3, 10, 4, 6, 3, 7, 20, 5, 2
Safia records the sizes in this grouped frequency table.

Button size (mm)	Frequency
1–5	
6–10	
11–15	
16–20	

a Which class contains
  i a 4 mm button
  ii a 10 mm button?
b How many buttons are in the group 6–10 mm?
c Which is the **modal class**?

Key point
The **modal class** is the group of data with the highest frequency.

51

3 Mark recorded the colour of cars passing the school one morning.

red   blue   red   black   red   white   silver   red
blue   green   red   green   blue   blue   green   black
red   black   silver   black   green   blue   black   red

He plans to do a longer survey the next day.
Copy and complete this **data collection sheet** for his survey.

Car colour	Tally	Frequency
red		
blue		

Discussion Would it be useful to have a row for 'other colours'?

Key point

A **data collection sheet** is a table or chart for collecting **data**. It has a tally column and a frequency column.

Q3 hint

Include all the colours.

4 **Problem-solving** Fernando asked some of his classmates how many text messages they sent last week. These are his results.

12   8   23   15   18   24   23   24
10   17   22   6   7   14   18   23

a Copy and complete this data collection sheet for his data.

Number of text messages	Tally	Frequency
0–4		
5–9		

b How many of his classmates did he ask?
c What is the modal class?

Discussion When is it useful to group data?

Q4c hint

What is the highest value in the frequency column?
Which group is it in?

5 **Problem-solving / Reasoning** Simon and Tara did a survey of the number of books owned by students in their class.
They designed these data collection sheets to collect their results.
What is wrong with each table?

Simon's table

Number of books	Tally	Frequency
0–10		
10–20		
20–30		
30–40		

Tara's table

Number of books	Tally	Frequency
0–10		
11–30		
31–40		

Discussion Can the table cover *every* possible number of books?

6 Here are 20 students' test scores.

153   142   135   143   152   155   154   156   132   138
141   148   149   152   156   162   159   151   158   160

a What is
  i the lowest score
  ii the highest score?
b Draw a data collection sheet for this data with equal class intervals.

Q6b hint

You should have 4, 5 or 6 classes.

7 In a probability experiment, a dice is rolled 50 times.
Design a data collection sheet to record the numbers rolled.

8 Kim measured 20 Year 8 students' heights to the nearest centimetre.
These are her results.

153 142 135 143 152 155 154 156 132 138
141 148 149 152 156 162 159 151 158 160

Kim is going to collect 100 Year 8 students' heights.
Design a data collection sheet she could use.

9 **Real / Problem-solving** James records the number of people in cars passing the school in the morning and afternoon. The table shows his results.

Number of people	am	pm
1	5	3
2	7	12
3	10	8
4	11	4
5	2	6
more than 5	1	0

  a In the morning, how many cars had 3 people?

  b In the afternoon, how many cars had 5 people?

  c Did James record more cars in the morning or the afternoon?
    Show your working to explain.

10 **Problem-solving / Real** Design a data collection sheet to collect data on Year 8 and Year 9 students' favourite sports.

11 Ask 20 people in your class to write as many words as they can beginning with the letter B in one minute.
Design a data collection sheet to record the number of words they write, using appropriate groups with equal class intervals, such as 1–10, 11–20 and so on.

12 **Explore** What data is collected in the National Census?
How is the data grouped?
What have you learned in this lesson to help you answer this question? What other information do you need?

13 **Reflect** Louise and Jez are collecting data about the ages of people in their town.
Louise creates this data collection sheet.

Age (years)	Tally
0–10	
11–20	
21–30	
31–40	

Jez makes this data collection sheet.

Age (years)	Tally
0–40	
41–80	
81–120	

Think about why people want to collect information about people's ages. Whose data collection sheet would be more useful? Explain.

Key point

You can use a data collection sheet to record results from an experiment.

Q8 hint

Include a 'less than ☐ cm' class for shorter people and a 'greater than ☐ cm' class for taller people.

Key point

A table can show two sets of data.

Q10 hint

Record the Year 8 and Year 9 data in separate columns.

Explore

Reflect

3.2 Interpreting bar charts

You will learn to:
* Interpret complex bar charts.

Why learn this?
Diagrams and charts make it easier to spot patterns in data.

Fluency
Start with 0.
Count up in steps of 2, steps of 5, steps of 10.

Explore
How could a sports team use charts to measure its performance?

Exercise 3.2

1 The bar chart shows the number of items recycled by a family in one week.

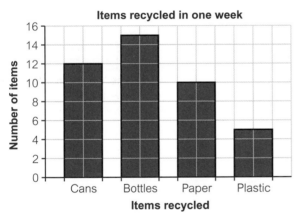

a How many cans were recycled?

b How many plastic items were recycled?

c How many items were recycled in total?

d How many more bottles were recycled than paper items?

2 This bar chart shows the number of phone calls made by a Year 8 class last month.

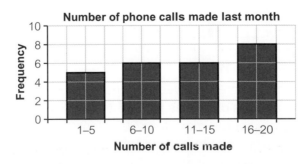

a What values are included in the class 6–10?

b How many students made between 1 and 5 phone calls?

c How many students made more than 10 phone calls?

d What is the modal class?

Warm up

3 The **dual bar chart** shows the colours of students' mobile phone covers.

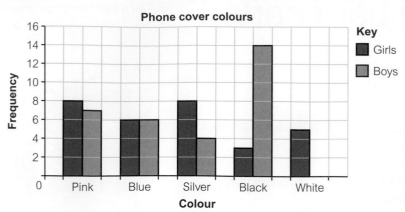

Key point

A **dual bar chart** shows two sets of data.

a How many girls have a black mobile phone cover?
b Which is the most popular colour for boys?
c Why does white only have one bar?
d How many students have a pink mobile phone cover?
e How many more girls have a silver mobile phone cover than boys?

Q3a hint

What colour bar represents girls?

4 **Problem-solving** This dual bar chart shows the number of texts and emails Charley sent each day.

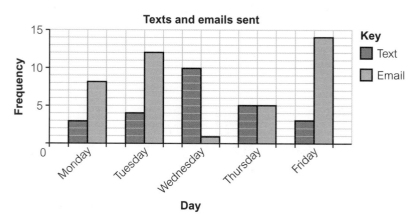

a How many emails did she send on Tuesday?
b On which day did she send an equal number of texts and emails?
c How many texts did Charley send during the week?
d Charley says that she sends twice as many texts as emails.
Is she correct? Show your working to explain.

5 **Real** This dual bar chart shows students' scores in two maths tests.

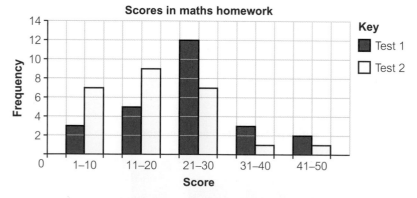

a How many students scored between 11 and 20 in Test 1?
b What is the modal class of scores for Test 2?
c How many students scored more than 30 in Test 2?
d **Problem-solving** The pass mark for each test is 20.
How many students passed each test?

Discussion Can you tell how many students scored more than 15 marks on Test 1? Explain.

6 Real / Problem-solving This **compound bar chart** shows the number of medals a team won in their last five competitions.

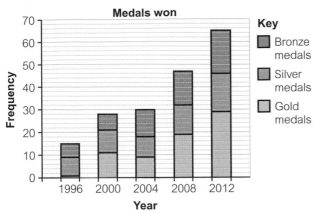

Key point

A **compound bar chart** combines different sets of data in one bar.

a In which year did they win the most medals in total?

b How many medals did they win in 2004?

c How many bronze medals did they win in 2000?

d How many more medals did they win in 2004 than in 1996?

e How many more silver medals did they win in 2012 than in 2004?

f Jane says, 'In 2012 they won more than three times as many medals than in 1996'. Is she correct? Show your working to explain.

7 This compound bar chart shows the sales of computer games, in thousands.

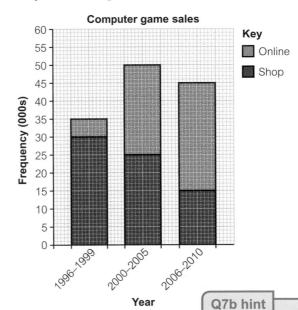

a How many shop sales were made between 2000 and 2005?

b How many online sales were made between 1996 and 1999?

c In which years were online sales most popular?

d In which years were online sales and shop sales equal?

e How many online sales were made between 2000 and 2010?

Discussion Can you see a pattern in the number of online sales? Describe the pattern.

Q7b hint

Start at the bottom of the red section and count up.

8 Explore How could a sports team use charts to measure its performance?

Is it easier to explore this question now you have completed the lesson? What further information do you need to be able to answer this?

9 Reflect Which did you find easier, working out the modal class from a table (as in lesson 3.1) or from a bar chart (as in this lesson)?

Think carefully about how you learn in all your subjects. Do you understand things better when there is a picture or a diagram?

3.3 Drawing bar charts

You will learn to:
- Draw bar charts for more than one set of data.

Why learn this?
Television companies use charts to show viewer numbers.

Fluency
Which is
- a dual bar chart
- a compound bar chart?

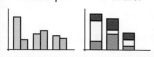

Explore
How has the population of the UK changed since 1950?

CONFIDENCE

Exercise 3.3

Warm up

1 This frequency table shows the number of coins some Year 7 and Year 8 students had on them one day.
   a How many
      i Year 7 students had between 4 and 7 coins
      ii Year 8 students had between 8 and 11 coins?
   b What was the modal class of number of coins for Year 8 students?
   c How many Year 7 students were surveyed?

Number of coins	Year 7	Year 8
0–3	8	10
4–7	4	5
8–11	6	2
12–15	3	3

2 Copy and complete the dual bar chart for the data in Q1.

Q2 hint

How many Year 7s had 8–11 coins?

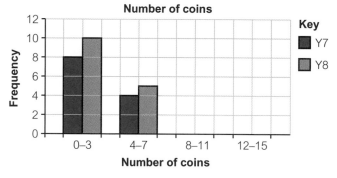

3 **Real** The table shows the number of drinks sold in Carmen's Café one week.

Day	Hot	Cold
Monday	10	8
Tuesday	2	12
Wednesday	5	6
Thursday	4	5
Friday	9	10

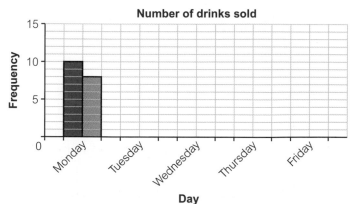

   a Does the blue bar in the chart represent hot or cold drinks?
   b Copy and complete the dual bar chart to show the data.

c Give your bar chart a key.

d Which day had the greatest difference between the number of hot drinks sold and the number of cold drinks sold?

Discussion What does 'Frequency' mean on the vertical axis?

4 **Real** The table shows the ages of the people in a tennis club and a badminton club.

Age (years)	Tennis	Badminton
10–19	10	8
20–29	20	25
30–39	18	20
40–49	15	15
50–59	8	12
60–69	5	8

a Look at all the groups. What is the highest frequency?

b Draw a pair of axes on graph paper. Label the vertical axis so it includes the highest value.

c Draw a dual bar chart to show the data.

Discussion Saima says, 'There are more people in the tennis club under the age of 40 than in the badminton club.' Is she correct? Explain.

Q4c hint

Give your bar chart a key and a title. Label the axes.

5 **Problem-solving** Jane recorded two friends' video game scores.

Karon

21 17 28 32 45 28 32 43 38 46 55 38 27 33

Alex

43 22 31 34 32 45 42 11   8   17 28 38 55 36

a Copy and complete this frequency table.

Score	Frequency	
	Karon	Alex
0–9		
10–19		
20–29		
30–39		
40–49		
50–59		

b Construct a dual bar chart for this data.

c What was the modal class of scores for

  i Karon

  ii Alex?

Discussion Who do you think was better at the video game?

6 **Problem-solving** 105 boys and 105 girls from Year 8 were asked some information about their favourite type of film.

	Thriller	Comedy	Animation	Drama
Boys	25	30	40	10
Girls	30	25	35	15

Draw a dual bar chart for this data.

Q6 hint

Use the horizontal axis for the type of film.

Worked example

This frequency table shows the numbers of packets of different flavour crisps sold in one week.

	Mon	Tues	Wed	Thurs	Fri
Plain crisps	10	5	6	8	9
Other flavours	12	10	2	3	2

Draw a compound bar chart to show this data.

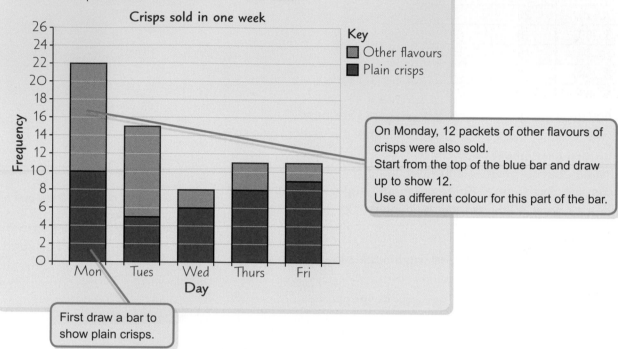

Key
- ■ Other flavours
- ■ Plain crisps

On Monday, 12 packets of other flavours of crisps were also sold.
Start from the top of the blue bar and draw up to show 12.
Use a different colour for this part of the bar.

First draw a bar to show plain crisps.

---

7 Robin asked 20 Year 8 students and 20 Year 9 students how they usually listen to music.

	CD	Download	Online
Year 8	6	12	10
Year 9	4	10	14

a Copy and complete this compound bar chart for the data.

b What is the most popular way of listening to music for Year 9s?

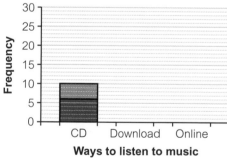

Ways to listen to music

8 Explore How has the population of the UK changed since 1950? Is it easier to explore this question now you have completed the lesson? What further information do you need to be able to answer this?

9 Reflect Make a list of the questions from this lesson you found easiest to answer.
What made them easier for you?
Make a list of the questions from this lesson you found hardest to answer.
What made them harder for you?

3.4 STEM: Pie charts

You will learn to:
• Interpret pie charts.

Why learn this?
Scientists draw pie charts to show compositions of different soils.

Fluency
What is
• half of 8000
• 3 × 40
• double 15000?
Order these fractions.
$\frac{1}{2}$ $\frac{1}{10}$ $\frac{1}{3}$ $\frac{1}{4}$

Explore
How could a scientist use pie charts to show the different types of animals on Earth?

Exercise 3.4: Scientific pie charts

1 a What fraction is
   i red   **ii** blue?
   b What percentage is
   i red   **ii** blue?

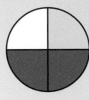

Warm up

2 STEM On the Moon there is a powdery 'soil' called regolith.
The pie chart shows the composition of regolith.
Write the different materials in order from the
greatest proportion to the least.

Composition of Moon regolith

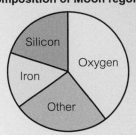

Worked example

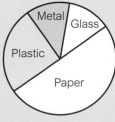

This **pie chart** shows the types of waste recycled in one town.
The town recycles 10 000 tonnes of paper. How many tonnes of waste does it recycle in total?

Paper = $\frac{1}{2}$ of pie chart

Paper = 10 000 tonnes = $\frac{1}{2}$ of all waste

Total recycled = 10 000 × 2 = 20 000 tonnes

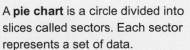

Key point
A **pie chart** is a circle divided into slices called sectors. Each sector represents a set of data.

3 Real In one day, John recorded the number of items he threw away. Here is a pie chart of his data.

Waste in one day

Key
- Plastic/glass
- Paper
- Organic

a What fraction of his waste was paper?

b What fraction was organic?

c He threw away 40 organic items. How many items did he throw away altogether?

d How many plastic items did he throw away?

4 STEM This pie chart shows the proportions of food types to make up a healthy diet.

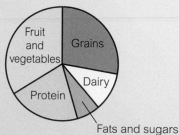

Use the words and fractions in the cloud to complete the sentences.

$\frac{1}{3}$ grains

fats and sugars $\frac{1}{2}$

a Approximately _____ of your food should be fruit and vegetables.

b Just over $\frac{1}{4}$ of your food should be _____.

c More than _____ should be made up of fruit, vegatables and grains.

d The smallest category should be _____.

5 STEM The pie chart shows the composition of a soil sample.

Soil composition

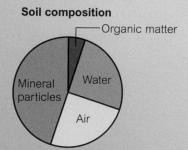

a What makes up the largest proportion of soil?

b What percentage of soil is

  i water   ii air?

c The mass of the soil sample is 2.8 kg. What is the combined mass of minerals and organic matter in the sample?

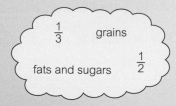

Q5a hint

Which is the largest sector?

Topic links: Fractions, Percentages, Angles

Subject links: Science (Q2–7)

6 STEM This pie chart shows the different sources of energy used to generate electricity in a city.

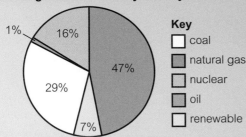

Sources of energy used to generate electricity in a city

1% 16% 47% 29% 7%

Key
- ☐ coal
- ☐ natural gas
- ☐ nuclear
- ☐ oil
- ☐ renewable

a Which is the most common energy source?

b What percentage of the energy comes from fossil fuels (gas, coal and oil)?

7 STEM / Problem-solving The pie chart shows the proportion of living species currently known.

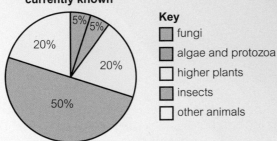

Number of living species currently known

5% 5% 20% 20% 50%

Key
- ☐ fungi
- ☐ algae and protozoa
- ☐ higher plants
- ☐ insects
- ☐ other animals

a Which type of species is the mode?

b There are approximately 70 000 species of fungi. How many species of algae and protozoa are there?

c How many species of insects are there?

Q7c hint

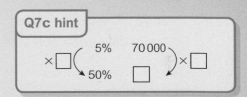

$\times \square \left(\begin{array}{c} 5\% \\ \searrow \\ 50\% \end{array} \right)$ $\begin{array}{c} 70\,000 \\ \square \end{array} \times \square$

8 Explore How could a scientist use pie charts to show the different types of animals on Earth?
What have you learned in this lesson to help you answer this question?
What other information do you need?

9 Reflect Charlie says that fractions help you to interpret pie charts (as in Q3 and Q4). What other areas of maths help you to interpret pie charts?
What maths skills do you need to draw pie charts?

Explore

Reflect

3 Check up

Log how you did on your Student Progression Chart.

Collecting data

1 A food delivery shop recorded the time it took to deliver the food from the time it was ordered.

Here are the delivery times in minutes during one day.

27   30   45   8   29   42   42
45   56   26   23   30   13

a What is wrong with this grouped frequency table?

Time (minutes)	Tally	Frequency
0–10		
10–20		
20–30		
30–40		
40–50		

b Draw a better frequency table and use the data to complete the table.

2 Claire wants to find out which of these drinks the students in her class prefer.

  orange   lemon   water   strawberry

Design a data collection sheet to collect this information.

Bar charts

3 This dual bar chart shows the eye colours of some boys and girls in Year 8.

a How many boys have blue eyes?

b For which eye colour are there equal numbers of boys and girls?

c How many students were surveyed altogether?

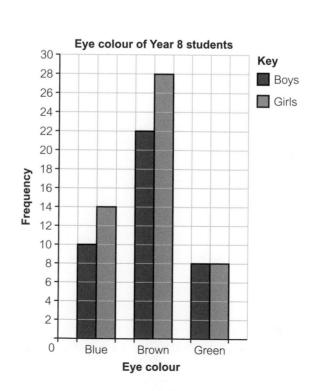

4 Copy and complete the dual bar chart of ages of teachers in a school.

Age (years)	Male	Female
21–30	3	6
31–40	4	4
41–50	8	5
51–60	5	4
61–70	3	4

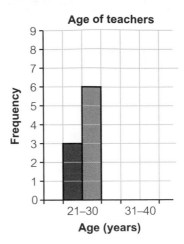

Age of teachers

5 This compound bar chart shows the results for a school's football and hockey teams.

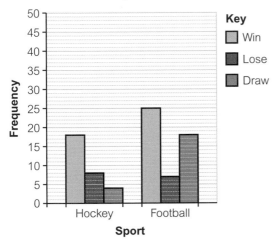

Key
- Win
- Lose
- Draw

a How many games did each team play?

b How many games did the hockey team win?

c How many games did the football team win?

d Which team was more successful?
Show your working to explain your answer.

Pie charts

6 This pie chart shows UK carbon emissions by source.
  a Which source produces the largest proportion of carbon emissions?
  b What percentage of the carbon emissions is produced by residential sources?
  c The UK produces two million tonnes of carbon emissions per week. How many tonnes are from transport? Give your answer as a fraction of 1 million.

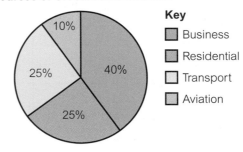

Sources of UK carbon emissions

Key
- Business
- Residential
- Transport
- Aviation

7 How sure are you of your answers? Were you mostly

😞 **Just guessing** 😐 **Feeling doubtful** 🙂 **Confident**

What next? Use your results to decide whether to strengthen or extend your learning.

Challenge

8 Design a data collection sheet to discover if your class is getting enough sleep.

> **Q8 hint**
>
> Collect data to the nearest hour.
> What other information do you need?

Master
P51

Check
P63

STRENGTHEN

Extend
P69

Test
P73

3 Strengthen

You will:
• Strengthen your understanding with practice.

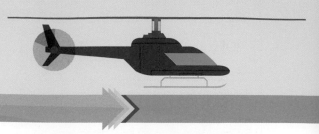

Collecting data

1 Shanaya finds these animals while pond dipping.

minnow	water boatman	tadpole
minnow	tadpole	minnow
tadpole	tadpole	water boatman
pond skater	tadpole	

Copy and complete this data collection sheet.

Type of animal	Tally	Frequency
minnow		

2 Wendy is designing a data collection sheet to find out the main method of transport students use to travel to school.

a Write down four ways students might travel to school.

b Draw a data collection sheet for Wendy including all your travel methods from part **a**, and a row called 'other'.

> **Q2b hint**
>
> Remember to include a tally column and a frequency column.

3 Greg wants to design a data collection sheet for the number of eggs laid by his hens.

a Which of these lists of classes have

  i equal width groups plus a 'greater than' class

  ii no overlaps

  iii space to record all possible data?

A

Number of eggs
0–2
2–4
4–6
>6

B

Number of eggs
1–2
3–4
5–6
>6

C

Number of eggs
0–1
2–3
4–5
>5

D

Number of eggs
0
1–2
2–4
4–5

b Which list is the best one?

> **Q3b hint**
>
> Which list has all of **i**, **ii** and **iii**?

4 Aimee records the number of items in people's shopping baskets.

3	24	6	4	15	2	1	19
13	3	5	5	7	4	12	8
10	2	3	9	2	3	4	18
12	6	20	13	17	23	20	25

a What is the smallest number of items?

b What is the largest number of items?

c Write five equal-sized classes to group this data.

> **Q4c hint**
>
> How big should the classes be?

Bar charts

1 Danielle surveyed her classmates to find out how many cousins they have.

Number of cousins	Frequency
0–4	3
5–9	5
10–14	7
15–19	4
20–24	1

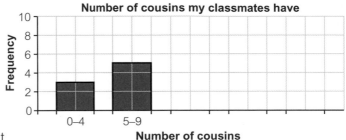

a Copy and complete the grouped bar chart.

b Which group is the modal class?

c How many students have more than 14 cousins?

2 The table shows the number of adults and children visiting a sports centre during the summer.

	Adults	Children
June	25	30
July	30	40
August	20	40

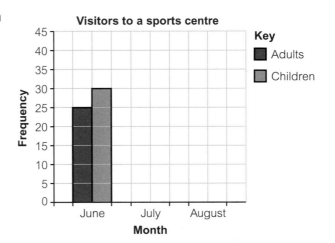

a How many adults visited the centre in June?

b Copy and complete the dual bar chart. Draw the blue bar for adults in July first.

c In which month was there the largest difference between adults and children?

> **Q2c hint**
>
> Which month has the greatest difference in the heights of the bars?

3 The table shows the scores of Year 8 and Year 9 students in a spelling test.

Scores in a spelling test	Year 8	Year 9
0–6	4	5
7–13	10	9
14–20	6	8
21–27	5	3

a How many students took part in the test?

b Copy the grid below and draw a dual bar chart.

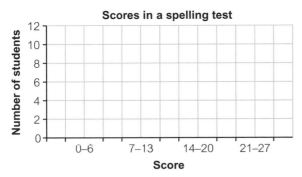

c How many Year 9 students scored 21 or more?

d How many students altogether scored 21 or more?

4 The dual bar chart shows the items Kalim and Rebecca recycled in one month.

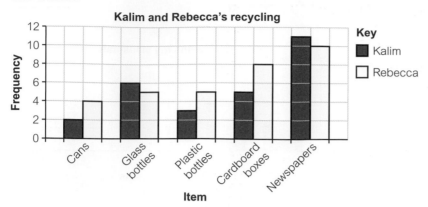

Kalim and Rebecca's recycling

Key
■ Kalim
☐ Rebecca

Item

a How many plastic bottles did Kalim recycle?
b Which items did Rebecca recycle the most?
c Who recycled more newspapers?
d How many cans were recycled altogether?

Q4 hint

Look at the chart carefully.
Make sure you understand the key.
From the top of each bar, look across to the frequency to see how many of that item were recycled.

5 The table shows the number of bicycles sold in a shop during 3 months.

a Copy and complete this compound bar chart.

	Apr	May	Jun
Adult bicycles	10	15	12
Child bicycles	15	10	12

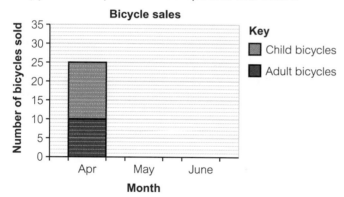

Bicycle sales

Key
☐ Child bicycles
■ Adult bicycles

Month

Q5a hint

How many adult bicycles were sold in May? Draw the blue bar that height. Start at the top of the blue bar and count up 10 for the child bicycles. Draw the red bar to that height.

b How many bicycles were sold in April altogether?
c In which month were most bicycles sold?
   How can you tell?
d In which month were most adult bicycles sold? How can you tell?
e In which month were more child than adult bicycles sold?

Q5e hint

Which month has a taller red bar than blue bar?

6 The chart shows the amount of time two students, Atifa and Joanne, spent talking, texting and playing games on their mobile phones one day.

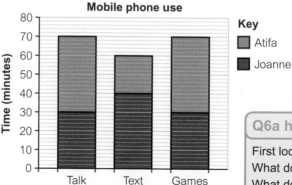

Mobile phone use

Key
■ Atifa
■ Joanne

Phone use

a How long did Joanne spend talking?
b How long did Atifa spend texting?
c Who spent the most time playing games?
d How many minutes altogether did Atifa spend talking, texting and gaming?

Q6a hint

First look at the key.
What does red represent?
What does blue represent?

Pie charts

1 The pie chart shows some students' favourite pets.

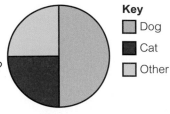

Key
- Dog
- Cat
- Other

  a What is the most common favourite pet?

  b What fraction of the students prefer dogs?

  c There are 20 students in the class. How many of them prefer dogs?

  d How many students like cats best?

Q1d hint

What fraction liked cats?

2 Tina asked some students to pick a colour. The pie chart shows the results.

Key
- Green
- Blue
- Red
- Yellow

  a What fraction of the students chose green?

16 students chose green.

  b Sketch or trace the pie chart. Write 16 in the green sector.

  c How many students chose blue? Write this number in the sector.

  d How many chose
    i red   **ii** yellow?
    Write these numbers in the sectors.

  e How many students were asked?

Q2c hint

The blue sector is half the size of the green sector

3 The pie chart shows the favourite drinks of a football team.

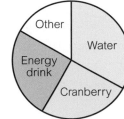

Other, Water, Energy drink, Cranberry

  a What is the most popular drink?

  b The manager buys 1000 bottles of drink. How many bottles of energy drink should he buy?

Q3b hint

What fraction of the team prefer the energy drink? Work out this fraction of 1000.

4 **STEM** This pie chart shows how people in a town accessed the internet in 2013.

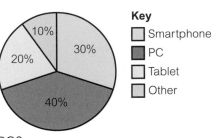

10%, 30%, 20%, 40%

Key
- Smartphone
- PC
- Tablet
- Other

  a What was the most common way of accessing the internet?

  b What percentage of people accessed the internet using a smartphone?

  c 3000 people surveyed answered 'other'. How many people used a PC?

Q4c hint

$\times \square \underset{40\%}{\overset{10\%}{\curvearrowright}} \square \overset{3000}{\underset{}{\curvearrowright}} \times \square$

Enrichment

1 Alex wants to find out how many students have a school dinner, a packed lunch or go home for lunch.

  a Design a data collection sheet to collect this information.

  b Ask 20 students in your class and complete the data collection sheet.

  c How many students in your class have school dinners?

Q1a hint

You could draw a frequency table to collect this data.

2 **Reflect** For these strengthen lessons, copy and complete these sentences.

I found questions ____ easiest. They were on ____ (list the topics)

I found questions ____ most difficult. I still need help with ____ (list the topics)

Reflect

3 Extend

You will:
- Extend your understanding with problem-solving.

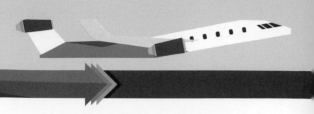

1 The table shows the results of a survey of the hair colours of boys and girls in Year 8.

	Boys	Girls
black		
brown		
fair	7	10
red	4	8
other	2	2

a Copy and complete the frequency table from the dual bar chart.

b Copy and complete the dual bar chart.

c For which hair colour was the difference between boys and girls largest?

d For which category was the number of boys and girls equal?

e What was the total number of girls surveyed?

f What is the modal hair colour for girls?

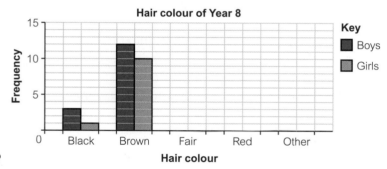

2 The bar chart shows the number of homeworks missed during one term in classes 8W and 8T.

a What is the range for the numbers of homeworks missed in 8W?

b How many students missed a homework in 8W?

c Copy and complete the statements below to find the total number of homeworks missed in 8W.

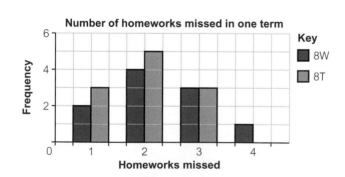

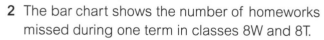2 students missed 1 piece → 2 pieces missed

4 missed 2 pieces → 8 pieces missed

3 missed 3 pieces → ☐ pieces missed

☐ missed 4 pieces → ☐ pieces missed

Total = ☐

d Find the mean number of homeworks missed in 8W.

e Find the mean and range for the number of homeworks missed in 8T.

Q2a hint

Range = largest value − smallest value

Q2d hint

Mean
= total number of homeworks missed
÷ total number of students

3 James and Alyssa played the hand game of rock, paper, scissors.
They put their results in a table.

	James	Alyssa
Win		
Lose	8	5
Draw	2	2

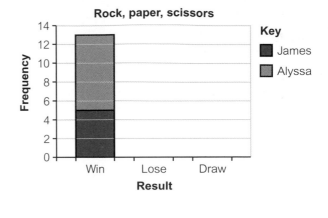

Rock, paper, scissors

a Copy and complete the compound bar chart and the table.

b What do you notice about the total numbers of games won and lost?

4 **Problem-solving** Martha is going to do an experiment where she will record the colours spun on a spinner.
Design a table that Martha could use to record her results.

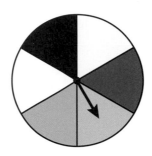

5 **Real** The bar chart shows the number of gold, silver and bronze medals won by three countries' teams in a sports contest.

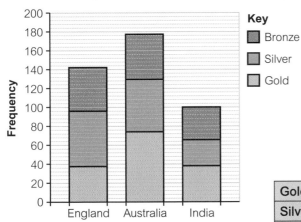

Key
Bronze
Silver
Gold

Copy and complete this table.

	England	Australia	India
Gold			
Silver			
Bronze			

6 **Real** The bar charts show the games won by two tennis players from 2011 to 2013.

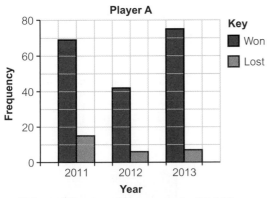

Player A

Key
Won
Lost

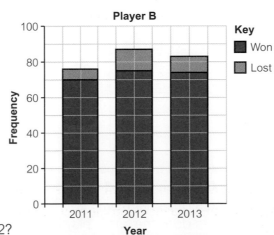

Player B

Key
Won
Lost

a Who played more games in 2011?

b How many games did player A play in 2012?

7 The compound bar chart shows the percentage of items sold in a museum shop one weekend.
  a On which day was the greater percentage of gifts sold?
  b On which day were equal percentages of gifts and drinks sold?

  Discussion Laura said that they sold more gifts on Sunday than on Saturday. Discuss why this may not be correct.

Percentage of items sold in a museum during a weekend

8 Problem-solving The pie charts show how Year 8 and Year 9 students at Hightown School travel to school.
There are 80 students in Year 8 and 50 students in Year 9.

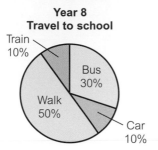 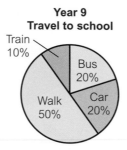

  a What percentage of students in Year 8 walk to school?
  b How many students in Year 8 walk to school?
  c How many students in Year 9 walk to school?

9 Problem-solving The pie charts show two families' average weekly spending.

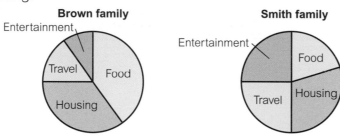

  a Which family spends the larger proportion of their money on food?
  b The Smiths say they spend more money on entertainment each week than the Browns. Explain why the Smiths may be wrong.

> **Q9b hint**
>
> Do you know how much each family spends?

10 The pie chart shows a family's Playstation use.
  a Which member of the family plays the most?
  b Measure the angle of each sector of the pie chart and complete the table below.

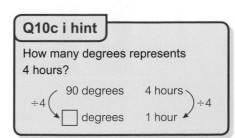

Playstation use

Family member	Angle
Dad	
Mum	
Mark	
Nathaniel	
Gemma	

  c Gemma spends 4 hours a week using the Playstation.
    i How many hours does her dad play?
    ii How many hours does her mum play?
    iii How many hours does the family play in total each week?

> **Q10c i hint**
>
> How many degrees represents 4 hours?
>
> ÷4 (90 degrees → ☐ degrees)   4 hours → 1 hour) ÷4

11 **Real** These pie charts show the formats for listening to music in 2000 and 2010.

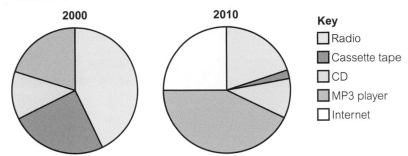

Key
- ☐ Radio
- ◼ Cassette tape
- ☐ CD
- ◼ MP3 player
- ☐ Internet

Write the missing words in this report on how formats for listening to music have changed from 2000 to 2010.

In 2010, most people listened to music using ....

In 2000, most people listened to music by ....

In 2000, about $\frac{1}{4}$ of people used the .... to listen to music.

In 2000, people did not use the .... to listen to music but in 2010, about a $\frac{1}{4}$ of people used the .... to listen to music.

12 Caitlin played some games of football in a tournament. The percentage of games she won, lost and drew are shown in the table.
  a Draw a pie chart to show this information.
  b How many degrees does 50% represent?

Result	Number of games
win	50%
lose	25%
draw	25%

Q12a hint

Draw a circle using compasses.

Caitlin played another tournament.
The number of games that she won, lost and drew are shown in the table.
  c How many games did she play in the second tournament?
  d Copy and complete:

Result	Number of games
win	12
lose	6
draw	18

$\div \square \left(\overset{\square \text{ games}}{\underset{1 \text{ game}}{}} \quad \overset{360°}{\underset{\square°}{}} \right) \div \square$

  e Copy and complete the table showing the angles you will need to draw in the pie chart.
  f Draw an accurate pie chart for this data.

Result	Number of games	Angle
win	12	12 × ☐° =
lose	6	6 × ☐° =
draw	18	☐ × ☐° =

13 The table shows the composition of the atmosphere on Mars.

Element	Percentage
nitrogen	2.7
carbon dioxide	95
argon	1.6
other	0.7

Use a spreadsheet to create a pie chart for the data.

14 **Reflect** In this unit you have used lots of different types of charts. Copy and complete this list of charts you have used, and write an example of the type of data you can show using each chart.

Q14 hint

Look back over your work from this unit for examples.

Dual bar charts: comparing boys' and girls' heights at different ages

Pie charts:

Reflect

3 Unit test

Log how you did on your Student Progression Chart.

1 Design a data collection sheet to find out your class's favourite pizza topping.

2 This pie chart shows the types of cake on a stall.

   a Which type of cake is the mode?

   b Jonah says, 'There are more brownies than all the other cakes put together.' Is he correct? Explain.

   c There were 12 cupcakes on the stall. How many cakes were there altogether?

Cakes on stall

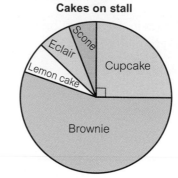

3 Jodie did a survey of students' favourite subjects. The pie chart shows her results.

   a What fraction of the students asked chose maths?

   b 15 students chose science.

     i How many students liked maths?

     ii How many students were there altogether?

Favourite subjects

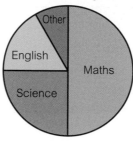

4 **Real** The pie chart shows the causes of animal extinction.

   a What has been the main cause of animal extinction?

   b Write the missing words and fractions in these sentences.

     About _____ of species have been made extinct through hunting. _____ and _____ have been the main causes of extinction.

Known cause of animal extinction

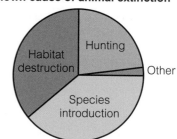

5 The dual bar chart shows the scores of a Year 8 class and a Year 9 class in a unit test.

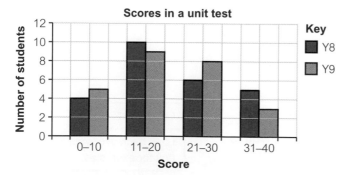

How many Year 9s scored more than 20?

6 The table shows the number of students who were late in two Year 8 classes one week.

Number of students late	8W	8R
Monday	3	5
Tuesday	4	4
Wednesday	1	2
Thursday	0	1
Friday	1	1

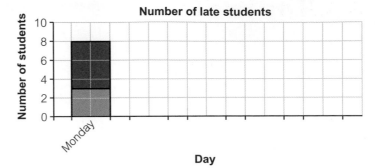

a Copy and complete the compound bar chart.

b What is the difference in the total number of students late in 8R and 8W?

c Write a sentence comparing the numbers of late students in 8R and 8W.

7 Jacqui asked her friends how many texts they had sent one day. Here are her results.

| 8 | 15 | 22 | 13 | 12 | 21 | 19 | 12 | 25 | 21 | 18 | 17 | 12 |
| 2 | 4 | 12 | 13 | 18 | 22 | 21 | 17 | 16 | 12 | 3 | 5 |

a Copy and complete this grouped frequency table.

Number of texts	Tally	Frequency
1–5		
6–10		
11–15		
16–20		
21–25		

b How many friends did she ask?

c What is the modal class?

d How many friends sent less than 16 texts?

Challenge

8 a Design a data collection sheet for finding out the favourite _____ of people in your class.

b Choose a way of representing the information you could collect.

c Write a comment on your findings.

> **Q8a hint**
>
> Do you want to know their favourite sport? Colour? Shop? Food?

9 Reflect Think back to when you have struggled to answer a question in a maths test.

a Write two words that describe how you felt.

b Write two things you could do when you're finding it difficult to answer a question.

c Imagine you have another maths test and you do the two things you wrote in part **b**. How do you think you might feel then?

4.1 Simplifying expressions

You will learn to:
- Simplify expressions by collecting like terms.

Why learn this?
Engineers designing theme park rides simplify expressions to work out forces.

Fluency
Work out
- $3 + 5$
- $4 - 6$
- $-2 + 5$
- $-2 - 5$

Explore
What expressions will simplify to give $20x + 12y$?

CONFIDENCE

Exercise 4.1

Warm up

1 Match each yellow card with its correct simplified blue card.

| $2x + 5x$ | $8x - 2x$ | $3x + x$ | $12x - 7x$ |

| $4x$ | $5x$ | $6x$ | $7x$ |

Q1 hint
Write your answers as $2x + 5x = \square$

2 Simplify
  a $5x + 6x + 3x$ **b** $8m + 2m - 3m$
  c $9y - 4y + 2y$ **d** $4z + 5z - z$
  e $12p - 2p - 5p$ **f** $9w - 7w + 4w - 5w$

3 Work out each subtraction.
   The first one is done for you.
  a $3 - 5 = -2$ $3b - 5b = -2b$
  b $4 - 9$ $4a - 9a$
  c $8 - 12$ $8x - 12x$
  d $5 - 3 - 10$ $5y - 3y - 10y$

Key point
When you subtract numbers you can have negative answers.
The same is true for algebra.

4 Simplify
  a $2 \times x$ **b** $6 \times y$
  c $b \div 3$ **d** $c \div 5$
  e $c \times d$ **f** $p \times q$
  Discussion Does $a \times 4$ simplify to $4a$ or $a4$?
  Does $c \times b$ simplify to cb or bc? What are the rules?

Q4 hint
$5 \times a$ simplifies to $5a$
$a \div 5$ simplifies to $\frac{a}{5}$
$a \times b$ simplifies to ab

5 Simplify
  a $z \times 5$ **b** $a \times 11$
  c $z \times y$ **d** $r \times p$

Topic links: Multiplication facts to 12 × 12, Negative numbers, Perimeter

6 Match each blue card with its equivalent yellow card.

| $a \times 4$ | $4 + a$ | $a \div 4$ | $4 \div a$ | $a \times b$ | $b + a$ |

| $\dfrac{a}{4}$ | ab | $4a$ | $a + b$ | $a + 4$ | $\dfrac{4}{a}$ |

Q6 hint

$4 + a$ is the same as $a + 4$

Worked example

Simplify
a $3 \times 4y$
b $10x \div 2$

a $3 \times 4y = 12y$

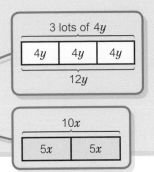

3 lots of $4y$

| $4y$ | $4y$ | $4y$ |
$12y$

b $10x \div 2 = 5x$

$10x$
| $5x$ | $5x$ |

7 Simplify
a $5 \times 2x$ **b** $4 \times 6y$
c $3p \times 5$ **d** $9t \times 7$
e $12x \div 6$ **f** $15y \div 5$
g $\dfrac{10m}{2}$ **h** $\dfrac{6r}{3}$

Worked example

Simplify $2b + 3r + 5b$

$2b + 3r + 5b = 2b + 5b + 3r$

$= 7b + 3r$

Think of some blue and red tiles.
The question is:

You can add together the blue tiles, but you can't add the blue tiles to the red tiles.
The answer is:

Key point

Like terms contain the same letter (or contain no letter). For example, $5x$ and $7x$ are like terms, but $4x$ and $3y$ are not like terms. You can **simplify** an expression by collecting like terms.

8 Simplify by collecting **like terms**.
a $4r + 5b + 6r$
b $8a + 3c + 5a$
c $3t + 9 + 7t + 2$
d $7x + 3y + 2x + y$

Q8c hint

$3t$ and $7t$ are like terms.
9 and 2 are like terms.

9 **Problem-solving** Copy and complete this addition pyramid.
Each brick is the sum of the two bricks below it.

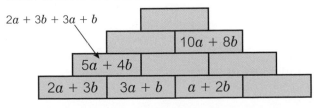

$2a + 3b + 3a + b$

| $10a + 8b$ |
| $5a + 4b$ |
| $2a + 3b$ | $3a + b$ | $a + 2b$ |

10 Simplify by collecting like terms.

   a $8g + 5h - 3g = 8g - 3g + 5h = \square g + 5h$
   b $6x - 2y - 3x = 6x - 3x - 2y = \square x - 2y$
   c $9d + 4k - 5d - 2k$
   d $5x - 3y - 2x$
   e $4a + 5b - 8a$
   f $7n + 5p - 5n - 8p$
   g $7w + 3u - 6u - 6w$

Q10e hint

$4 - 8 = -4$

11 Which two of these expressions simplify to give the same answer?

   A $6x + 4y - 10x - 7y + 5x$

   B $2x + 6x + y - 7x - 5y$

   C $2x + 7y - x - 8y - 2y$

12 **Reasoning** **Show that** the perimeter of this triangle is $16w + 15z$.

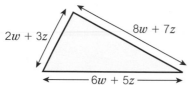

$2w + 3z$ $8w + 7z$ $6w + 5z$

Q12 Literacy hint

Show that means you need to show your working.

Investigation   **Problem-solving**

Work with a partner to solve this puzzle.
Here are 10 dominoes.

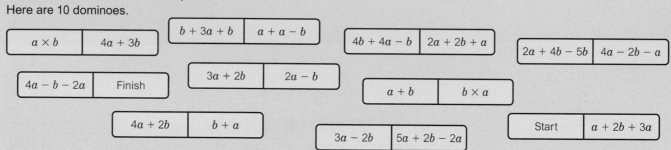

$a \times b$	$4a + 3b$
$b + 3a + b$	$a + a - b$
$4b + 4a - b$	$2a + 2b + a$
$2a + 4b - 5b$	$4a - 2b - a$
$4a - b - 2a$	Finish
$3a + 2b$	$2a - b$
$a + b$	$b \times a$
$4a + 2b$	$b + a$
$3a - 2b$	$5a + 2b - 2a$
Start	$a + 2b + 3a$

The dominoes need to be placed end to end to match equivalent expressions.
The first two dominoes are:

| Start | $a + 2b + 3a$ | $4a + 2b$ | $b + a$ |

1 Work out the order of the 10 dominoes.
2 Is there only one way the dominoes can be linked? Explain your answer.

---

13 **Explore** What expressions will simplify to give $20x + 12y$?
   Is it easier to explore this question now you have completed the lesson?
   What further information do you need to be able to answer this?

14 **Reflect** Rhys says, 'Simplifying in maths means writing more simply.'
   Do you agree with Rhys?
   Write down a question (and answer) from this lesson to show why you
   agree or disagree.
   Fatima says, 'Simplifying always involves like terms.'
   Do you agree with Fatima?
   Write down a question (and answer) from this lesson to show why you
   agree or disagree.

Explore

Reflect

4.2 Functions

You will learn to:
- Find outputs and inputs of function machines
- Construct functions.

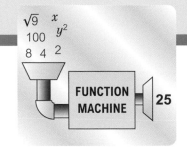

Why learn this?
Function machines can be used to write rules to solve problems.

Fluency
Work out the missing numbers.
- $3 + 4 = \square$
- $6 + \square = 11$
- $\square - 3 = 7$
- $20 - \square = 12$

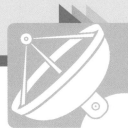

Explore
How can you use a function machine to work out the mass of gold in a necklace that isn't all gold?

Exercise 4.2

1 Work out
   a 7×1000
   b 23×1000
   c $3000 \div 1000$
   d $5500 \div 1000$

2 Work out the outputs of each function machine.

   a
   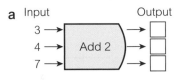
   Input: 3, 4, 7 → Add 2 → Output

   b
   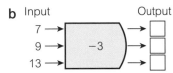
   Input: 7, 9, 13 → −3 → Output

   c
   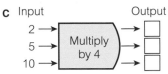
   Input: 2, 5, 10 → Multiply by 4 → Output

   d
   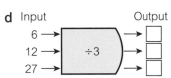
   Input: 6, 12, 27 → ÷3 → Output

3 Write down the function for each machine.

   a
   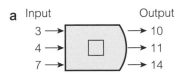
   Input: 3, 4, 7 → □ → Output: 10, 11, 14

   b
   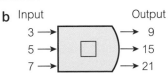
   Input: 3, 5, 7 → □ → Output: 9, 15, 21

4 Write down the missing function for each **inverse function** machine.

   a
   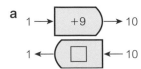
   $1 \rightarrow +9 \rightarrow 10$
   $1 \leftarrow \square \leftarrow 10$

   b
   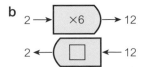
   $2 \rightarrow \times 6 \rightarrow 12$
   $2 \leftarrow \square \leftarrow 12$

   c
   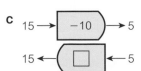
   $15 \rightarrow -10 \rightarrow 5$
   $15 \leftarrow \square \leftarrow 5$

   d
   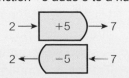
   $8 \rightarrow \div 4 \rightarrow 2$
   $8 \leftarrow \square \leftarrow 2$

Key point
The function +5 adds 5 to a number.

$2 \rightarrow +5 \rightarrow 7$
$2 \leftarrow -5 \leftarrow 7$

The **inverse function** is −5 because it reverses the effect of adding 5.

Warm up

Worked example

Work out the missing input for this function machine.

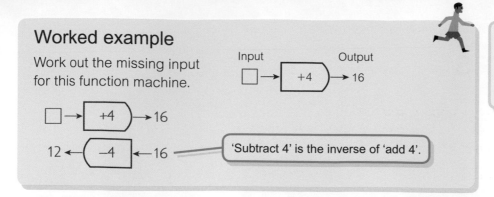

'Subtract 4' is the inverse of 'add 4'.

Key point

You can use the inverse function to find the input of a function machine when you know the output.

5 Work out the missing inputs for these function machines.

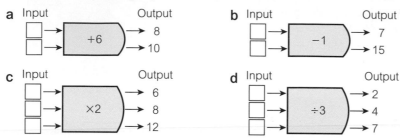

a
Input → +6 → Output
8
10

b
Input → −1 → Output
7
15

c
Input → ×2 → Output
6
8
12

d
Input → ÷3 → Output
2
4
7

6 **Problem-solving** Work out the missing inputs for these function machines.

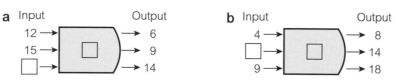

a
Input → [ ] → Output
12 → 6
15 → 9
[ ] → 14

b
Input → [ ] → Output
4 → 8
[ ] → 14
9 → 18

Q6a Strategy hint

Work out a function that takes the input 12 and gives the output 6. Does this function work for input 15 and output 9?

7 **Problem-solving** Copy and complete the table of inputs and outputs for this function machine.

[ ] → ×3 → [ ]

Input	Output
0	
	15
6	
	27

8 Write down the missing function for this function machine.

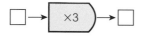

Input: metres → [ ] → Output: centimetres

Q8 hint

How do you convert metres to centimetres?

9 **Real** To change a measurement in cm³ to a measurement in litres, divide by 1000.

a Write down the missing function for this function machine.

Input: cm³ → [ ] → Output: litres

b Kelly wants to fill three plant pots with compost.
The plant pots hold 2000 cm³, 4500 cm³ and 9200 cm³.
Use the function machine from part **a** to work out the number of litres of compost each pot needs.

c A shop sells compost in three different size bags.
The bags contain 8 litres, 12 litres and 20 litres.
How many cm³ of compost does each bag contain?

Topic links: Multiplication facts to 12 × 12, Negative numbers, Dividing by 1000, Converting between cm³ and litres, Decimals, Ratio

Subject links: Science (Q11)

10 Draw three different function machines with these outputs.

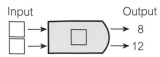

Input   Output
→ 8
→ 12

For each machine, write in the function and the inputs.

Discussion Did you draw the same function machines as others in your class? Explain how you decided on your function machines.

11 **STEM** The ratio of the mass of aluminium to other materials in a plasma TV is $1:4$.

a What fraction of the mass of the TV is aluminium?

b The mass of a plasma TV is 10 kg.
What is the mass of aluminium in this TV?

c Write down the missing function for this function machine.

Input   Output

mass of TV → □ → mass of aluminium

d Two different plasma TVs have masses of 15 kg and 25 kg.
Use the function machine from part **c** to work out the mass of aluminium in each TV.

e The mass of aluminium in a different plasma TV is 7 kg.
What is the mass of the TV?

12 Work out the missing outputs and inputs for each function machine.

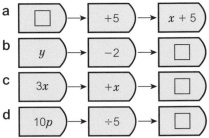

a $\square$ → $+5$ → $x+5$

b y → -2 → $\square$

c $3x$ → $+x$ → $\square$

d $10p$ → $\div 5$ → $\square$

13 **Explore** How can you use a function machine to work out the mass of gold in a necklace that isn't all gold?
Is it easier to explore this question now you have completed the lesson? What further information do you need to be able to answer this?

14 **Reflect** After this lesson Nigel says, 'I can use inverse functions to check whether I have done a calculation properly.'
Write down a calculation and check it using an inverse function.
When else do you think inverse functions might be useful?

4.3 Solving equations

You will learn to:
- Solve simple equations and check the solution is correct
- Understand the difference between an expression and an equation, and identify the unknown in an equation.

CONFIDENCE

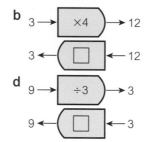

Why learn this?
Scientists solve equations to work out the time it will take a space rocket to travel a certain distance.

Fluency
When $x = 10$, work out
- $x + 6$
- $x - 3$
- $4 \times x$
- $x \div 2$

Explore
How long will it take to do a charity walk?

Exercise 4.3

Warm up

1 Write down the missing function for each inverse function machine.

a $3 \rightarrow +2 \rightarrow 5$

$3 \leftarrow \square \leftarrow 5$

b $3 \rightarrow \times 4 \rightarrow 12$

$3 \leftarrow \square \leftarrow 12$

c $10 \rightarrow -4 \rightarrow 6$

$10 \leftarrow \square \leftarrow 6$

d $9 \rightarrow \div 3 \rightarrow 3$

$9 \leftarrow \square \leftarrow 3$

2 Work out the missing inputs for these function machines.

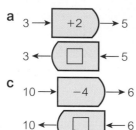

a Input $\rightarrow -5 \rightarrow$ Output 0, 8

b Input $\rightarrow +2 \rightarrow$ Output 10, 17

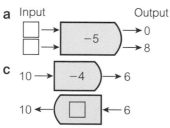

c $10 \rightarrow -4 \rightarrow 6$

$10 \leftarrow \square \leftarrow 6$

d $9 \rightarrow \div 3 \rightarrow 3$

$9 \leftarrow \square \leftarrow 3$

3 Work out the missing number in each calculation.
   a $\square + 2 = 5$ b $6 - \square = 4$ c $3 \times \square = 15$ d $\square \div 2 = 3$

4 Write down whether each of these is an **expression** or an **equation**. The first one is done for you.

   a $x + 5$ is an expression
   b $x + 5 = 14$
   c $5a + 4b$
   d $3d + 2c - 8d$
   e $4m = 16$
   f $30 = 3x - 9$
   g $d + \dfrac{d}{2}$
   h $24 = 5x + 3x$

Discussion What is the difference between an equation and a formula?

Key point

An **expression** contains letters and numbers. An **equation** contains numbers, one unknown letter and an = sign.

Subject links: Science (Q9)

5 Reasoning In the equation $4x - 7 = 31$, x is called the **unknown**.

a Write down the unknown in each of these equations.

   i $5y + 3 = 18$ **ii** $7t = 21$ **iii** $4 = v - 9$

b Write your own equation with an unknown of

   i x **ii** y **iii** z

Discussion Why is it called an unknown?

Q5 hint

In the equation $4x - 7 = 31$, x is the **unknown**.

Worked example

Solve the equation $x + 7 = 12$.

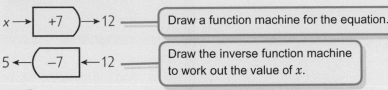

$x \rightarrow \boxed{+7} \rightarrow 12$ — Draw a function machine for the equation.

$5 \leftarrow \boxed{-7} \leftarrow 12$ — Draw the inverse function machine to work out the value of x.

$x = 5$

Check: $x + 7 = 5 + 7 = 12$ ✓ — Check by substituting $x = 5$ back into $x + 7$.

Key point

To **solve** an equation means to work out the value of the unknown number. The **solution** is the value for the unknown.

6 Solve these equations. Check your **solutions**.

  a $x + 4 = 10$ **b** $y + 3 = 15$

  c $z + 9 = 11$ **d** $n - 1 = 5$

  e $m - 3 = 7$ **f** $p - 10 = 6$

Q6 Strategy hint

Draw a function machine.

7 Solve these equations. Check your solutions.

  a $2x = 8$ **b** $10v = 80$

  c $3y = 21$ **d** $12k = 36$

  e $\dfrac{p}{4} = 6$ **f** $\dfrac{u}{2} = 11$

  g $\dfrac{x}{5} = 10$ **h** $\dfrac{m}{3} = 12$

Q7a hint

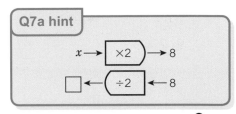

$x \rightarrow \boxed{\times 2} \rightarrow 8$

$\square \leftarrow \boxed{\div 2} \leftarrow 8$

8 Finance Priya works out her **gross income** each month using this rule:

    gross income − tax = take-home pay

At the end of one month Priya pays £130 tax and her take-home pay is £1220.

She writes this equation: $G - 130 = 1220$

Solve the equation to work out Priya's gross income this month.

Q8 Literacy hint

Gross income is the amount you earn before tax is paid.

9 STEM An engineer uses this equation to work out the time it takes, in seconds, a car to accelerate from 0 to 60 miles per hour:

    $60 = 5t$

Solve the equation to work out the value of t.

10 Explore How long will it take to do a charity walk?

Is it easier to explore this question now you have completed the lesson?
What further information do you need to be able to answer this?

11 Reflect Look back at the hint in Q6. Did using a function machine help you to solve the equations?

If not, what other method did you use?
Compare your methods with others in your class.

Explore

Reflect

4.4 Using brackets

You will learn to:
- Use brackets with numbers and letters.

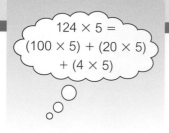

$$124 \times 5 =$$
$$(100 \times 5) + (20 \times 5)$$
$$+ (4 \times 5)$$

Why learn this?
Using brackets can often make mental calculations easier.

Fluency
Work out
- 6×5
- 3×9
- 4×2
- 3×20
- 5×70

What is 370p in £s?

Explore
How could you multiply a number by 27 in your head?

Exercise 4.4

1 Simplify

  a $6 \times x$ **b** $3 \times y$ **c** $4 \times z$

2 Work out

  a $2 \times 3 + 4 \times 3$ **b** $6 \times 5 \times 2$

Q2 hint

Do Multiplication and Division before Addition and Subtraction.

3 Work out the area of each rectangle.

  a

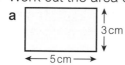

3 cm

5 cm

  b

8 cm

10 cm

Area = length × width
      = 5 × 3
      = □ cm²

4 **Reasoning** Copy and complete the workings to find the area of these green rectangles.

  a

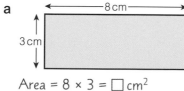

8 cm

3 cm

Area = 8 × 3 = □ cm²

  b

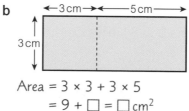

3 cm · 5 cm

3 cm

Area = 3 × 3 + 3 × 5
      = 9 + □ = □ cm²

Key point

When you multiply out a bracket, multiply every number inside the bracket by the number outside the bracket.

  c What do you notice about your answers to parts **a** and **b**?

  Discussion Why are the answers to parts **a** and **b** the same?

Worked example

Work out $4 \times (10 + 6)$

$4 \times (10 + 6) = 4 \times 10 + 4 \times 6$
             $= 40 + 24$
             $= 64$

Think of working out the area of a rectangle.

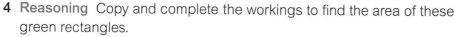

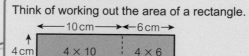

10 cm · 6 cm

4 cm

| 4 × 10 | 4 × 6 |
| 40 | 24 |

Total area = 64 cm²

Topic links: Area, Using formulae   **Subject links:** Science (Q10)

5 Work out by multiplying out the brackets.
 a $5 \times (3 + 9)$ **b** $2 \times (8 + 5)$ **c** $3(10 + 7)$
 d $6(4 + 12)$ **e** $7(10 - 8)$ **f** $8(11 - 3)$

Q5c hint

$3(10 + 7)$ means $3 \times (10 + 7)$.
You don't need to write the × sign.

6 **Real** Jules runs a market stall selling fruit.
 She sells pineapples for 85p each.
 A customer buys 7 pineapples.
 Copy and complete the working to show
 how Jules calculates the total price.

$$7 \times 85 = 7 \times (\square + 5)$$
$$= \square + \square$$
$$= \square \text{ pence}$$
$$= £\square$$

7 **Problem-solving** Match each blue rectangle card to its equivalent
 yellow oval card.

 A $\boxed{2 \times 4 + 2 \times 3}$ **i** $(4(3 + 9))$

 B $\boxed{7 \times 3 + 7 \times 2}$ **ii** $(3(2 + 7))$

 C $\boxed{4 \times 3 + 4 \times 9}$ **iii** $(2(4 + 3))$

 D $\boxed{3 \times 2 + 3 \times 7}$ **iv** $(9(4 + 7))$

 E $\boxed{9 \times 4 + 9 \times 7}$ **v** $(7(3 + 2))$

8 Sort these calculations into equivalent pairs.

 $\boxed{7 \times 15}$ $\boxed{4 \times 13}$ $\boxed{4 \times 23}$ $\boxed{3 \times 44}$ $\boxed{5 \times 17}$

 $(5(7 + 10))$ $(7(5 + 10))$ $(4(3 + 10))$ $(4(20 + 3))$ $(3(40 + 4))$

 Discussion Where else don't you need to write a × sign?

Key point

You can multiply out or **expand**
expressions with brackets.

9 **Expand** the brackets.
 a $2(x + 5)$ **b** $4(y + 6)$ **c** $7(z + 1)$
 d $9(3 + p)$ **e** $6(4 + q)$ **f** $10(8 + r)$

Q9a hint

$2(x + 5) = 2 \times x + 2 \times 5$
$= 2x + \square$

10 **STEM** An engineer uses this formula to work out the distance
 travelled by a car in 10 seconds,
 $s = 5(u + v)$
 where s is the distance, u is the starting speed and v is the finishing
 speed.
 a Expand the bracket.
 b Work out the value of s when
  i $u = 4$ and $v = 10$ **ii** $u = 12$ and $v = 20$ **iii** $u = 0$ and $v = 15$

Q10a hint

$s = 5(u + v)$
$s = \square + \square$

11 **Explore** How could you multiply a number by 27 in your head?
 Is it easier to explore this question now you have completed the lesson?
 What further information do you need to be able to answer this?

12 **Reflect** Kali and Sophie answer this question:
  Work out $v(100 - r)$ when $v = 10$ and $r = 2$.

 Kali
 $10(100 - 2) = 10 \times 100 - 10 \times 2$
 $= 1000 - 20$
 $= 980$

 Sophie
 $10(100 - 2) = 10 \times 98$
 $= 980$

 Whose method would you use? Why?

Explore

Reflect

Master
P75

CHECK

Strengthen
P87

Extend
P91

Test
P95

4 Check up

Log how you did on your
Student Progression Chart.

Functions

1 Write down the missing function for each inverse function machine.

a
$3 \rightarrow$ | +7 | $\rightarrow 10$

$3 \leftarrow$ (□) $\leftarrow 10$

b
$8 \rightarrow$ (÷2) $\rightarrow 4$

$8 \leftarrow$ (□) $\leftarrow 4$

c
$21 \rightarrow$ (−8) $\rightarrow 12$

$20 \leftarrow$ (□) $\leftarrow 12$

d
$7 \rightarrow$ (×3) $\rightarrow 21$

$7 \leftarrow$ (□) $\leftarrow 21$

2 Work out the missing inputs for these function machines.

a Input   Output

□ →
□ → | +9 | → 10
      → 13

b Input   Output

□ → (−3) → 2

c Input   Output

□ →
□ → (×6) → 12
      → 24

d Input   Output

□ → (÷3) → 1

3 a Write down the missing function
for this function machine.

b A piece of wood measures 12 cm.
Use the function machine from part **a** to work out the length
of the wood in mm.

c A different piece of wood is 370 mm long.
How long is this piece of wood in cm?

Input   Output

centimetres → (□) → millimetres

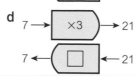

Expressions and equations

4 Simplify
  a $5 \times z$ **b** $v \div 3$ **c** $q \times 4$ **d** $x \times y$

  e $t \times f$ **f** $3a \times 5$ **g** $12b \div 4$ **h** $\dfrac{15a}{5}$

5 Simplify
  a $3r + 4b + 2r$ **b** $2a + 4c + 2a + c$ **c** $5t + 7 + 3 + 8t$
  d $10x + 6y - 4x$ **e** $9a + 6b - b - 3a$ **f** $8m + 6n - 5m - n$

6 Simplify
  a $5x + 3y - 7x$ **b** $8x + 3y - 5x - 5y$

7 Solve these equations.
  a $x + 2 = 6$ **b** $y - 1 = 9$

  c $4z = 24$ **d** $\dfrac{m}{4} = 5$

Brackets

8 Work out
   a $4 \times (2 + 7)$
   b $3(9 + 5)$

9 Match each pink rectangular card to its equivalent yellow hexagonal card.

A $\boxed{4 \times 5 + 4 \times 3}$ **i** $3(6 + 4)$

B $\boxed{5 \times 3 + 5 \times 6}$ **ii** $4(5 + 3)$

C $\boxed{3 \times 6 + 3 \times 4}$ **iii** $5(3 + 6)$

10 Expand
   a $3(x + 2)$
   b $2(y + 1)$
   c $5(4 + a)$
   d $7(3 + b)$

11 **How sure are you of your answers? Were you mostly**
   ☹ **Just guessing**   😐 **Feeling doubtful**   ☺ **Confident**
   What next? Use your results to decide whether to strengthen or extend your learning.

Reflect

Challenge

12 a Write two different functions for this function machine.

Input   Output
$2 \rightarrow \boxed{} \rightarrow 10$

b Use your answers to part **a** to work out two different inputs for this function machine.

Input   Output
$2 \rightarrow$
$\boxed{} \rightarrow$ $\boxed{}$ $\rightarrow 10$
$\rightarrow 25$

13 Joe and Leah solve these equations.
   $x + 10 = 32$
   $y - 9 = 11$
   $5z = 40$

Joe says   I think that $x + y + z = 52$

Leah says   I think that $x + y + z = 50$

Who is correct? Explain why.

> **Q13 hint**
>
> Solve the equations to find the values of x, y and z, and then add the three values together.

Master
P75

Check
P85

STRENGTHEN

Extend
P91

Test
P95

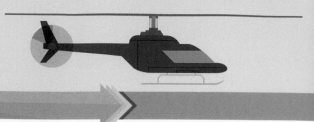

4 Strengthen

You will:

• Strengthen your understanding with practice.

Functions

1 Copy and complete these statements using the words in the cloud.

   a The **inverse** of add is ____

   b The inverse of subtract is ____

   c The inverse of multiply is ____

   d The inverse of divide is ____

subtract
add
divide
multiply

Q1 Literacy hint

An **inverse** operation is the opposite operation.

2 a Write down the inverse operation of

    i add 3   **ii** subtract 3   **iii** multiply by 3   **iv** divide by 3.

   b Work out the missing input for each of these function machines.

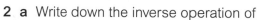

Q2b hint

Use the inverse operations from part **a**.

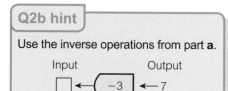

3 Work out the missing outputs and inputs for these function machines.

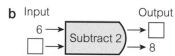

Q3 hint

First find the inverse operation.

4 Work out the missing outputs and inputs for these function machines.

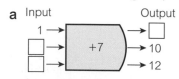
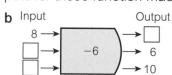

5 Write down the missing function for this function machine.

   Input   Output
   centimetres → ☐ → metres

Q5 hint

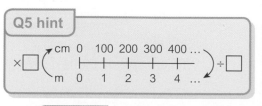

6 Three trees measure 500 cm, 700 cm and 900 cm in height.
Copy and complete this function machine to work out the height of each tree in metres.

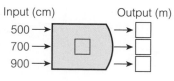

Q6 hint

Use your answer to Q5 to help.

7 A ticket for a football match costs £20.

a Work out the missing values.

1 ticket costs £20

2 tickets cost 2 × £20 = £☐

3 tickets cost 3 × £20 = £☐

4 tickets cost 4 × £20 = £☐

b Write down the missing function for this function machine.

c Use the function machine in part **b** to work out the total cost of 5 tickets, 6 tickets and 10 tickets.

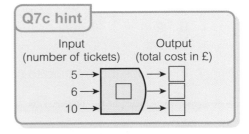

Input → ☐ → Output

number of tickets → total cost in £

Q7c hint

Input (number of tickets)   Output (total cost in £)

5 → ☐ → ☐

6 → ☐ → ☐

10 → ☐ → ☐

Expressions and equations

1 Work out each subtraction. Use the number line to help.

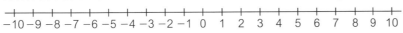

−10 −9 −8 −7 −6 −5 −4 −3 −2 −1 0 1 2 3 4 5 6 7 8 9 10

a   **i** $4 - 6$ **ii** $3 - 7$

    iii $5 - 10$ **iv** $7 - 5 - 6$

b Use your answers to part **a** to simplify these expressions.

    i $4x - 6x$ **ii** $3x - 7x$

    iii $5x - 10x$ **iv** $7x - 5x - 6x$

Q1a i hint

−6

−4 −3 −2 −1 0 1 2 3 4 5 6

Q1b i hint

−6x

−4x −3x −2x −x 0 x 2x 3x 4x 5x 6x

2 Match each blue rectangle card to its equivalent yellow oval card.

A $8y - 10y$ **i** $-10y$

B $4y - 14y$ **ii** $-3y$

C $2y + 3y - 8y$ **iii** $-8y$

D $12y - 5y - 15y$ **iv** $-2y$

3 Simplify

a $8 \times b$ **b** $6 \times c$ **c** $x \times 3$ **d** $y \times 2$

e $a \times b$ **f** $x \times y$ **g** $m \times l$ **h** $d \times c$

Q3 hint

Don't write the × signs.

Write numbers before letters.

Write the letters in alphabetical order.

4 Put these cards into pairs of equivalent expressions.

A $y \div 2$ **B** $y \div 8$ **C** $y \div 4$ **D** $y \div 7$ **E** $y \div 5$

i $\dfrac{y}{4}$ **ii** $\dfrac{y}{5}$ **iii** $\dfrac{y}{2}$ **iv** $\dfrac{y}{8}$ **v** $\dfrac{y}{7}$

Q4 hint

$\dfrac{y}{4}$ means $y \div 4$

5 Simplify

a $6 \times 2y$ **b** $4 \times 5x$

c $7t \times 3$ **d** $2h \times 8$

e $8p \div 4$ **f** $9y \div 3$

g $18h \div 6$ **h** $\dfrac{6q}{3}$

i $\dfrac{10x}{2}$ **j** $\dfrac{12n}{4}$

Q5a hint

$6 \times 2 \times y$

$= 12 \times y$

Q5e hint

$8 \div 4 = 2$

$8p \div 4 = \square p$

Q5h hint

$\dfrac{6q}{3} = 6q \div 3 = \square q$

6 Simplify by collecting like terms.

   a $5r + 3r$

   b $5r - 3r$

   c $8b + 2b$

   d $8b - 5b$

   e $4r + 3y + 2r + y$

   f $4r + 3y - 2r - y$

   g $6g + 5b + 2g + 3b$

   h $6g + 5b - 2g - 3b$

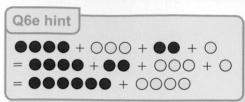

7 Ellen uses this method to simplify the expression $8x + 5y - 12x$

$$(8x) + 5y (- 12x) = 8x - 12x + 5y$$
$$= -4x + 5y$$
$$= 5y - 4x$$

Simplify these expressions.

   a $6x + 3y - 9x$

   b $5a + 4b - 8a$

   c $6z + 8w - 12w$

   d $9x + 2y - 3x - 7y$

   e $7a + 5b + a - 9b$

   f $8p + 5q - 20p - 3q$

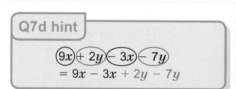

8 Draw function machines for

   a $x + 6$

   b $y - 2$

   c $5m$

   d $\dfrac{t}{2}$

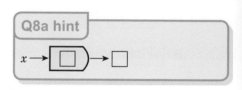

9 Nikole and Pritesh use different methods to solve an equation.

Nikole uses a function machine.   Pritesh uses a 'missing number' method.

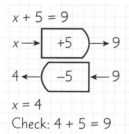

$x + 5 = 9$
$\square + 5 = 9$
$4 + 5 = 9$
$x = 4$

Solve these equations. Use Nikole's method or Pritesh's method.
Check your solutions.

   a $x + 6 = 10$

   b $y + 4 = 15$

   c $x - 3 = 5$

   d $y - 1 = 9$

   e $4x = 12$

   f $6y = 30$

   g $\dfrac{x}{3} = 2$

   h $\dfrac{c}{5} = 3$

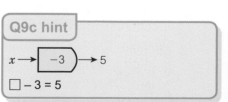

Brackets

1 You can use a multiplication grid to work out $6 \times (4 + 9)$ like this:

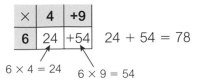

×	4	+9
6	24	+54

$24 + 54 = 78$

$6 \times 4 = 24$ $6 \times 9 = 54$

Work out

a $3 \times (5 + 12)$

b $4(8 + 9)$

c $7(7 + 5)$

Q1b hint

×	8	+9
4	☐	+☐

2 Copy and complete.

a $3 \times 2 + 3 \times 5 = 3(☐ + ☐)$

b $6 \times 4 + 6 \times 9 = 6(☐ + ☐)$

c $8 \times 3 + 8 \times 2 = ☐ (☐ + ☐)$

d $5 \times 6 + 5 \times 3 = ☐ (☐ + ☐)$

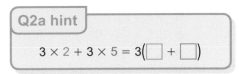

Q2a hint

$3 \times 2 + 3 \times 5 = 3(☐ + ☐)$

3 Expand

a $8(x + 9)$

b $4(y + 3)$

c $3(8 + w)$

d $6(4 + z)$

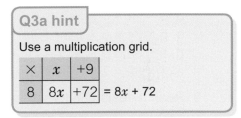

Q3a hint

Use a multiplication grid.

×	x	+9
8	$8x$	+72

$= 8x + 72$

Enrichment

1 Sort these cards into pairs that have the same answer.

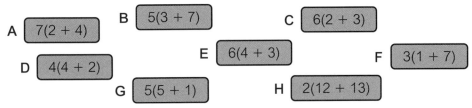

A $7(2 + 4)$ **B** $5(3 + 7)$ **C** $6(2 + 3)$

D $4(4 + 2)$ **E** $6(4 + 3)$ **F** $3(1 + 7)$

G $5(5 + 1)$ **H** $2(12 + 13)$

2 Here are six equations.

$x + 32 = 42$ $x - 7 = 2$ $6x = 66$ $x + 15 = 23$ $x - 4 = 8$ $\frac{x}{10} = 1$

Which equation has the solution with

a the smallest value of x

b the biggest value of x?

3 **Reflect** In these strengthen lessons you have used number lines, function machines and circle diagrams to help answer questions. Which of these methods have you found the most useful? Is there another method you found helpful when working on these strengthen lessons? If so, describe it in your own words.

Master
P75

Check
P85

Strengthen
P91

EXTEND

Test
P95

4 Extend

You will:
- Extend your understanding with problem solving.

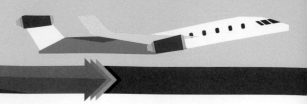

1 Work out
   a 4(10 – 3)
   b 5(8 – 2)
   c 3(5 + 7 + 8)
   d 4(7 + 2 – 5)

2 Work out
   a 9 × 23 = 9 × (20 + 3) = 9 × 20 + 9 × 3 = □ + □ = □
   b 8 × 42 = 8 × (40 + 2)
   c 6 × 34 = 6 × (□ + □)
   d 5 × 58 = 5 × (60 – 2)
   e 7 × 69 = 7 × (□ – □)

> **Q1c hint**
>
> 3(5 + 7 + 8) = 3 × 5 + 3 × 7 + 3 × 8

> **Q2b hint**
>
> Use the same method as in part **a**.

3 **Real** It costs £38 for one person to go horse riding.
   Copy and complete the working to calculate how much it costs
   a family of 5 to go horse riding.
   5 × 38 = 5 × (□ – □) = □ – □ = £□

4 **Real** A ticket for a music festival costs £134.
   Copy and complete the working to calculate how much it costs
   6 friends to go to the music festival.
   6 × 134 = □ × (□ + □ + □) = □ + □ + □ = £□

5 Match each blue card to its equivalent yellow and pink cards.

   A $\boxed{5 \times 62}$ **i** $\boxed{5(50 - 2)}$ **1** $\boxed{6 \times 60 - 6 \times 3}$

   B $\boxed{4 \times 52}$ **ii** $\boxed{6(60 - 3)}$ **2** $\boxed{5 \times 60 + 5 \times 2}$

   C $\boxed{5 \times 48}$ **iii** $\boxed{5(60 + 2)}$ **3** $\boxed{4 \times 50 + 4 \times 4}$

   D $\boxed{6 \times 57}$ **iv** $\boxed{4(50 + 4)}$ **4** $\boxed{4 \times 50 + 4 \times 2}$

   E $\boxed{4 \times 54}$ **v** $\boxed{4(50 + 2)}$ **5** $\boxed{5 \times 50 - 5 \times 2}$

6 **Reasoning** Kim and Leon both work out 7 × 68.
   Kim says: I think it's easier to work out 7 × (60 + 8).
   Leon says: I think it's easier to work out 7 × (70 – 2).

   a Work out 7 × 68 using
      i Kim's method
      ii Leon's method.
   b Do you think Kim's or Leon's method is easier? Explain why.

Topic links: Perimeter, Working with decimals and fractions,
Ratio, Negative numbers, Fractions and percentages

Subject links: Science (Q18)

7 Problem-solving Here are some algebra cards.

$\boxed{12x}$ $\boxed{8x}$ $\boxed{11x}$ $\boxed{7x}$ $\boxed{5x}$ $\boxed{2x}$

Work out which of the cards simplify to the answers given.

a $\quad\boxed{} - \boxed{} = -3x$

b $\quad\boxed{} - \boxed{} + \boxed{} = -3x$

c $\quad\boxed{} - \boxed{} - \boxed{} = -3x$

Q7 Strategy hint
Keep trying different cards until you find the ones which work.

8 Which of these expressions simplify to give $-2x - 3y$?

A $\boxed{6x + 4y - 8x - 7y}$ B $\boxed{4x + 7y - 6x - 9y}$

C $\boxed{12x + 3y - 10x - 6y}$ D $\boxed{x + 2y - 3x - 5y}$

9 Simplify these expressions.
   a $\quad 7g + 9 + 2h + 4 + 3g + 6h$ b $\quad 12x + 7y + 5z - 10x - 4y - 10z$

Q9a hint
$7g + 3g + 2h + 6h + 9 + 4$
$= \boxed{}g + \boxed{}h + \boxed{}$

10 Write an expression for the perimeter of each shape.
Write each expression in its simplest form.

a   b

Q10a hint
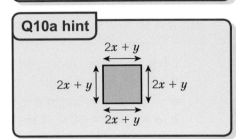

11 Problem-solving In this algebra wheel the terms in opposite circles multiply to give the expression at the centre.
Write down the missing numbers from these algebra wheels.

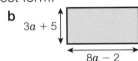

$x \times 12 = 12x$
$2x \times 6 = 12x$
$3x \times 4 = 12x$

a 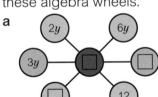   b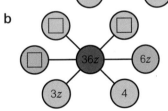

Q11a hint
Work out the expression at the centre first.
$2y \times 12 = \boxed{}$

12 Work out the missing outputs and inputs for these function machines.

a 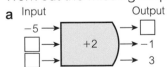   b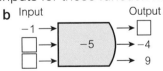

13 Work out the missing outputs and inputs for these function machines.

a 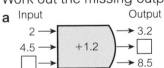   b

14 Problem-solving Use the numbers from the cloud to complete this function machine.

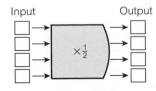 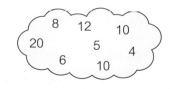

Q14 hint
Multiplying by $\frac{1}{2}$ is the same as finding half of an amount, or dividing by 2.

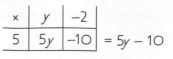

15 You can use a multiplication grid to expand $5(y - 2)$ like this:

×	y	-2
5	$5y$	-10

$= 5y - 10$

Expand
a $3(y - 4)$ **b** $5(x - 6)$ **c** $2(9 - v)$
d $8(3 - w)$ **e** $4(6y + 2)$ **f** $3(7y - 4)$

16 Solve these equations.
a $14 = d + 3$ **b** $a - 9 = -2$ **c** $2f = 38$
d $\frac{r}{4} = 15$ **e** $6 = t - 9$ **f** $60 = \frac{t}{3}$

17 Jade uses this formula to work out her total pay:
total pay (P) = wages (W) + tips (T)
a Work out P when $W = £35$ and $T = £9$.

$P = W + T$
$= \square + \square = £\square$

b Work out W when $P = £58$ and $T = £12$.

$P = W + T$
$58 = W + 12$
$W = £\square$

Q17b hint

Solve the equation $58 = W + 12$

18 **STEM** The formula used to work out the force (F) on an object is
$F = ma$
where m is the mass and a is the acceleration of the object.
Work out the value of
a F when $m = 5$ and $a = 3$
b a when $F = 30$ and $m = 6$
c m when $F = 54$ and $a = 9$?

Q18 hint

$F = ma$ means $F = m \times a$
Substitute in the numbers you know and then work out the one you don't know.

19 **Problem-solving** Here are four formula cards.

$A = B + 3$	$B = 3C$	$B + D = A$	$A + B + E = 20$

Copy and complete this table to show the values of A, B, C, D and E.

A	B	C	D	E
9				

Q19 hint

Start by using $A = 9$ in the first formula to work out the value of B.

20 The diagram shows some angles on a straight line.
a Write and simplify an expression for the sum of these angles.
b Use your expression to write an equation for the sum of these angles.
c Solve your equation to find x.
d Copy this diagram and write the angles in degrees.

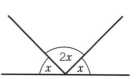

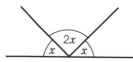

21 **Modelling** An author earns 10% of the total value of her book sales.
a What is 10% as a fraction?
b Write an expression for the amount the author earns when the total value of her book sales is v.
c How much will the author earn when the total value of her book sales is £20 000?
d What must the total value of the author's book sales be for her to earn £8000?

Q21b hint

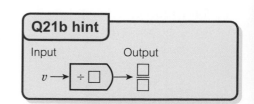

22 Real To convert a distance in miles to a distance in kilometres you use this rule:

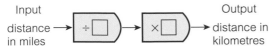

Divide the distance in miles by 5 then multiply the result by 8.

a Complete this function machine to convert a distance in miles to a distance in kilometres.

Input
distance → ÷ ☐ → × ☐ → Output distance in
in miles   kilometres

b Tyler is going to take part in two charity cycle rides.
The first is 20 miles and the second is 45 miles.
Use the function machine in part **a** to work out distance in kilometres of each charity cycle ride.

23 A basketball club sell tickets to home supporters and away supporters in the ratio 3 : 1.
   a Work out the number of tickets sold to home supporters when there are 200 tickets. Write down all the steps in your working.
   b Complete the function machine to work out the number of tickets sold to home supporters.

Input
total number → ÷ ☐ → × ☐ → Output tickets sold to
of tickets   home supporters

> **Q23a hint**
> What fraction are sold to home supporters?

> **Q23b hint**
> Look at the method you used in part **a**.

   c For two different basketball matches there are a total of 180 and 260 tickets. Use the function machine in part **b** to work out the number of tickets sold to home supporters for each match.

Investigation   **Reasoning**

Look at the number grid on the right.
There are green and yellow L shapes on the grid.
You can work out the L-value of a shape using this rule:
    L-value = total of bottom numbers − top number
So the yellow L-value is 12 + 13 − 7 = 18.

1	2	3	4	5
6	7	8	9	10
11	12	13	14	15
16	17	18	19	20
21	22	23	24	25

1 Work out the green L-value.
2 Choose two more L shapes on the grid and work out their L-values.
   What do you notice about each L-value and the number at the top of the L shape?
3 Complete this rule: L-value = top number + ☐
4 a Copy and complete the expressions in this L shape.
   b Write an expression for the L-value of this L shape.
      Simplify your expression.
5 What do you notice about your answers to parts 4b and 3?
6 What will be the L-value of the L shape that has 42 as its top number?

> **Part 2 hint**
> What is the difference between the L-value and the number at the top of the L shape?

> **Part 4b hint**
> $n + 5 + n + ☐ − n = ☐ + ☐$

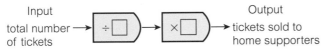

n

$n + 5$ | $n + ☐$

---

24 Reflect In these extend lessons you have used lots of different maths topics. Look back at your work and make a list of the topics you have used, and the questions that used them.
You might begin: Expanding brackets, Q1.

4 Unit test

Log how you did on your Student Progression Chart.

1 Work out

  a $3 \times (4 + 5)$ **b** $4(8 + 3)$ **c** $7(10 - 2)$

2 Simplify

  a $4x - 7x$ **b** $9y + y - 15y$

  c $a \times b$ **d** $c \div 4$

  e $e \times d$ **f** $7 \times 2n$

  g $\dfrac{20m}{5}$

3 Simplify

  a $4x + 6y + 9x$ **b** $11a + 9c + 3a + c$

  c $4g + 9 + 6 + 4g$ **d** $13x + 11y - 3x$

  e $7n + 8p - p - 5n$

4 Simplify

  a $8x - 3y - 3x$ **b** $9w + 4z - 11w$

  c $7a + 4b - 5a - 5b$ **d** $3x - 7y + 2y - 6x$

5 Match each blue rectangular card to its equivalent orange pentagonal card.

  A $\boxed{8 \times 5 + 8 \times 4}$ **i** $5(8 + 4)$

  B $\boxed{6 \times 4 + 6 \times 8}$ **ii** $8(5 + 4)$

  C $\boxed{5 \times 8 + 5 \times 4}$ **iii** $6(4 + 8)$

6 Write down the missing function for each inverse function machine.

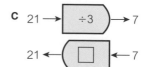

  a $3 \to \boxed{\times 6} \to 18$
      $3 \leftarrow \boxed{\square} \leftarrow 18$

  b $9 \to \boxed{-2} \to 7$
      $9 \leftarrow \boxed{\square} \leftarrow 7$

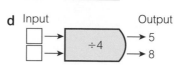

  c $21 \to \boxed{\div 3} \to 7$
      $21 \leftarrow \boxed{\square} \leftarrow 7$

  d $6 \to \boxed{+8} \to 14$
      $6 \leftarrow \boxed{\square} \leftarrow 14$

7 Work out the missing inputs for these function machines.

  a Input $\boxed{\square}\to \boxed{+12} \to$ Output 14, 18

  b Input $\boxed{\square}\to \boxed{-5} \to$ Output 0, 8

  c Input $\boxed{\square}\to \boxed{\times 6} \to$ Output 18, 36

  d Input $\boxed{\square}\to \boxed{\div 4} \to$ Output 5, 8

8 Solve these equations.

   a $y + 9 = 20$ **b** $x - 5 = 13$

   c $6w = 30$ **d** $\frac{u}{8} = 3$

9 Expand

   a $4(x + 3)$ **b** $8(2 + y)$

   c $3(a - 5)$ **d** $7(3 - b)$

10 This formula is used to work out the distance (d) an object travels

    $d = s \times t$

   where s is the speed of the object and t is the time the object takes.

   Work out the value of

   a d when $s = 7$ and $t = 5$

   b t when $d = 50$ and $s = 10$

   c s when $d = 48$ and $t = 8$.

11 **a** Write down the missing function for this function machine.

    b Three bags of rice have masses of 5 kg, 2 kg and 1.5 kg. Use the function machine in part **a** to work out the mass of each bag of rice in grams.

    c A recipe uses 800 g of rice. How much rice is this in kg?

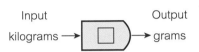

Input   Output

kilograms → ▢ → grams

Challenge

12 Copy this secret code box. The code spells the name of a place.

				G				
$8x - 8y$	$8x - 4y$	$8y - 4x$	$8x - 4y$	$4x - 8y$	$8x + 4y$	$8x + 8y$	$4x + 8y$	$8x - 4y$

Simplify each expression in the green box, then find its equivalent expression in the secret code box. Write the letter above the equivalent expression in the secret code box.

The first one is done for you.

$2y + 4x - 10y = 4x - 8y$, so G = $4x - 8y$

What is the name of the place in the code?

Now write your own secret code questions and code box.

G	$2y + 4x - 10y$
N	$8(x + y)$
O	$12x + 3y - 4x + y$
A	$4(2x - y)$
I	$x + 9y - y + 3x$
T	$3x + 10y - 7x - 2y$
P	$15x - 2y - 6y - 7x$

13 **Reflect** The work in this unit is all about algebra.

   This might be the first time you have used algebra since Year 7.

   Write down one thing you liked doing in this unit.

   What did you like about it?

   Write down one thing you found difficult in this unit.

   Ask your teacher or a classmate to explain it to you if you still find it difficult.

Reflect

5.1 Adding and subtracting decimals

You will learn to:
- Add and subtract decimal numbers.

CONFIDENCE

Why learn this?
Architects must measure accurately and be able to add and subtract decimals to ensure that their calculations are correct.

Fluency
What is the value of the 3 in
- 327
- 0.32
- 53.61
- 9432?
What is the mean of 3, 4 and 8?

Explore
How could you add £9.99 to any amount?

Exercise 5.1

Warm up

1 Work out
  a 423 + 574   **b** 59 + 472   **c** 5.8 + 9.3

2 Work out
  a 392 − 181   **b** 927 − 88   **c** 9.2 − 7.6

3 Work out
  a 21.54 + 9.34   **b** 9.8 + 12.17   **c** 0.9 + 8.32
  d 2.45 + 8.7   **e** 19.2 + 7.81   **f** 3.25 + 19
  Discussion Why is 19 the same as 19.0?

4 Work out
  a 3.2 + 19.4 + 7.37
  b 21.3 + 34 + 0.37

> **Q3a hint**
> Write as a column addition.
> ```
>   21.54
> +  9.34
> ───────
> ```

> **Q3b hint**
> Line up the decimal points, the tenths with the tenths, the hundredths with the hundredths, and so on.
> ```
>    9.18
> + 12.17
> ───────
> ```

> **Q3f hint**
> Write 19 as 19.00

> **Q4a hint**
> Write the three numbers as a column addition.

Worked example

Work out 14.7 − 7.43

```
  14.7
−  7.43
```
Line up the decimal points, the tenths with the tenths, and the hundredths with the hundredths.

```
  14.70
−  7.43
```
Write a zero in any spaces that are empty.

```
  14.70
−  7.43
───────
   7.27
```
Subtract column by column, starting on the right. Borrow a tenth from the tenths column to make 6 tenths and 10 hundredths. Continue in the same way for each column, borrowing 1 from the next column where necessary.

Topic links: Averages

5 Work out

  a 12.8 − 0.32

  b 18.5 − 9.43

  c 15.6 − 0.79

  d 24 − 3.45

  e 52 − 44.91

6 Work out

  a 9.3 subtract 7.77

  b 4.2 less than 9.81

  c 23.2 more than 8.53

  d the difference between 9 and 3.72

  e the sum of 8.45 and 19.8.

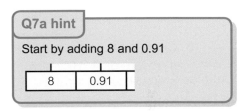

Q6d,e hint

To find the difference, subtract the smaller number from the larger number.
To find the sum, add the numbers together.

7 In these addition pyramids, the number in each brick is the sum of the 2 bricks below it.
Copy and complete each pyramid.

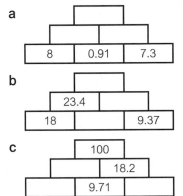

Q7a hint

Start by adding 8 and 0.91

| 8 | 0.91 | |

Q7b hint

Start by working out 23.4 − 18.
Which brick does this number go in?

8 Work out

  a 3.2 + 0.91 − 2.4

  b 19 + 7.3 − 0.48

  c 12 − 0.54 + 7.2

  d 28.6 − 9.8 − 12.3

  e 19 + 5.4 − 16.2 + 0.11

Q8a hint

Work from left to right. Work out 3.2 + 0.91 first, then subtract 2.4

Q8c hint

Work out 12 − 0.54 first.

9 **Real** A supermarket lists the prices of basic items.

Loaf of bread	£0.98
1 pint of milk	£0.50
Jar of coffee	£2.00
Cucumber	£0.48
Packet of tea	£1.49

  a How much would each of these shopping lists cost?

    i 2 jars of coffee, 1 packet of tea, 2 pints of milk

    ii 3 loaves of bread, 1 cucumber and 1 jar of coffee

  b How much change would you get from £20 for each list?

10 **Real / Problem-solving** A roll of fabric is 5 m long.
A shop sells 3.25 m to a customer.
How much is left?

11 Real / Problem-solving A rope is 20 m long.
A fisherman cuts off 2 pieces measuring 3.91 m and 8.7 m.
a What is the total length he cuts off?
b How much rope is left?

12 Real / Problem-solving A medicine bottle contains 200 ml of liquid.
A nurse gives his patient 3 doses of 7.5 ml.
How much is left in the bottle?

13 Real / Problem-solving Julia ran four 200 m races.
Her times were 29.3 s, 28.96 s, 27.2 s and 34.54 s.
What was her mean time?

14 In a shop all the items cost £0.99 or £1.99.
Jake buys 3 items costing £0.99 and 1 item costing £1.99.
Work out the total cost of his shopping.
Discussion What method did you use?
Can you think of another method?

15 Choose two numbers from the box that have
   a a sum of 9.28
   b a difference of 4.4
   c a sum of 14.46
   d a difference of 5.17.

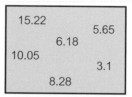

15.22
5.65
6.18
10.05
3.1
8.28

Investigation   **Problem-solving**

Work out a solution to this addition pyramid.

16 Explore How could you add £9.99 to any amount?
Look back at the maths you have learned in this lesson.
How can you use it to answer this question?

17 Reflect Sasha says, 'Adding and subtracting decimals is just
like adding and subtracting big whole numbers.'
Look back at the worked example in this lesson.
Do you agree with Sasha?
Write down one thing that is similar when adding or subtracting
decimals and whole numbers.
What is important to remember when adding or subtracting
decimals?

5.2 Multiplying decimals

You will learn to:
• Multiply decimals.

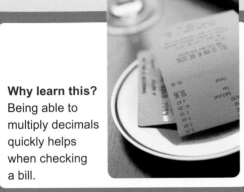

Why learn this?
Being able to multiply decimals quickly helps when checking a bill.

Fluency
Double
• 24
• 18
• 32

Explore
Two decimals multiplied together always give a decimal answer. Is this true?

Exercise 5.2

1 Work out
  a 8^2
  b 13^2
  c 15^2

2 Work out
  a 3.2×9
  b 9.8×7
  c 4×3.6
  d 3×6.9

3 Copy and complete.
  a $13 \times 10 = \square$
  b $27 \div 10 = \square$
  c $29 \div \square = 2.9$
  d $4 \div \square = 0.4$
  e $762 \div 100 = \square$
  f $428 \div \square = 4.28$

4 Work out
  a 16×0.5
  b 24×0.5
  c 38×0.5
  d 0.5×62
  e 0.5×800
  f 87×0.5
  g 0.5×23
  Discussion What method could you use to multiply by 0.25?

5 Work out
  a 0.25×8
  b 36×0.25
  c 0.25×40
  d 100×0.25

6 Work out
  a 16×0.2
  b 45×0.2
  c 0.2×84
  d 0.2×56
  Discussion What method could you use to multiply by 0.4? … by 0.8?

7 Work out
  a 30×0.4
  b 11×0.8
  c 12×0.3
  d 20×0.6

8 Real A sheet of paper is 0.2 mm thick.
  How thick is a booklet of 63 sheets?

Warm up

Q2a hint
First work out
$$\begin{array}{r} 32 \\ \times\ 9 \\ \hline \end{array}$$

Key point
$0.5 = \frac{1}{2}$, so multiplying by 0.5 is the same as multiplying by $\frac{1}{2}$, which is the same as dividing by 2.
For example,
$14 \times 0.5 = 14 \times \frac{1}{2} = 14 \div 2 = 7$

Key point
$0.2 = \frac{2}{10}$, so multiplying by 0.2 is the same as multiplying by 2 and then dividing by 10.
For example, to work out 18×0.2
$18 \times 2 = 36 \qquad 36 \div 10 = 3.6$
So $18 \times 0.2 = 3.6$

Worked example

Work out 11 × 3.5

11 × 3.5 = 11 × (3 + 0.5) ← Partition 3.5 into 3 + 0.5

       = 11 × 3 + 11 × 0.5

       = 33 + 5.5 ← Add the two answers together.

       = 38.5

Key point

You can use **partitioning** to make some calculations easier. Partitioning splits a number into its place value components.

9 Work out

  a 24 × 1.5   **b** 5.5 × 12

  c 4.1 × 25   **d** 42 × 1.2

  e 2.2 × 36

10 A bottle holds 2.5 litres. How much juice is needed to fill 75 bottles?

Worked example

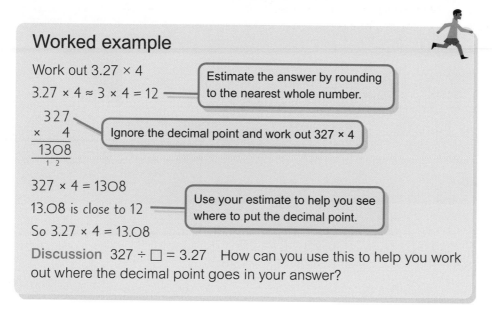

Work out 3.27 × 4

3.27 × 4 ≈ 3 × 4 = 12 ← Estimate the answer by rounding to the nearest whole number.

```
  327
×   4      ← Ignore the decimal point and work out 327 × 4
-----
 1308
   1 2
```

327 × 4 = 1308

13.08 is close to 12 ← Use your estimate to help you see where to put the decimal point.

So 3.27 × 4 = 13.08

Discussion 327 ÷ □ = 3.27   How can you use this to help you work out where the decimal point goes in your answer?

11 Work out

  a 9.23 × 7   **b** 8.21 × 9

  c 8.54 × 4   **d** 3.01 × 8

  e 0.79 × 3   **f** 9.99 × 6

Q11 hint

Don't forget to estimate the answer first.

12 Real Music downloads cost £0.99 per song.
How much will 7 songs cost?

13 Real A book is 1.23 cm thick.
How high will a stack of 4 books be?

14 Real Anstey needs 9 pieces of ribbon 1.25 cm long.
What is the total length of ribbon she needs?

15 Real A shop sells cans of cola for £0.45 each.
They are also available as multipacks of 6 cans for £3.00.
Which is the cheaper way of buying cola?

Worked example

Work out 0.02×0.4

$2 \times 4 = 8$ ← Ignore the decimal points and work out 2×4

$8 \div 1000 = 0.008$ ← $2 \div 100 = 0.02$, and $4 \div 10 = 0.4$, so work out $8 \div 1000$ (which is $8 \div 100 \div 10$) to get the final answer.

So $0.02 \times 0.4 = 0.008$

16 Match each multiplication to the correct answer.

A 15   **B** 0.15   **C** 0.015   **D** 1.5

a 0.3×0.5
b 3×0.5
c 3×5
d 0.05×0.3

Discussion Count the number of digits after the decimal point in both numbers in each question part. Do the same for the answers. What do you notice?

17 Work out
a 0.9×0.1
b 0.2×0.05
c 0.09×8
d 0.3×0.07
e 0.02×0.8
f 0.7×5
g 0.9×0.3

18 Square these numbers.
The first one has been started for you.
a $0.2^2 = 0.2 \times 0.2 =$
b 0.9^2
c 0.5^2
d 0.7^2
e 0.11^2

19 **Explore** Two decimals multiplied together always give a decimal answer. Is this true?
Is it easier to explore this question now you have completed the lesson?
What further information do you need to be able to answer this?

20 **Reflect** Look back at the worked examples in this lesson.
They show you different ways to multiply decimals.
Which method do you prefer?
Try your favourite method on one part from Q9, Q11 and Q17.
Does it work for all of them?

5.3 Ordering and rounding decimals

You will learn to:
- Round decimals
- Order decimals.

CONFIDENCE

Why learn this?
Knowing which is the smallest number can help you choose the cheapest deal.

Fluency
What is the value of the digit 2 in
- 0.276
- 31.82
- 1.082?
Which number has the most hundredths?
- 3.17
- 3.19
- 3.12

Explore
Why do shops use prices like £999.99?

Exercise 5.3

1 For each number in parts **a** to **f**, round the number to
  i the nearest whole number
  ii 1 decimal place.
  a 3.72
  b 9.57
  c 12.49
  d 237.81
  e 4.59
  f 5.65

Warm up

2 Write < or > between each pair of numbers.
  a 3.1 ☐ 3.7   **b** 9.08 ☐ 9.05
  c 4.59 ☐ 4.6   **d** 6.72 ☐ 6.27

3 Write these numbers in **ascending** order.
  3.45   3.4   3.05   3.04   3.1

4 Round each number to 2 decimal places.
  a 7.926
  b 9.353
  c 4.325
  d 8.897
  e 0.2946
  f 0.2954

5 Work out each calculation.
  Give your answers to 2 decimal places.
  a £52.70 ÷ 18   **b** £35.45 ÷ 3
  c 19.2 m ÷ 18   **d** 15 litres ÷ 52

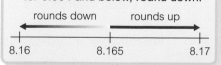

Q3 Literacy hint
Ascending order is from smallest to largest.

Key point
When rounding to 2 decimal places, look at the thousandths:
- for 0.005 and above, round up
- for 0.004 and below, round down.

rounds down ← | → rounds up
8.16 —— 8.165 —— 8.17

Q4a hint
There are 6 thousandths (7.92**6**), so round up.

Q4d hint
Always write the second decimal place, even if it's zero, to show that you've rounded to 2 decimal places.

Topic links: Division, Averages

6 Real A plank of wood 3 m long is cut into 7 equal pieces.
How long is each piece?
Give your answer to 2 decimal places.

7 Real A bottle contains 800 ml. An equal amount is poured into each
of 9 glasses.
How much is in each glass?
Give your answer to 2 decimal places.

8 Problem-solving The weekly wages of 4 people working for the
same company are
£252.40   £318.80   £297.50   £302.25
What is their mean wage?

Investigation   Reasoning / Real / Finance

A restaurant bill comes to £145.70
6 people split the bill equally.
1 How much should they each pay?
2 Multiply your answer to part **1** by 6.
3 Is there enough to pay the bill?
Comment on your answer.
4 Repeat parts **1** to **3** for a total bill of £186.25 divided between 7 people.

---

9 Write < or > between each pair of numbers.
a 3.203 ☐ 3.029
b 4.3507 ☐ 4.532
c 21.722 ☐ 22.99
d 123.88 ☐ 123.96
e 0.2455 ☐ 0.2551
f 0.7324 ☐ 0.73505

10 Write each set of numbers in ascending order.
a 3.524   3.504   3.554   3.004
b 231.4   232.9   200.9   231.01
c 41.259   40.995   41.529   41.292
d 0.2325   0.2352   0.2035   0.22252

11 Real The 4 heaviest fish caught in an angling competition weighed

A 1.835 kg   **B** 1.892 kg

C 1.839 kg   **D** 1.799 kg

Which were the 2 heaviest fish?

12 Explore Why do shops use prices like £999.99?
Look back at the maths you have learned in this lesson.
How can you use it to answer this question?

13 Reflect Alison says, 'In this lesson I drew a bar 10 units long, and
used it to help me work out whether to round up or down, and to
order decimals.'
What strategies did you use in this lesson?
For example, did you imagine the numbers on a number line?

> **Key point**
>
> When comparing the size of two
> decimal numbers
> • first compare the whole number
>   parts
> • then, if they are equal, compare
>   the tenths
> • then, if they are equal, compare
>   the hundredths
> … and so on.
> If there is no digit in a column, its
> value is 0 and it does not change
> the overall size of the number.
> For example,
> 2.3 = 2.30 = 2.300 = …

5.4 STEM: Problem-solving with decimals

You will learn to:

- Solve problems involving decimals.

CONFIDENCE

Why learn this?
Our currency uses the decimal system, so we need to be able to handle decimal numbers every day.

Fluency
Estimate
- £0.99 × 8
- £6.99 × 7
- £2.49 × 4

Explore
How could you estimate the price of your shopping?

Warm up

Exercise 5.4: Decimals in science and technology

1 Work out

  a 3.2 + 19.57   **b** £19.50 + £12

  c 4.5 − 3.98   **d** £30 − £23.45

2 Work out

  a 7 × 3.2   **b** 0.3 × 0.4   **c** £0.50 × 5

3 Work out

  a 40 ÷ 8   **b** 19 ÷ 2   **c** 42 ÷ 5

4 Reasoning / Finance   This board shows the prices of drinks in a coffee shop.

  a Which is the cheapest drink on the menu?

  b Which is cheaper

    • 1 latte and 1 cappuccino, or

    • 1 tea and 1 Americano?

  c How much change do you get from £10 when you buy a hot chocolate and a latte?

  d List all the possible combinations of 2 drinks you could buy for £5 or less.

Tea	£1.80
Cappuccino	£2.99
Latte	£2.75
Americano	£2.95
Hot chocolate	£2.45

Q4d hint

The two drinks can be the same.

5 Problem-solving   An MP3 player costs £14.98 in Shop A and £13.97 in Shop B.

  a How much cheaper is the MP3 player in Shop B?

An online company sells the same MP3 player for £12.84, but charges £1.99 postage.

  b Where is it cheapest to buy the MP3 player? Show your workings.

6 Problem-solving / STEM   An engineer cuts a piece of metal into 6 pieces. Each piece measures 0.8 m. How long was the original piece of metal?

Topic links: Averages, Estimation, Area

Subject links: Geography (Q10, Q11), Computing (Q12), Science (Q14), Cookery (Q15)

7 **STEM** A sheet of steel 9 m long is cut into 18 pieces.
How long is each piece in metres?

8 **Real** Estimate the price of
a 2 DVDs, each costing £3.49
b 10 cars priced at £9999.99
c 5 MP3 players costing £12.89 each
d 9 USB sticks costing £2.12 each.

Q8 hint
Round the prices and then multiply.

9 **STEM** The 4 members of a team flew a paper aeroplane distances
of 2.5 metres, 1.58 metres, 2.26 metres and 1.3 metres.
a What was the total distance for the team?
Another team's total distance was 8.45 metres.
b What was the difference in distance between the two teams?

10 **Real / STEM** Charlie measures the total rainfall over 5 days.

Monday	Tuesday	Wednesday	Thursday	Friday
0.52 mm	2.5 mm	3.2 mm	2.1 mm	0.68 mm

Work out the mean rainfall.

11 **STEM / Problem-solving** A rain gauge collects 3.3 mm of water.
The next day, 0.49 mm evaporates. On the third day, 5.66 mm of rain
falls. What is the reading on the rain gauge?

Q11 Literacy hint
When water evaporates, it changes
from a liquid to a gas.

12 **Real / STEM** Bruce has 149.6 MB free on his computer disk.
He deletes a file that is 3.72 MB and creates a 2.35 MB file.
How much space does he have on his computer disk now?

13 Work out the area of each rectangle.

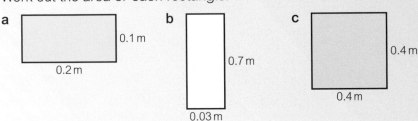

Q13 hint
Area = ☐ × ☐ = ☐ m²

14 **STEM** A chemical reaction needs 0.5 teaspoons of baking soda for
every 10 ml of vinegar.
If you use 50 ml of vinegar, how much baking soda should you add?

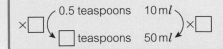

Q14 hint
Multiply each part by the same
number to get the same proportions.

15 **Real** A recipe needs 2 tablespoons of syrup for every 100 g of oats.
Alice uses 25 g of oats.
How much syrup does she need?

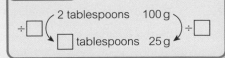

Q15 hint

16 **Explore** How could you estimate the price of your shopping?
Look back at the maths you have learned in this lesson.
How can you use it to answer this question?

17 **Reflect** In this lesson you have solved problems using multiplication,
division, addition and subtraction of decimals.
Which questions did you find easiest? What made them easy?
Which question did you find the most difficult?

Explore

Reflect

Master
P97

CHECK

Strengthen
P109

Extend
P113

Test
P117

5 Check up

Log how you did on your
Student Progression Chart.

Adding and subtracting decimals

1 Work out
a 3.2 + 9.45
b 1.92 + 14.6

2 Work out
a 3.5 − 1.42
b 10 − 0.87

3 Work out
a 9.61 + 0.7 + 15
b 9.5 + 3.2 − 0.34

4 A DVD costs £5.20 in one shop. In another shop it costs £3.59.
What is the difference in price?

5 Three pieces of wood measure 0.32 m, 1.4 m and 0.5 m.
What is the total length?

Multiplying decimals

6 Work out
a 0.5 × 18
b 700 × 0.5
c 0.2 × 14
d 27 × 0.2

7 Work out
a 0.3 × 15
b 90 × 0.8

8 Work out
a 25 × 3.2
b 2.5 × 15

9 Work out
a 5.27 × 6
b 3 × 0.29

10 A piece of string is cut into 8 pieces. Each piece measures 0.24 m.
How long was the original piece of string?

11 A chemical is mixed with water in the ratio 0.5 : 1.
The mixture contains 4 litres of the chemical.
How much water was used?

12 Work out the area of this rectangle.

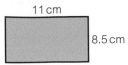

11 cm

8.5 cm

13 Work out
  a 0.3^2
  b 0.6^2

14 Work out
  a 0.2×0.03
  b 0.08×0.1

Rounding and ordering decimals

15 Round each number to 2 decimal places.
  a 8.505
  b 7.398
  c 9.2949

16 Write these numbers in ascending order (from smallest to largest).

  0.405   4.15   0.5405   4.1005   0.05   0.4051

17 **How sure are you of your answers? Were you mostly**
  ☹ **Just guessing**   😐 **Feeling doubtful**   ☺ **Confident**
  What next? Use your results to decide whether to strengthen or extend your learning.

Challenge

18 The **product** of two numbers is 2.4
  List pairs of numbers that they could be.
  How many pairs can you find?

19 Some of the digits are missing from these calculations.
  Work out what they are.

  a   2 . ☐ 1
      − 0 . 7 ☐
      ‾‾‾‾‾‾‾‾‾
        1 . 7 2

  b   ☐☐ . 1
      −   8 . ☐☐
      ‾‾‾‾‾‾‾‾‾‾‾
        8 7 . 3 3

> **Q18 Literacy hint**
> The **product** of two numbers is the result of the two numbers multiplied together.

Reflect

Master
P97

Check
P107

STRENGTHEN

Extend
P113

Test
P117

5 Strengthen

You will:
- Strengthen your understanding with practice.

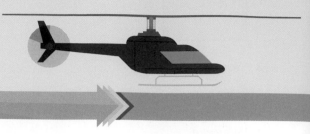

Adding and subtracting decimals

1 Work out

a 9.4 + 8.27

```
 U . t h
 9 . 4 0
+8 . 2 7
_____
   .
```

b 8. 62 + 23

```
 T U . t h
   8 . 6 2
+2 3 . 0 0
_____
     .
```

Q1a hint

9.40 is the same as 9.4

2 Work out

a 8.21 + 7.9
b 3.89 + 59
c 19.54 + 0.98

Q2 hint

Use the method in Q1.

3 Work out

a 5.84 − 2.3

```
 U . t h
 5 . 8 4
−2 . 3 0
_____
   .
```

b 18.7 − 3.24

```
 T U . t h
 1 8 . 7 0
−  3 . 2 4
_____
     .
```

Q3a hint

2.30 is the same as 2.3

4 Work out

a 19.73 − 8.5
b 28.9 − 3.72
c 14 − 9.73

Q4 hint

Use the method in Q3.

5 Work out

a 2.47 + 9.8
b 2.47 + 9.8 + 0.35

Q5b hint

You've already worked out
2.47 + 9.8, so add 0.35 to your
answer to part **a**.

2.47	9.8	0.35

6 Work out

   a 3.45 + 9.7 + 0.11

   b 3.67 − 1.9 + 8.6

   c 19.57 − 14.9 − 2.03

   d 12 + 8.03 − 9.6

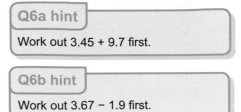

Q6a hint

Work out 3.45 + 9.7 first.

Q6b hint

Work out 3.67 − 1.9 first.

7 On Monday William earns £50. On Tuesday he earns £14.92.
How much does he earn in total?

8 Sid buys an MP3 player that costs £12.57.
How much change does he get from £20?

Multiplying decimals

 1 a Work out $\frac{1}{2}$ of 26.

   b Work out 0.5 × 26 on your calculator.
What do you notice?

2 Work out

   a 0.5 × 34 = $\frac{1}{2}$ of ☐ = ☐

   b 0.5 × 400 = $\frac{1}{2}$ of ☐ = ☐

   c 6.4 × 0.5

3 Work out

   a 9 × 0.2

   b 0.2 × 14

   c 36 × 0.2

   d 41 × 0.2

   e 0.4 × 7

   f 0.6 × 3

   g 8 × 0.05

4 a Work out 7 × 45

   b Copy and complete the number pattern.

     7 × 45 = ☐

     7 × 4.5 = ☐

     7 × 0.45 = ☐

5 Work out

   a 9 × 0.36

   b 8.23 × 8

   c 4.21 × 6

6 Jago works 8 hours a day. He earns £7.75 an hour.
How much does he earn in a day?

7 Bart is paid £6.45 per hour. How much does he earn for a 7-hour shift?

8 Work out

   a 36 × 3.5

   b 24 × 4.5

   c 73 × 2.2

   d 5.2 × 31

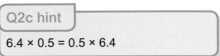

Q1a hint

$\frac{1}{2}$ of 26

$\frac{1}{2}$ of 20 $\frac{1}{2}$ of 6

☐ + ☐

Q2c hint

6.4 × 0.5 = 0.5 × 6.4

Q3a hint

Use a number pattern.
9 × 2 = 18, 9 × 0.2 = ☐

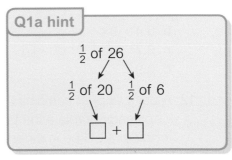

Q4a hint

Use the grid method or the column
method.

×	40	5
7	☐	☐

   45
× 7
‾‾‾‾

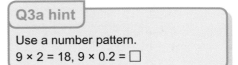

Q6 hint

☐ × ☐ = £☐

Q8a hint

36 × 35 = ☐
36 × 3.5 = ☐

9 Copy and complete this number pattern.
$4 \times 3 = \square$
$0.4 \times 3 = \square$
$0.04 \times 3 = \square$

10 Work out
  a 0.03×5
  b 0.06×7
  c 0.05×0.7
  d 0.03×0.4
  e 0.9×0.08

Q10a hint

Use a number pattern.
$3 \times 5 = \square$, $0.3 \times 5 = \square$, $0.03 \times 5 = \square$

11 Work out
  a 0.3×0.3
  b 0.4×0.4
  c $0.7^2 = 0.7 \times 0.7 = \square$
  d 0.9^2

Q11a hint

$3 \times 3 = \square$, $0.3 \times 3 = \square$, $0.3 \times 0.3 = \square$

12 A paint stripper contains 0.5 litres of white spirit and 3.5 litres of water. Copy and complete the table to show how much of each ingredient will be in different sized bottles.

Q12 hint

The size of bottle has been multiplied by 2, so do the same to the amount of white spirit.

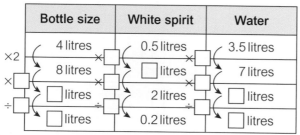

Bottle size	White spirit	Water
4 litres	0.5 litres	3.5 litres
8 litres	☐ litres	7 litres
☐ litres	2 litres	☐ litres
☐ litres	0.2 litres	☐ litres

13 Squash is mixed with water in the ratio 1 : 3.5.
The mixture contains 7 litres of water. How much squash is used?

Q13 hint

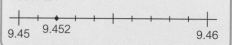

14 Pink paint is mixed from red paint and white paint in the ratio 0.25 : 1.
How much white paint is mixed with 2 litres of red paint?

Q14 hint

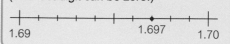

Rounding and ordering decimals

1 Round each number to 2 decimal places.
  a 9.452
  b 5.439
  c 2.825
  d 5.0308
  e 0.9871
  f 1.697
  g 0.295
  h 9.3038

Q1a hint

Which number, to 2 decimal places, is it closer to?

9.45   9.452   9.46

2 Copy this number line.

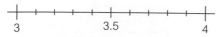

  a Mark 3.206 and 3.6 on the number line.
  b Which is larger, 3.206 or 3.6?

Q1f hint

Your answer must have 2 decimal places.
(The last digit can be zero.)

1.69   1.697   1.70

3 Which is the larger number in each pair?

   a 4.25   4.5

   b 8.032   8.3

   c 12.1542   12.136

   d 0.34911   0.4391

   e 0.92379   0.92397

Q3a hint

First compare the units: 4.25 and 4.5
Both are the same so continue comparing.
Next compare the tenths: 4.25 and 4.5

4 Problem-solving One number in each list is in the wrong place. Write each list in the correct order.

   a 0.3   0.17   0.89   0.92

   b 3.5   3.92   3.903   3.99

   c 0.29   0.293   0.281   0.296

   d 13.4   14.5   19.234   19.1

Q4 Strategy hint

Are they in order (smallest to largest)?

Enrichment

1 Reasoning Each brick in the pyramid is found by adding together the 2 bricks below it.
Work out the value of the top brick in each pyramid.

a   **b**   **c**

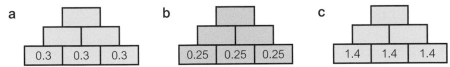

How could you find the top brick in each pyramid *without* doing any addition?
Use your method to find the top brick in a pyramid whose bottom 3 bricks each are 2.39

2 **Reflect** These strengthen lessons have shown different methods for working with decimals. Look back at the questions that used
  • bar models
  • number lines
  • multiplication using a grid.
Did any of these methods help you?
If so, which was the most helpful?
Did you use the method for any other questions?

5 Extend

You will:
* Extend your understanding with problem-solving.

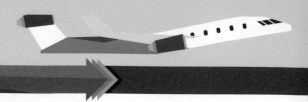

1 Every day a plant grows 0.2 mm.
How much will it grow in 5 days?
Give your answer in cm.

2 Here are two ways of working out 16 × 0.5

    A   16 × 5 ÷ 10   **B**   B 16 ÷ 2

Complete both calculations.
Which is the easier way of working out 16 × 0.5?

3 Find the missing values in the function machines.

  a   Input   Output
       0.81 → +3.2 → ☐

  b   Input   Output
       7.1 → ×6 → ☐

  c   Input   Output
       ☐ → ÷3.85 → 9

  d   Input   Output
       ☐ → −0.37 → 8.9

4 In these number wheels, each pair of opposite numbers **sums** to the total in the red circle.
Copy and complete the wheels.

> **Q4 hint**
>
> **Sum** means 'add to'.

  a   (0.51)   ( )
    ( )   5   (2.87)
    (3.7)   ( )

  b   (4.6)   (0.4)
    ( )   ( )   (3.94)
    ( )   (1.09)

5 Work out

  a −0.34 × 5   **b** −9 × 1.64
  c 8 × −3.79   **d** 9.61 × −3
  e −12.17 × 5   **f** 20.09 × −9

> **Q5 hint**
>
> negative × positive = negative

Topic links: Averages, Surface area of cuboids, Volume, Negative numbers, Priority of operations, Units, Function machines, Formulae, Angle properties

Subject links: Science (Q8, Q10, Q25)

6 Here is a list of decimal numbers.

    0.62   0.4   0.55   0.55   0.88

Work out

a the mode

b the median

c the mean.

7 Ruby carries out an experiment testing students' reaction times.
She records the time students take to press a buzzer after they see a
light come on. Here are the reaction times, in seconds, of 7 students.

    0.42   0.2   0.24   0.45   0.11   0.18   0.3

Work out

a the mean reaction time

b the median reaction time

c the range.

Give your answers to 2 decimal places.

8 **STEM** The ratio of oxygen to nitrogen in air is 1 : 4. An air cylinder
used for scuba diving contains 3.6 litres of nitrogen.

a How much oxygen does the cylinder contain?

Divers also use nitrox cylinders. The ratio of oxygen to nitrogen in a
nitrox mixture is 9 : 16. One cylinder contains 5.4 litres of oxygen.

b How much nitrogen does it contain?

9 Work out the size of the missing angles.

a 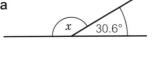   **b** 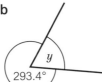   **c**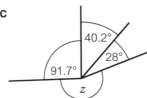

10 **STEM** The metal magnesium burns with oxygen to produce
magnesium oxide.
Julie burns 2.6 g of magnesium and gets 4.11 g of magnesium oxide.
How much oxygen combines with the magnesium?

11 Work out

a 15.9 − 4.72 − 6.35 + 8.4

b 79.05 + 291.68 − 157.3 + 65

12 **STEM** To calculate the distance travelled (in metres) you can use
the formula

    distance = speed × time

Work out the distance travelled when

a speed = 0.45 m/s, time = 8 seconds

b speed = 2.37 m/s, time = 7 seconds

c speed = 9 m/s, time = 8.05 seconds.

13 The prices of 7 different cars are

    £2456   £5000   £1999   £3245   £4529   £3949   £6288

Work out the mean price of the cars.

> **Q13 hint**
>
> Round your answer sensibly.

14 The heights of 6 different plants, in cm, are

3.6   0.91   8.4   2.03   7.21   4.85

a Work out the mean height.

b What is the range of heights?

15 A holiday for 9 people costs a total of £2000.
Work out the cost per person.

16 Work out the area and perimeter of each shape.

a
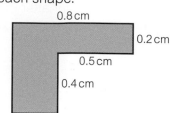

b

> **Q16b hint**
>
> To find the area, split the shape into 2 rectangles.

17 Ahmed and Sean do a sponsored walk to raise money for their two charities. They share the money between the charities where the ratio of Ahmed's charity to Sean's charity is 3 : 4. Sean's charity gets £156.60.
How much does Ahmed's charity get?

18 Work out

a 0.8^2

b $\sqrt{0.25}$

> **Q18b hint**
>
> □ × □ = 0.25

19 A square has area $0.09\,\text{m}^2$.
Work out

a the length of one side

b the perimeter.

20 Find the missing value in each function machine.

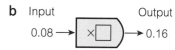

a   Input   Output
0.02 → ×0.5 → □

b   Input   Output
0.08 → ×□ → 0.16

c   Input   Output
□ → ×0.03 → 0.006

d   Input   Output
0.1 → □ → 0.01

21 Work out the surface area of this cube.

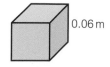
0.06 m

22 A cuboid has side lengths 1 m, 0.4 m and 0.6 m.
Work out its surface area.

> **Q22 Strategy hint**
>
> Sketch the cuboid first.

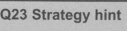

23 Write these capacities in ascending order of size (smallest first).

4.5*l*   3562 m*l*   4.09*l*   4.599*l*   4500 m*l*   3.9*l*

> **Q23 Strategy hint**
>
> Convert them to the same units.
> 1000 m*l* = 1 *l*

24 Write these lengths in ascending order of size.

3.5 m   453 cm   4.205 m   0.6 m

35 cm   3.209 m   4350 mm

25 STEM These are the 8 most common metals in the Earth's crust, by mass.
Put them in **descending** order, with the commonest metal first.

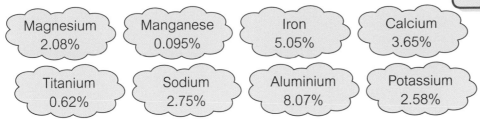

Q25 Literacy hint
Descending order is from largest to smallest.

Magnesium 2.08%   Manganese 0.095%   Iron 5.05%   Calcium 3.65%

Titanium 0.62%   Sodium 2.75%   Aluminium 8.07%   Potassium 2.58%

26 A cube has side length 0.2 m.
Work out its volume.

0.2 m

27 Work out the volume of this cuboid.
Give your answer in cubic metres.

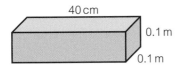
40 cm
0.1 m
0.1 m

28 Work out
  a $0.2 \times 0.5 + 7.3$
  b $9.4 - 4 \times 0.3$
  c $18 \div 6 + 3.49$
  d $0.03 + 0.02 \times 0.4$
  e $0.4 \times 8 - 0.81$

Q28 Strategy hint
Multiplication and division, then addition and subtraction.

29 a The product of two numbers is 0.36 and the sum is 1.2.
    What are they?
  b The product of two numbers is 0.15 and the sum is 0.8.
    What are they?

Investigation   Problem-solving

1 Start with a 2-digit number with 2 decimal places, e.g. 0.49
2 Reverse the digits to make another 2-digit number with 2 decimal places.
3 Find the difference between the two numbers.
4 Use the answer to part **3** and repeat parts **2** and **3**. Do this 10 times. Write the sequence of numbers that you get.
5 Repeat all this for two different starting numbers.
6 Comment on the sequences you made.

30 Reflect This unit is about decimals. What other areas of maths have
you used in these extend lessons?
Make a list like this:
Multiplying by negative numbers, Q5
Ratio, Q8

Reflect

5 Unit test

Log how you did on your Student Progression Chart.

1 Work out
   a 3.4 + 5.91
   b 0.89 + 18.2

2 Work out
   a 68 × 0.5
   b 0.5 × 900
   c 0.2 × 43

3 Two books are 0.67 cm and 3.4 cm thick.
   How much space will they take up on a bookshelf?

4 Work out
   a 0.54 × 8
   b 3.24 × 9

5 Work out
   a 3.9 − 0.34
   b 18 − 0.47
   c 9.18 − 7.2

6 A 5 m length of cloth has 3.72 m cut off.
   How much is left?

7 A recipe needs 0.5 g of ginger for every 2.5 g of garlic.
   For 4 people the recipe needs 10 g of garlic.
   How much ginger is needed?

8 Ethanol is put into two test tubes in the ratio 1 : 3.
   There is 52.5 ml in the first test tube.
   How much is in the second test tube?

9 Work out
   a 9.2 + 0.35 + 18
   b 9.6 − 0.58 + 18.4

10 Work out
   a 3.5 × 27
   b 94 × 4.2

11 Sweets cost £0.02 each.
   How much will 37 cost?

12 34 bricks 8.5 cm long are laid end to end.
   How long is the row?

13 Round each number to 2 decimal places.
   a 18.925
   b 256.9142
   c 7.2985

14 Work out
  a 0.08×0.9
  b 0.7×0.05

15 Work out
  a 0.4^2
  b 0.1^2

16 Write these numbers in ascending order (from smallest to largest).

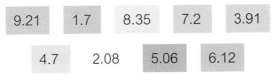

| 3.8 | 3.04 | 3.42 | 3.244 | 4.32 | 3.402 |

17 Work out the area and perimeter of this rectangle.

0.7 m

0.3 m

Challenge

18 Here are some numbers.

| 9.21 | 1.7 | 8.35 | 7.2 | 3.91 |

| 4.7 | 2.08 | 5.06 | 6.12 |

Choose the pair with
  a the sum closest to 10
  b the difference closest to 5.

19 **Reflect** Put these topics in order, from easiest to hardest.
  (You could just write the letters.)
  A Writing decimals in order
  B Adding decimals
  C Subtracting decimals
  D Multiplying decimals
  E Dividing decimals
  F Rounding decimals
  Think about the two topics you said were hardest.
  What made them hard?
  Write at least one hint to help you for each topic.

6.1 Measuring and drawing angles

You will learn to:
- Use a protractor to measure and draw obtuse and reflex angles
- Estimate the size of reflex angles.

CONFIDENCE

Why learn this?
Reflex angles are used to describe bearings in a westerly direction.

Fluency
Subtract these angles from 360°.
- 40°
- 100°
- 130°

Name these angles.

Explore
Which angles describe SW, NW and other points of the compass?

Exercise 6.1

1 Measure these angles.

a

b

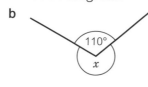

2 Use a ruler and protractor to draw each of these angles.

a

70°

b

c ∠ABC = 50°

3 Work out the size of angle x in each diagram.

a

40°

b

110°
x

Q3 hint

Angles round a point add up to 360°.

c

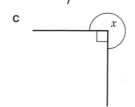
x

Warm up

Topic links: Bearings

Worked example

Measure the reflex angle shown by the red arc.

80°

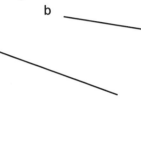

Measure the smaller angle.

Work out the size of the **reflex angle**.

360° − 80° = 280°

4 Measure each angle.

a

b

c

5 Draw these obtuse angles.

a

150°

b

120°

6 **i** Estimate the **bearing** of each ship.
  ii Measure the bearing with a protractor.

a N

b N

c N

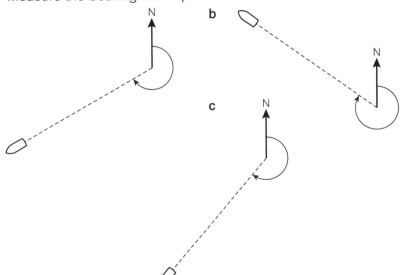

Worked example

Draw an angle of 200°.

$360° - 200° = 160°$

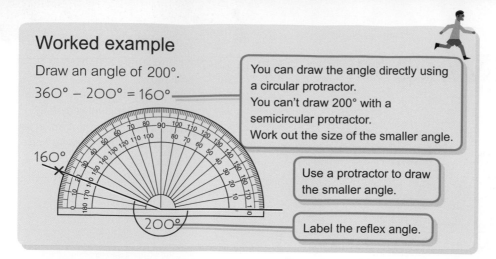

You can draw the angle directly using a circular protractor.
You can't draw 200° with a semicircular protractor.
Work out the size of the smaller angle.

Use a protractor to draw the smaller angle.

Label the reflex angle.

160°

200°

7 Draw these reflex angles.

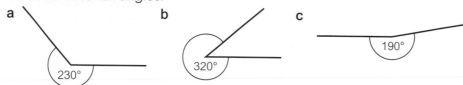

a   230°

b   320°

c   190°

8 a Are these angles acute, obtuse or reflex?

   i Angle ABC = 210°   **ii** ∠DEF = 140°

   iii GĤI = 340°   **iv** Angle JKL = 35°

   v ∠PQR = 27°   **vi** Angle XYZ = 305°

b Use a protractor to draw each angle in part **a**.

> **Q8 hint**
>
> Angle ABC can also be written ∠ABC or AB̂C.

> ### Investigation
> Reasoning
>
> **1 a** Describe each angle as acute or obtuse: 70° and 160°.
>   **b** Add the two angles together. Is the result acute, obtuse or reflex?
> **2** If you add an obtuse angle to an acute angle, do you always get a reflex angle?
>   Repeat part **1** several times using different angles.
> **3 a** Describe each angle as acute, obtuse or reflex: 60° and 300°.
>   **b** Subtract 60° from 300°. Is the result acute, obtuse or reflex?
> **4** If you subtract an acute angle from a reflex angle, do you always get a reflex angle?
>   Repeat part **3** several times using different angles.
>   **Discussion** What were your answers to parts **2** and **4**? Did everyone reach the same conclusion?

9 Explore Which angles describe SW, NW and other points of the compass?
Is it easier to explore this question now you have completed the lesson?
What further information do you need to be able to answer this?

10 Reflect 'Notation' means symbols. Mathematics uses a lot of notation.
For example:

   = means 'is equal to'

   ° means 'degrees'

   ⌐ means 'a right angle'

Look back at this lesson on angles. Write a list of the maths notation you used. Why do you think mathematicians use notation?
Could you have answered the questions in this lesson without understanding the maths notation?
What others subjects use notation?

Active Learn Pi 2, Section 6.1

6.2 Vertically opposite angles

You will learn to:

• Use vertically opposite angles.

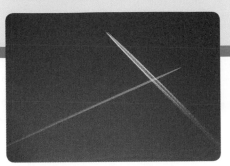

Why learn this?
Vertically opposite angles help you find missing angles where straight lines cross.

Fluency
Work out
• 90 + 65
• 180 – 50
• 360 – 150
What do angles round a point add up to?
What do angles on a straight line add up to?

Explore
How many pairs of vertically opposite angles are made when three lines cross?

Exercise 6.2

1 Work out the size of the angles marked with letters.

  a
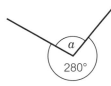

  b

2 Work out the size of the angles marked with letters.

  a

  b

  c

  d

Investigation   **Reasoning**

1 Draw two straight lines that cross each other.
2 Measure two **vertically opposite angles**.
   What do you notice?
3 Measure the other two vertically opposite angles.
   What do you notice?
4 Draw two more straight lines that cross.
   Repeat parts **2** and **3**.
5 Copy and complete the sentence:
   Vertically opposite angles are _____

Literacy hint

When two straight line cross, two pairs of **vertically opposite angles** are created.

3 Work out the size of the angles marked with letters.

  a

  b

  c

  d
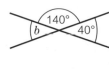

Worked example

Work out the size of the angles a and b.
Write any rules that you use.

$a = 40°$ (vertically opposite angles)
$b = 180° - 40° = 140°$ (angles on a straight line)

> Write down the rules you have used.

4 Work out the size of the angles marked with letters. Give reasons.

a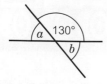

b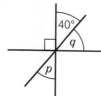

c

> **Q4 hint**
>
> Write the rules you use as reasons for your answer.

Discussion What reason did you give for angle b?
Could you have used another reason?

5 **Problem-solving** The diagram shows part of a wall trellis made out of identical rhombuses.

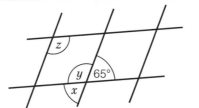

  a What is the size of angle x?
  b Work out the size of angle y.
  c Work out the size of angle z.

> **Q5 hint**
>
> Use the symmetry of a rhombus.

6 **Reasoning** Choose two pairs of angles from the cloud to show the angles in a pair of crossed lines.
Draw two diagrams showing crossed lines like this:
Label them with your pairs of angles.

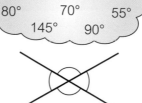

7 **STEM / Problem-solving** Light is **refracted** when it passes through a glass lens. Work out the angles x and y.

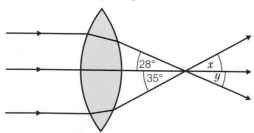

> **Q7 Literacy hint**
>
> When light **refracts**, the ray of light changes direction.

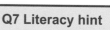

8 **Explore** How many pairs of vertically opposite angles are made when three lines cross?
Look back at the maths you have learned in this lesson.
How can you use it to answer this question?

9 **Reflect** Look back at Q4 and Q5 in this lesson.
In what order did you work out each angle?
Could you have worked out the missing angles in a different order?
Explain why or why not.

*Active*Learn   Pi 2, Section 6.2

Explore

Reflect

MASTER

Check
P131

Strengthen
P133

Extend
P137

Test
P141

6.3 Angles in triangles

You will learn to:
• Work out the size of unknown angles in a triangle.

Why learn this?
Surveyors use the angles in triangles to plot landscape features on a map.

Fluency
Work out
• 180 − 30 − 100
• 180 − 90 − 25
Which three of these numbers add up to 180?
• 30, 90, 50, 100

Explore
If you change one angle of a triangle, how does it change the other angles?

Exercise 6.3

1 Work out the size of angle a. Give a reason.

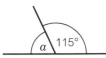

2 Use the correct notation to describe each angle of the triangle.

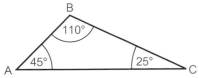

Q2 hint

$\angle ABC$ can also be written $A\hat{B}C$ or angle ABC.

3 Match the triangles to the names in the cloud.

a   b   c

equilateral
                scalene
    isosceles

Q3 hint

Equal sides are marked with a dash.

Warm up

Investigation   Reasoning

1 Draw a triangle with angles a, b and c.
2 Cut out the triangle and tear off each of the corners.
3 Arrange the three parts in a straight line so that the angles a, b and c meet.
4 What does this tell you about the angles in a triangle?
Does this work for all triangles?

Worked example

Work out the size of angle x.

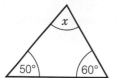

$x = 180° - 130° - 25°$ ————— Subtract the angles you know from 180°.

   $= 25°$

Key point

Angles in a triangle add up to 180°.

4 Work out the size of angle x in each triangle.

a

b

c

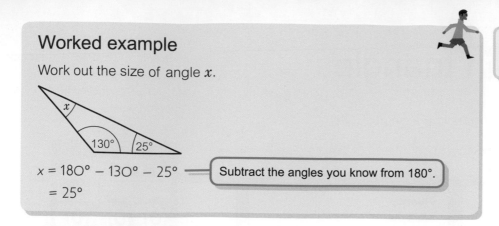

Q4a hint

$180° - 50° - 60° = \square°$

Discussion What is a quick way of finding the size of an unknown angle in a right-angled triangle?

5 **Sketch** each triangle.
Mark the angles you know.
Work out the size of the unknown angle.
  a ABC where ∠ABC = 55° and ∠BAC = 35°
  b PQR where ∠PQR = 65° and ∠QPR = 90°
  c DEF where ∠DFE = 40° and ∠FED = 100°

Q5 Literacy hint

A **sketch** is a rough diagram.
Draw the angles approximately
without a protractor.

Q5a hint

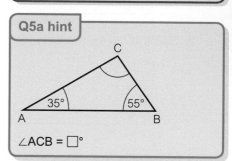

∠ACB = $\square°$

6 For each triangle
  i work out the size of the unknown angle
  ii write down the type of triangle: is it equilateral, isosceles, right-angled or scalene?

a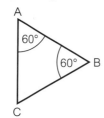

b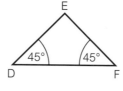

c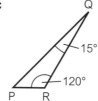

7 **Reasoning / Real** A sail-maker used this plan to mark out a sail on a sheet of cloth.

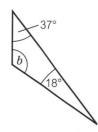

She checked the shape by measuring the angle b and found it to be 125°. Did she draw the sail correctly? Explain your answer.

8 Work out the size of the **exterior angle** in each diagram.

a 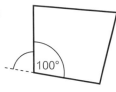   **b**   **c**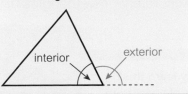

Key point

An **interior angle** is inside a shape.
An **exterior angle** is outside the shape on a straight line next to the interior angle.

interior   exterior

9 Work out the size of the marked exterior angle in each quadrilateral.

a   **b**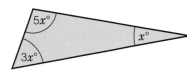

100°   120°

Q8a hint

$x = 180° - \square°$
(angles on a straight line)

10 a Draw a triangle.
  b Measure its interior angles. Mark them on your diagram.
  c For each interior angle, draw an exterior angle.
  d Work out the exterior angles. Mark them on your diagram.

11 The diagram shows a triangle.
  a Write an expression for the sum
    of the angles in the triangle.
    Show that your expression simplifies
    to $9x°$.
  b The sum of the angles in a triangle is 180°.
    Solve the equation $9x = 180$.
  c Copy and complete the working to calculate the sizes of the
    angles in the triangle.
    Use your answer to part **b**.
    $x = \square°$
    $3x = 3 \times \square = \square°$
    $5x = 5 \times \square = \square°$

$5x°$ $x°$ $3x°$

12 Explore If you change one angle of a triangle, how does it
change the other angles?
Choose some sensible numbers to help you explore this situation.
Then use what you've learned in this lesson to help you answer
the question.

13 Reflect William says, 'Interior angles are on the inside of a
shape and exterior angles are on the outside.'
Do you agree with William?
Write a better definition, in your own words, for interior and
exterior angles. You could draw a diagram to help with
your explanation.

Explore

Reflect

6.4 Drawing triangles accurately

You will learn to:
- Accurately draw triangles using a ruler and protractor.

CONFIDENCE

Why learn this?
Lots of bridges are built using triangles – architects need to be able to draw them accurately on the plan.

Fluency
- What is the sum of the angles of a triangle?
- Estimate the size of the three angles of this triangle.

Explore
How can you draw a kite and a rhombus?

Exercise 6.4

Warm up

1 a Sketch a triangle ABC with length AB 5 cm and ∠ABC 50°.
  b Label side AB with its length.
  c Label angle ABC 50°.

2 Draw a line AB 7.5 cm long.

3 Draw each angle.
  a 40°
  b 90°
  c 137°

Worked example

Make an accurate drawing of this triangle.

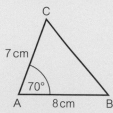

1 Use a ruler to draw the line AB 8 cm long.
2 Use a protractor to draw an angle of 70° at A. Draw a long line through the 70° mark.
3 Use a ruler to draw the line AC 7 cm long.
4 Draw in the third side of the triangle, from B to C.

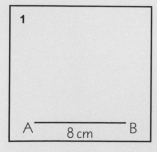

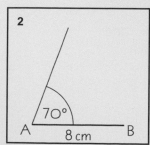

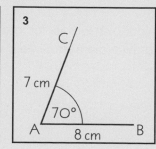

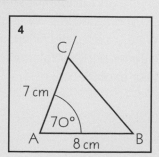

127

4 Use a ruler and protractor to draw these triangles accurately.

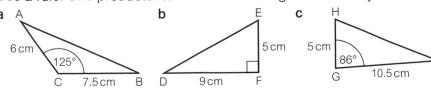

a A
6 cm
125°
C   7.5 cm   B

b   E
5 cm
D   9 cm   F

c H
5 cm
86°
G   10.5 cm   I

Q4 hint

Use the steps in the worked example. First draw and label a side with a length you know.

Discussion Does it matter where you draw the first line?

5 Use a ruler and protractor to draw the triangle ABC where AB = 9 cm, ∠CAB = 60° and AC = 7 cm.

Q5 Strategy hint

Make a sketch first. Label the sides and angles you know.

Worked example

Use a ruler and protractor to draw this triangle accurately.

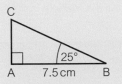

C
25°
A   7.5 cm   B

1 Use a ruler to draw the line AB 7.5 cm long.
2 Use a protractor to draw an angle of 90° at A.
   Draw a long line through the 90° mark.
3 Use a protractor to draw an angle of 25° at B.
   Draw a line through the 25° mark until it crosses the line from A. Label C.

1

A   7.5 cm   B

2

A   7.5 cm   B

3

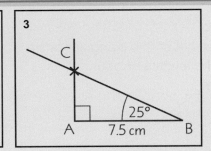

C

A   7.5 cm   25°   B

6 a Use a ruler and protractor to draw these triangles accurately.

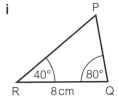

i   P
40°   80°
R   8 cm   Q

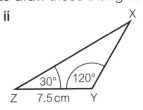

ii   X
30°   120°
Z   7.5 cm   Y

Q6 hint

Label the vertices (corners) of the triangle. Label the side and angles you know.

  b i Work out the size of the unknown angle in each triangle.
  ii Check your answer by measuring the angle.
  c i What kind of triangles are they?
  ii How can you use a ruler to check your answer?

Q6b i hint

What do the angles of a triangle add up to?

7 Use a ruler and protractor to draw the triangle ABC where AB = 9 cm, ∠CAB = 60° and ∠ABC = 50°.

8 Explore How can you draw a kite and a rhombus?
Is it easier to explore this question now you have completed the lesson?
What further information do you need to be able to answer this?

9 Reflect In this lesson you used two tools to help you draw triangles accurately – a ruler and a protractor.
Which did you find more difficult to use? Why?
Write down a hint or hints, in your own words, to help you use this tool in future.

6.5 Designing nets

You will learn to:
- Accurately draw a net of a 3D shape
- Investigate the sides of a right-angled triangle.

CONFIDENCE

Why learn this?
Product designers construct nets for boxes and packaging.

Fluency
Sketch a prism and a pyramid. What is a net of a 3D shape?

Explore
How can you tell if a triangle is right-angled?

Exercise 6.5

Warm up

1 Sketch a net of this triangular prism.
Label the lengths on your net.

6   10   12   8

2 Measure the length of each line accurately.
   a _____
   b _____

3 Use a ruler and protractor to draw this triangle accurately.

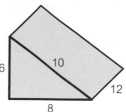

35°   35°
8 cm

4 The diagram shows the net of a right-angled triangular prism.

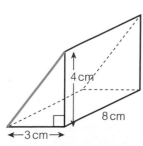

4 cm   8 cm   3 cm

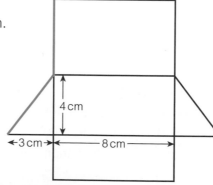

4 cm   3 cm   8 cm

   a Draw the net accurately on squared paper.
   b Label the lengths of the sides. Start with the bottom rectangle.

Q4a hint

You will need to measure the blue side of the triangle. Then you can draw the top rectangle of the net.

Topic links: Area and surface area, Nets, 3D shapes, Pythagoras' theorem

5 **STEM** Seb designs a box for tortilla chips.

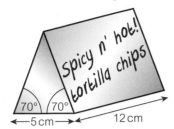
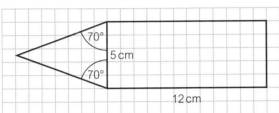

He has started to draw a net of the box on squared paper.

Q5 hint

Measure the sloping sides of the triangle.

Use a ruler and protractor to copy and complete the net.
Discussion Which part of the net did you draw first?

6 **STEM** A firework is in the shape of a square-based pyramid.
   a Draw a net of the pyramid.
   b Measure the sides and angles of the triangular faces.
      What do you notice?

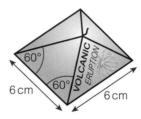

7 **Reasoning** The diagram shows a triangle with squares drawn on each side.
   a Work out the areas of each square.
      Add together the areas of the two smaller squares.
      What do you notice?
   b Repeat part **a** for this triangle.

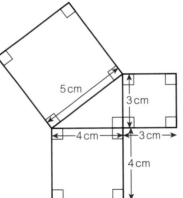

Q7 Strategy hint

Work out the area of each square.

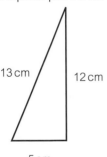

8 **Explore** How can you tell if a triangle is right-angled?
   Is it easier to explore this question now you have completed the lesson?
   What further information do you need to be able to answer this?

9 **Reflect** Chandni says, 'In this lesson I have used a lot of **spatial reasoning**.'
   Look back at your work this lesson.
   Which questions used spatial reasoning?
   Did you need to do anything different to answer these questions?

Q9 Literacy hint

Spatial reasoning means being able to imagine objects and shapes.

Explore

Reflect

Master
P119

CHECK

Strengthen
P133

Extend
P137

Test
P141

6 Check up

Log how you did on your
Student Progression Chart.

Measuring and drawing angles

1 Measure these angles.

a

b

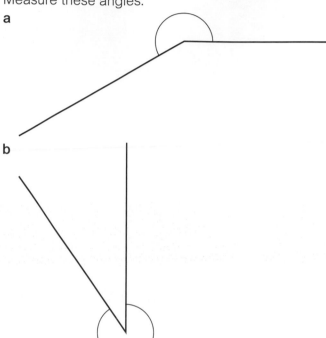

2 Use a ruler and protractor to draw an angle of
a 145°
b 300°.

Calculating angles

3 Work out the size of each labelled angle. Give a reason for each answer.

a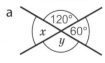

b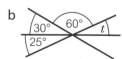

c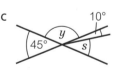

d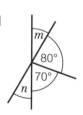

4 Work out the size of angle x.
Give a reason for your answer.

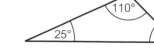

5 Work out the size of angles p and q. Give reasons for your answers.

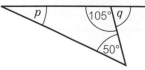

Drawing triangles and nets

6 **a** Use a ruler and protractor to draw this triangle accurately.

   b Measure the angle QPR.

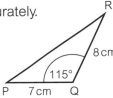

7 Use a ruler and protractor to draw this triangle accurately.

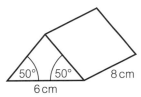

8 Draw an accurate net of this prism on squared paper.

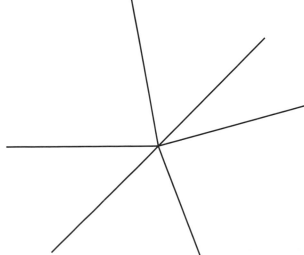

9 **How sure are you of your answers? Were you mostly**

   😞 **Just guessing**   😐 **Feeling doubtful**   🙂 **Confident**

   What next? Use your results to decide whether to strengthen or extend your learning.

Challenge

10 Sketch these diagrams. Use your knowledge of angle properties to work out which angles you need to measure and which you can calculate.

   i   **ii**

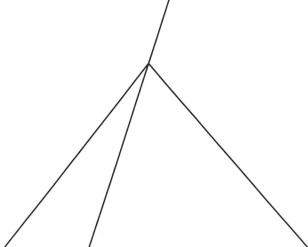

   a Write down the measured angles on your sketch.

   b Work out the sizes of the other angles.

   c Compare your answers with a classmate. Did you measure the same angles? Did you measure fewer or more?

6 Strengthen

You will:
- Strengthen your understanding with practice.

Measuring and drawing angles

1 Choose the best estimate for each angle.

a
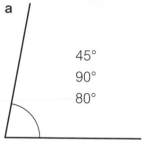
45°
90°
80°

b
95°   130°   180°

c
350°
345°
359°

2 Reasoning Becky says, 'The size of the angle marked in red is 70°.'
Give a reason why she is wrong.
What is the correct answer?

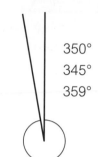

3 a Draw this angle accurately.
b Draw an angle of 110°.

105°

> **Q3b hint**
>
> Is it bigger or smaller than a right angle?

4 a Use your protractor to measure the red angle in each diagram.

A   B   C   D

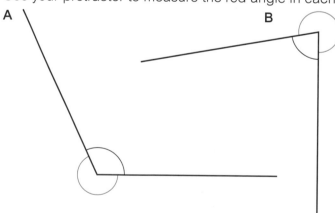
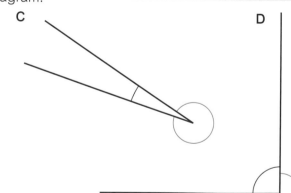

b Work out the size of the blue angle.
c Describe each angle as acute, right angle, obtuse or reflex.
d Copy and complete the table.

> **Q4b hint**
>
> Blue angle = 360° − red angle

Diagram	Red angle	Type of angle	Blue angle	Type of angle
A				
B				
C				
D				

5 Measure the marked angle in each diagram.

a

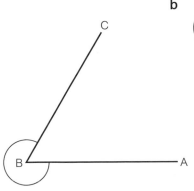

b

c

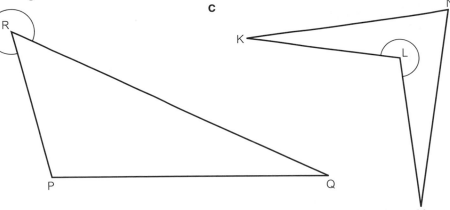

Discussion Does it matter whether you describe an angle as
∠ABC or ∠CBA?

6 a Work out the size of the red angle in each diagram.

i

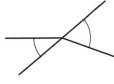
310°

ii

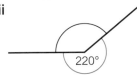
220°

iii

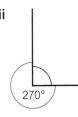
270°

Q5 Strategy hint

Measure the smaller angle.
Subtract from 360°.

b Use a ruler and protractor to draw the smaller (red) angle.
c Mark the reflex angle on your diagram.

7 Use a ruler and protractor to draw these reflex angles.
   a 320°   **b** 200°   **c** 295°

Q7a hint

Sketch the reflex angle.
Work out the
smaller angle

320°

Calculating angles

1 Use a ruler to decide if the marked angles are vertically opposite
angles.

a

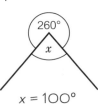

b

c

Q1 hint

These are not vertically opposite
angles because the red line is not
straight.

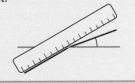

2 Stephanie has worked out the size of some angles.

a

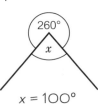
260°
x

x = 100°

b

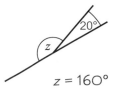
y
35°

y = 35°

c

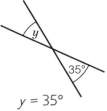
20°
z

z = 160°

Choose one of these reasons for each answer.
• Vertically opposite angles are equal.
• Angles on a straight line add up to 180°.
• Angles round a point add up to 360°.

3 Work out the size of each labelled angle. Give reasons for your answers.

a 　b 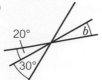　c 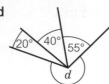　d

4 Copy and complete the working to find the size of angles a, b and c.

$a = \square$ (vertically opposite angles)

$b = \square$ (angles on a straight line)

$c = \square - 15 = \square$ (vertically opposite angles)

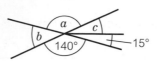

Q3 hint

Use the reasons from Q2.

5 Work out the size of the missing angle in each triangle.

a 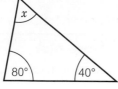　b　c

Q5 hint

Angles in a triangle add up to 180°.
$180° - \square - \square = \square$

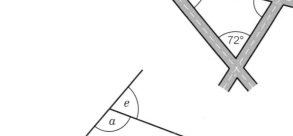

6 **Real** The runways at RAF Great Dunmow made a triangle.
 a Work out the size of the unknown angle.
 b What kind of triangle is it?

7 a Measure the interior angles of this triangle.
　　Check that they add up to 180°.
 b Measure the exterior angles.
 c Work out
　　i $a + e$　　ii $c + f$　　iii $b + d$
　　What do you notice?

8 Work out the size of angle z.

Drawing triangles and nets

1 Three students were asked to draw a triangle ABC where
　AB = 8 cm, BC = 7 cm and ∠ABC = 85°.
　They each made a sketch of the triangle before drawing it accurately.

Q1 Strategy hint

Check your accurate drawing against the correct sketch.

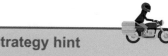

Karin　　　　Juan　　　　Eva

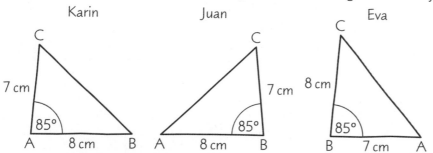

 a Only one of the sketches is correct. Who drew the correct sketch?
 b Draw a line AB 8 cm long.
 c Use a protractor to draw the given angle ∠ABC.
 d Draw in the other lines needed to complete the triangle accurately.

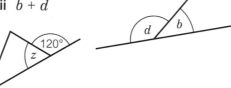

2 Make an accurate drawing of this triangle.

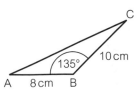

Q2 hint

Follow the steps in Q1.

3 Draw this triangle accurately.

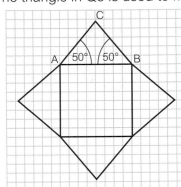

Q3 Strategy hint

Draw both angles.
Extend the lines until they cross.

4 The triangle in Q3 is used to make the nets below.

i

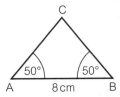

ii

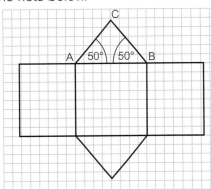

a Name the 3D solid that each net makes.

b Draw the nets on squared paper.
Use a ruler and protractor to draw the triangles.

c Cut out each net. Fold it up to make a solid.
Stick the edges together with tape.

Q4b ii hint

The edges of the rectangles must
have the same length as the side AC
of the triangle.
Measure them carefully so that the
net will fit together.

Enrichment

1 a Work with a partner. Each person draws a reflex angle.
Make sure the lines are long enough to measure the angle.

b **i** Ask your partner to estimate the size of your angle.

ii Measure your angle to check their answer.

c **i** Use a ruler and protractor to draw your partner's angle on tracing
paper.

ii Place your tracing on top of their angle to check your accuracy.

2 **Reflect** Look back at your work in these strengthen lessons.
For each section, choose statement A, B or C for how you felt about it
before and after the lessons.
A: ...difficult   B: ...OK   C: ...easy

	Before the lesson I found it ...	After the lesson I found it ...
Measuring and drawing angles		
Calculating angles		
Drawing triangles and nets		

If you find everything easy – well done!
If you still find something difficult, ask your teacher or a classmate for help.

Reflect

6 Extend

You will:
• Extend your understanding with problem-solving.

1 Measure the reflex angle at the centre of this circle.

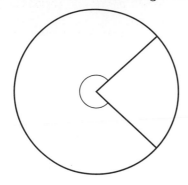

2 The pie chart shows the security strength of internet passwords.

Strength of password

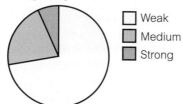

☐ Weak
▨ Medium
▦ Strong

a Estimate the angle of each sector.
b Decide whether each statement is true or false.
   i More than half of passwords are weak.
   ii At least a quarter of passwords are medium.
   iii Less than one third of passwords are medium or strong.
   iv One tenth of passwords are strong.

> **Q2b iii hint**
>
> What is $\frac{1}{3}$ of 360°?

3 Work out the size of the labelled angles.

a 60°, x, x, x
b 20°, y, y, 140°
c 35°, 60°, z

> **Q3 hint**
>
> Angles marked with the same letter are equal.

4 **Problem-solving** The diagram shows a silver brooch.

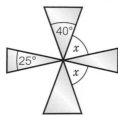

40°, x, 25°, x

Work out the size of angle x.

Topic Links: Pie charts, Line symmetry, Coordinates

5 STEM / Problem-solving The diagram shows part of an indoor TV aerial. The aerial has one line of symmetry.
Use a ruler and protractor to draw the aerial.

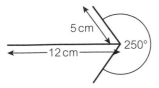

Q5 hint

Sketch the diagram. Mark the line of symmetry. Work out the angles.

6 ABCD is a rectangle.

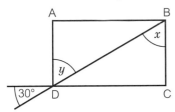

Q6 hint

Look for right angles, vertically opposite angles and angles in triangles.

Work out the size of angles x and y. Give reasons.

7 Problem-solving Two of the angles of some triangles are given below.
Decide if each triangle is isosceles, equilateral, right-angled or scalene. Give reasons.

  a 50°, 40°   **b** 110°, 20°   **c** 40°, 70°

Q7 Strategy hint

Sketch the triangle and work out the missing angle.

8 STEM The diagram shows a tooth of a band-saw blade.

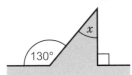

Q8 Strategy hint

Sketch the diagram. Label the angles as you work them out.

Work out the size of angle x.

9 Bunting is made from isosceles triangles.

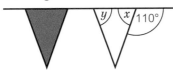

Work out the size of angles x and y. Give reasons for your answers.

10 Problem-solving a Copy the diagram.

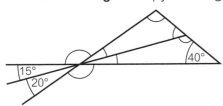

  b Work out the size of all the missing angles.
    Mark them on your diagram.

11 Work out the size of the angles marked with letters, in alphabetical order.
Choose one of these reasons for each answer.

  • Angles on a straight line add up to 180°.
  • Angles of a triangle add up to 180°.
  • Vertically opposite angles are equal.

12 **Real / Problem-solving** The diagram shows a cuboid box with the open lid resting on the ground.

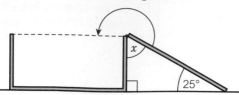

a Work out the size of angle x.
b Work out the size of the angle the lid will move through when it is closed.

13 The diagram shows a game to test hand-eye coordination.

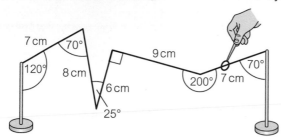

Use a ruler and protractor to draw the metal wire.

14 **Reasoning** One angle of a triangle is 42°.
Use a ruler and protractor to draw a possible triangle
a with all its angles acute
b with an obtuse angle
c that is right-angled
d that is isosceles.

Q14 Strategy hint
Make a sketch of each triangle first. Mark the size of the angles on your sketch.

15 a Draw these axes on squared paper.

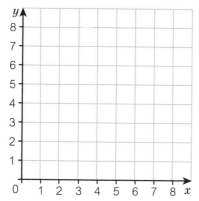

b Plot the points A(1, 1) and B(8, 1)
c ABC is a triangle where ∠ABC = 63° and ∠BAC = 63°.
  i Use a ruler and protractor to draw the triangle.
  ii Write the coordinates of point C.

16 a Use a ruler and protractor to draw this quadrilateral on squared paper.

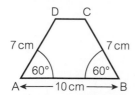

b What is the name of this quadrilateral?
c Measure the other two angles.

Q16a hint
Draw AB 10 cm long. Use your protractor to draw two 60° angles. Draw the sides BC and AD 7 cm long. Draw CD.

17 Use a ruler and protractor to draw these triangles.

a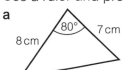

b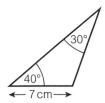

c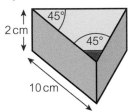

18 Problem-solving Use a ruler and protractor to draw this triangle.

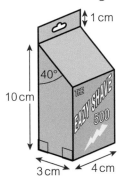

19 STEM Use a ruler and protractor to draw an accurate net of this open box.

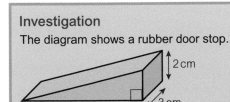

20 STEM The diagram shows a box containing an electric razor.

Draw a net for the box. Include the tab for hanging the box up in a shop. Use squared paper.

Q17a hint
Start with a side you know.

Your triangle doesn't have to be in the same position as in the diagram.

Q18 Strategy hint
Work out the size of the unknown angle.

Investigation   Problem-solving / STEM

The diagram shows a rubber door stop.

Sketch a box that will hold 10 door stops.
Draw a net of the box.
Compare your box with a classmate's. Did you choose the same design?

21 Reflect Look back at Q18.
What did you need to do first to be able to draw the triangle?
Why couldn't you draw the triangle just using the information in the question?

Master
P119

Check
P131

Strengthen
P133

Extend
P137

TEST

6 Unit test

Log how you did on your
Student Progression Chart.

1 Measure this angle.

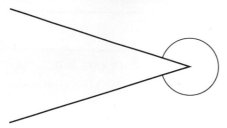

2 Draw an angle of
  a 108°
  b 195°.

3 Work out the size of the angles marked with letters. Give reasons.

  a

  b

  c

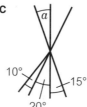

  d

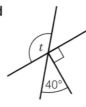

4 Work out the size of angle x.
  Give a reason.

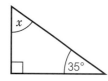

5 Work out the size of angles s and t.

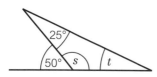

6 Use a ruler and protractor to draw this triangle accurately.

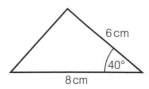

7 The triangle PQR has side PQ = 7 cm, ∠PQR = 80° and ∠QPR = 40°.
  Use a ruler and protractor to draw the triangle.

8 Draw the net of this square-based pyramid on squared paper.

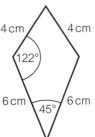

9 Use a ruler and protractor to draw this quadrilateral accurately.

Challenge

10 a This net is drawn on centimetre triangular grid paper.

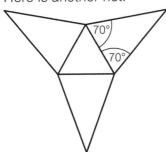

     i What are the sizes of the angles of the triangular faces?

    ii Describe the solid shape that is made when the net is folded up.

  b Here is another net.

     i Describe how the solid that this net forms is different from the one in part **a**.

    ii Make an accurate drawing of the net.

  c Design your own net using triangular grid paper.

11 Reflect This unit was all about angles and shapes. Joanna says, 'I'm glad I've learned more about triangles because I want to be an engineer.'

Ka says, 'I'm glad I've learned more about opposite angles because I want to be a joiner.'

What other professions can you think of that use angles and accurate drawings?

What job do you want to do? How will what you've learned in this lesson help?

7.1 Squares, cubes and roots

You will learn to:
- Calculate squares and square roots, mentally and using a calculator
- Calculate cubes and cube roots, mentally and using a calculator.

CONFIDENCE

Why learn this?
You can use square roots to work out the side length of a square when you know its area.

Fluency
Work out the area of each square.

 2 cm   4 mm   10 m

Explore
Do all numbers have a root?

Exercise 7.1

Warm up

1 Work out the volume of each cube.

a  3 cm   **b** 5 cm

 2 Work out

    a $\sqrt{36}$ **b** $\sqrt{81}$ **c** $\sqrt{100}$

3 Write down the first 10 square numbers.

4 Round each number to 1 decimal place.

    a 6.73   **b** 3.45   **c** 8.09

 5 Work out

    a $\sqrt{64}$ **b** $\sqrt{49}$ **c** $\sqrt{25}$

    d $\sqrt{16}$ **e** $\sqrt{4}$ **f** $\sqrt{9}$

6 A square has area 64 cm².
What is the length of its sides?

 7 Use the 'squared' key on your calculator to work out

    a 18^2 **b** 20^2 **c** 24^2

    d the 11th square number

    e the 15th square number

    f the 21st square number.

> **Key point**
>
> Finding the square root is the inverse of squaring.
> $\sqrt{}$ means 'the square root of'
> $64 = 8^2$
> so $\sqrt{64} = 8$

> **Q7 hint**
>
> Look for a key like $\boxed{x^2}$.

Topic links: Rounding to 1 decimal place, Area, Volume, Calculator skills, Calculating with decimals

Subject links: History (Q26)

8 a A square field is 22 m wide.
What is its area?

b A mouse mat measures 19 cm by 19 cm.
What is its area?

9 Work out
a 5.5^2 **b** 7.2^2
c 3.4^2 **d** 6.8^2

Q9 hint

Use the 'squared' key on your calculator.

10 Work out the square root of each number.
Round your answers to 1 decimal place.
a $\sqrt{50}$ **b** $\sqrt{200}$
c $\sqrt{375}$ **d** $\sqrt{480}$
e $\sqrt{468}$

Q10 hint

Use the 'square root' key on your calculator.
Look for a key like $\boxed{\sqrt{\ }}$ $\boxed{\sqrt{x}}$ or $\boxed{\sqrt{\Box}}$.

11 **Problem-solving** The area of a square paddock is 625 square metres.
What is the length of each side?

12 **Problem-solving** A theatre wants to arrange seats in a block that is as close to a square as possible. There should be the same number of seats in each row. There are 420 seats.
How many should be in each row?

13 **Problem-solving** A kitchen tile measures 15 cm by 15 cm.
What area will 100 tiles cover?

14 Work out
a $2^3 = 2 \times \Box \times \Box = \Box$
b $3^3 = \Box \times \Box \times \Box = \Box$
Discussion Why do you think these are called **cube numbers**?

Key point

When you multiply a number by itself three times, you get a **cube number**. You can write 2 × 2 × 2 more compactly as 2^3.

15 Work out
a 4^3 **b** 5^3
c 6^3 **d** 7^3
e 8^3 **f** 9^3

Q15 hint

Use the 'cubed' key on your calculator.
Look for a key like $\boxed{x^3}$ $\boxed{x^\Box}$ or $\boxed{y^x}$.
(You may need to use the 'shift' or '2nd function' key first.)

16 What is the volume of a cube with side length 15 cm?

17 Use a mental or written method to work out
a 30^2 **b** 50^2
c 40^2 **d** 80^2
e 1^3 **f** 10^3

Q17a hint

30 × 30 = 3 × 3 × 10 × 10

18 **Problem-solving**
a Sally squares a number and gets the answer 25.
What was the number?
b Reuben finds the square root of a number and gets the answer 6.
What was the number?

19 Work out these cube numbers.
Round decimal answers to 1 decimal place.
a 5.5^3 **b** 20^3 **c** 9.9^3

20 Work out these **cube roots**.

a $\sqrt[3]{1331}$ b $\sqrt[3]{3375}$

c $\sqrt[3]{9261}$ d $\sqrt[3]{15625}$

e $\sqrt[3]{1728}$

21 Work out

a $\sqrt[3]{64}$ b $\sqrt[3]{27}$ c $\sqrt[3]{1000}$

22 Work out each cube root.
Round your answers to 1 decimal place.

a $\sqrt[3]{100}$

b $\sqrt[3]{60}$

c $\sqrt[3]{78}$

d $\sqrt[3]{150}$

23 Reasoning The volume of a cube is 216 cm³.
What are the **dimensions** of the cube?

24 Reasoning

a Copy and complete the Venn diagram. Write each number in its correct place.

Square and cube numbers

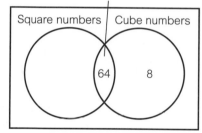

1   8   25   20   27   64   49   125   225   100   729   512   1331

b Which numbers are both square *and* cube numbers?

25 Explore Do all numbers have a root?
Choose some sensible numbers to help you explore this situation.
Use what you've learned in this lesson to help you answer the question.

26 Reflect The $\sqrt{\ }$ part of the root symbol began as an old-fashioned letter **r** in the 16th century. You could remember **r** for root!
List all the mathematics **notation** used in this lesson, and ways you might remember it.
Make sure you know what all the notation in this lesson tells you to do.

  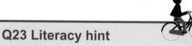
Explore

Reflect

7.2 Calculating with brackets and indices

You will learn to:
- Do calculations involving brackets and square numbers
- Use the brackets keys on a calculator
- Use index notation.

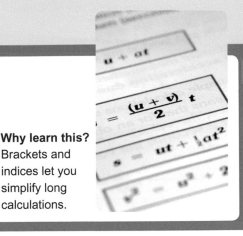

Why learn this?
Brackets and indices let you simplify long calculations.

Fluency

What is the area of this square?

7 cm

What is the volume of this cube?

3 cm

Explore
How do we use brackets in maths?

Exercise 7.2

1 Work out the value of
   a 9^2 **b** 10^3 **c** $\sqrt{36}$ **d** $\sqrt[3]{64}$

2 Work out
   a $3 + 4 \times 6$ **b** $5 \times 3 + 6$ **c** $10 \div 2 \times 3$ **d** $10 - 6 \div 3$

3 Work out each calculation using the **priority of operations**.
   a $(10 + 2) \times (3 + 6)$
   b $(20 - 10) \div (17 - 7)$
   c $5(3 + 4)$

4 **Reasoning** Put brackets into each pair of calculations to make the different answers correct.
   a $3 \times 4 + 6 = 30$ $3 \times 4 + 6 = 18$
   b $10 \div 2 + 8 = 1$ $10 \div 2 + 8 = 13$
   c $5 \times 3 + 8 = 23$ $5 \times 3 + 8 = 55$
   Discussion When there are no brackets, which answer in each pair is the correct one?

5 Write each multiplication as a **power** of the repeated number.
   a $2 \times 2 \times 2 = 2^\square$ **b** 3×3
   c $4 \times 4 \times 4$ **d** 5×5
   e $6 \times 6 \times 6$ **f** $10 \times 10 \times 10$
   g $10 \times 10 \times 10 \times 10 \times 10$

6 Work out the value of each power of 10.
   a $10^2 = 10 \times 10 = \square$ **b** 10^3
   c 10^4 **d** 10^5
   Discussion How does the power help you to know how many zeros the number will have?

Key point

It's important to use the correct **priority of operations** when you are doing calculations.
- **B**rackets
- **I**ndices (powers and roots)
- **D**ivision and **M**ultiplication
- **A**ddition and **S**ubtraction

Indices is the plural of index (say '**in**-di-seez').

Key point

The **index** or **power** of a number tells you how many times the number is multiplied by itself.
For example,
$3 \times 3 = 3^2$ $5 \times 5 \times 5 = 5^3$
$10 \times 10 \times 10 \times 10 = 10^4$

Q5a hint

How many 2s have been multiplied together?

Warm up

7 Work out
   a $5^2 + 4^3$
   b $\sqrt{9} \times \sqrt[3]{125}$
   c $4^2 - 2^3$
   d $\sqrt{100} - \sqrt[3]{64}$
   e $(3^2 + 2) - 4$
   f $3(11 - \sqrt[3]{125})$

Q7 hint

Follow the priority of operations.

8 Write as **ordinary numbers**.
   a $3 \times 10^3 = 3 \times \square = \square$
   b 6×10^2
   c $10^3 \times 12$
   d 25×10^2

Key point

An **ordinary number** is one without a power or index.
For example, 2^3 is 8, as an ordinary number.

9 Evaluate
   a $2^2 \times 3^2$ **b** $4^2 \times 1^3$
   c $6^2 \div 3^2$ **d** $5^2 \times 2^3$

Q9 Literacy hint

To **evaluate** means to work out the value.

10 Write each multiplication in **index notation**.
    The first one has been started for you.
   a $3 \times 3 \times 2 \times 2 \times 2 = 3^2 \times \square^3$
   b $4 \times 4 \times 4 \times 5 \times 5$
   c $10 \times 10 \times 10 \times 10 \times 6 \times 6$
   d $2 \times 3 \times 4 \times 3 \times 4 \times 2$
   e $5 \times 7 \times 10 \times 5 \times 10 \times 10$

Q10a hint

The index tells you how many times a number is multiplied by itself.

11 A small square is cut out of a larger square of metal.
    Work out the area of metal left.

8 cm

4 cm

Q10 Literacy hint

Index notation is the short way of writing a number being multiplied by itself.

Investigation   Reasoning

 1 Use your calculator to work out
     a $5 + 10 \times 3 - 6$
     b $4 \times 6 - 8 \div 4$
     c $8 \times (7 + 3)$
     d $(9 - 5) + 6 \times 3$
     e $10 \times 7 \div 2 + (6 - 2)$
   2 Compare your answers with someone else's.
     Are they the same?
   3 Does your calculator follow the priority of operations?
     How can you tell?

---

12 Explore How do we use brackets in maths?
    Look back at the maths you have learned in this lesson.
    How can you use it to answer this question?

13 Reflect Simone says, 'At first I kept going wrong because I multiplied the number and the index together. So then I started to work it out like this.'

$3^4 = 3 \times 3 \times 3 \times 3$

Look back at your work from this lesson.
Did you make the same mistake as Simone?
What did you do to make sure you didn't keep making the same mistake?

   Topic links: Calculator skills, Algebra    *Active* Learn   Pi 2, Section 7.2

Explore

Reflect

7.3 LCM and HCF

You will learn to:

- Find the factors of any whole number
- Use the lowest common multiple (LCM) and highest common factor (HCF) to solve problems.

Why learn this?
The lowest common multiple helps predict when orbiting satellites will line up.

Fluency
- What are the first 12 multiples of 2 and 10?
- What are the factors of 12?

Explore
How could you share out 30 blue balloons, 15 red balloons and 20 yellow balloons into several identical sets?

Exercise 7.3

1 a List the first 10 **multiples** of each number in the pair.
  i 3 and 5
  ii 4 and 6
 b What is the **lowest common multiple** of each pair of numbers?

2 For each pair of numbers in parts **a** and **b**
  i list all the **factors** of each number
  ii list the common factors of both numbers
  iii write the **highest common factor**.
 a 12 and 20
 b 18 and 32

3 a List the factors of 18 and the factors of 20.
 b Copy and complete the Venn diagram to show all the factors you have listed.
 c Use your Venn diagram to find the highest common factor of 18 and 20.

Factors of 18 and 20

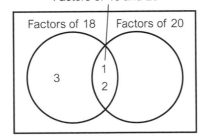

Factors of 18 | Factors of 20

3 | 1 2

4 a List the first 6 multiples of 10 and of 15
 b Copy and complete the Venn diagram to show all the multiples you have listed.
 c Use your Venn diagram to find the lowest common multiple of 10 and 15.

Multiples of 10 and 15

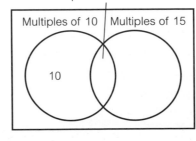

Multiples of 10 | Multiples of 15

10

> **Key point**
>
> A **multiple** of a number is the result of *multiplying* it by a whole number.
> The **lowest common multiple** of two (or more) numbers is the smallest number that is a multiple of both numbers.
> A **factor** is a number that *divides* exactly into another whole number.
> The **highest common factor** of two (or more) numbers is the largest number that is a factor of both numbers.

Warm up

5 Find the LCM of
   a 4 and 7   **b** 20 and 50   **c** 15 and 25
   Discussion How many multiples do you need to write?

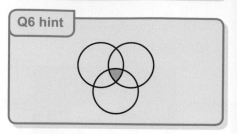

Q5 Strategy hint
For each pair, list some multiples of each number. Then draw and complete a Venn diagram.

6 a Find the common factors of 24, 30 and 36.
   b What is the HCF of 24, 30 and 36?

Q6 hint

7 Work out the LCM of 2, 3 and 5.

8 Real Two cyclists are cycling around an oval track.
One takes 5 minutes to do each circuit and the other takes 6 minutes.
They both start at 10 am.
When will they first cross the line at the same time?

Q8 hint
Use the LCM.

9 Real In a piece of music the cymbals play on every 8th beat and the
bass drum plays on every 3rd beat.
On which beats will both instruments play at the same time?

10 Real Three lighthouses protect a large coastal bay.
The first beams every 2 minutes, the second every 6 minutes and
the 3rd every 9 minutes.
After how many minutes will they all beam together?

11 Find the HCF of
   a 28 and 42
   b 25 and 35
   c 36 and 48
   d 12 and 60
   Discussion How can you tell if the HCF of a pair of numbers will
be one of those numbers?

Q11 hint
Use lists or a Venn diagram.

12 Problem-solving Two families have the same number of children.
The Bradley family has only twins and the Smith family has only
triplets.
How many children could be in each family?

13 Real / Problem-solving Bobbie is making identical table
decorations. She has 36 white flowers, 27 blue flowers and 18 lilac
flowers. She wants the number of each colour to be the same in all
the decorations. She wants to use all the flowers.
   a What is the greatest number of table decorations she can make?
   b How many flowers of each colour will be in each decoration?

Q13 hint
Use the HCF.

Investigation   **Reasoning / Problem-solving**
A netball club has 48 members. A football club has 60 members.
The two clubs are having a joint end-of-season meal. Here are the rules:
• The tables must all have the same number of people (2 or more)
• Netball and football players must not sit at the same table.
1 How many different ways could you seat these 2 clubs?
2 What is
   a the largest number
   b the smallest number of tables you might need?
3 Which arrangement do you think is best?
   Explain your reasons.

Part 1 hint
Use common factors.

Topic links: Venn diagrams

14 The diagram shows 3 swings with different length ropes, and the time it takes them to do a full swing.
All swings are pushed from vertical at the same time. How many seconds until they are all vertical at the same time again?

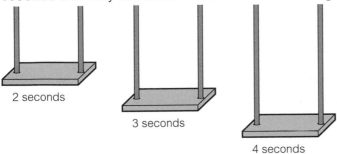

2 seconds

3 seconds

4 seconds

15 **Problem-solving / Reasoning** Work out the mystery numbers.
  a The LCM of two numbers is 15.
    What are the two numbers?
  b The HCF of two numbers is 10.
    What could the two numbers be?
  c The LCM of two numbers is 18.
    What could the two numbers be?
  d The HCF of two numbers is 8.
    What could the two numbers be?
  e A cube number has 9 as one of its factors.
    What could the cube number be?
  f A square number is a common multiple of 9 and 12.
    What could the square number be?

> **Q15a, b hint**
>
> Make sure there is not a higher common factor or a lower common multiple for the numbers you have found.

16 **Explore** How could you share out 30 blue balloons, 15 red balloons and 20 yellow balloons into several identical sets?
Look back at the maths you have learned in this lesson.
How can you use it to answer this question?

17 **Reflect** Write your own short definition for each mathematics word.
- highest
- lowest
- common
- factor
- multiple

Now use your definitions to write the meaning of each of these phrases in your own words.
- highest common factor
- lowest common multiple

7.4 Prime factor decomposition

You will learn to:
- Write the prime factor decomposition of a number.

Why learn this?
Computer programmers use prime factors to keep confidential information safe.

Fluency
- What are the prime numbers less than 20?
- What is the product of 3 and 6?

Explore
Can every number be written as the product of prime numbers?

CONFIDENCE

Exercise 7.4

Warm up

1 Use the words on the cards to complete these sentences.

factor | multiple | prime number

a 4 is a _____ of 24
b 48 is a _____ of 6
c 4 and 8 are both _____ of 2
d 4 and 8 are both _____ of 24
e 23 is a _____

Discussion Which number is a factor of every other **integer**?

2 From this set of numbers, write
a the **prime numbers**
b the factors of 12
c the multiples of 4

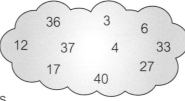

36 3 6
12 37 4 33
17 40 27

> **Key point**
> An **integer** (say 'in-ti-jer') is a whole number.
> A **prime number** is a whole number with only one pair of factors (itself and 1).

3 Write these products using powers.
a $2 \times 2 \times 5 \times 5 \times 5 = 2^2 \times \square^3$
b $7 \times 7 \times 7 \times 11 \times 11 = \square^\square \times \square^\square$
c $10 \times 10 \times 10 \times 6 \times 6 \times 6$
d $2 \times 5 \times 4 \times 5 \times 4 \times 2$

Investigation   Problem-solving

How many different numbers can you make by multiplying two prime numbers?
Use the prime numbers less than 20.
1 Start with 2: $2 \times 2, 2 \times 3, 2 \times 5, 2 \times 7, \ldots$
2 Then try 3: $3 \times 3, 3 \times 5, \ldots$
Discussion Which numbers less than 100 in the 11× table *cannot* be made from the product of just two prime numbers?

---

4 Reasoning Use prime numbers to complete these multiplications.
a $\square \times \square = 77$
b $\square \times \square = 26$
c $\square \times \square = 85$
d $\square \times \square \times \square = 30$
e $\square \times \square \times \square = 110$

5 **i** List the factors of each number.
   ii Write the **prime factors** of each number.
   a 18   **b** 10   **c** 19   **d** 22

Worked example

Write 200 as the **product** of its prime factors.

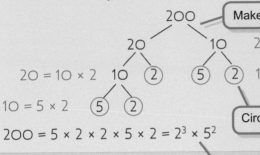

Make a factor tree using pairs of factors.

$200 = 20 \times 10$

$20 = 10 \times 2$

$10 = 5 \times 2$

$200 = 5 \times 2 \times 2 \times 5 \times 2 = 2^3 \times 5^2$

Circle the prime factors.

$10 = 5 \times 2$

Collect the prime factors from the diagram.
Then write them in size order with the smallest first, using index notation.

---

6 a Copy and complete each factor tree.
   Then use it to write 12 as the product of its prime factors.

   i 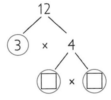   **ii**

   $12 = 2 \times \square \times \square$

   b Write 12 as the product of its prime factors using index notation.
   Discussion Does it matter which factor pair you start with on the factor tree?

7 a Copy and complete this factor tree for 20.
   b Write 20 as the product of its prime factors
      using index notation.

8 Draw factor trees to write each number as the product of its prime factors.
   a 16   **b** 18   **c** 30   **d** 32   **e** 40
   Discussion Look at your answers for 16 and 32.
   What do you notice about the product?

9 Ned finds that the prime factor decomposition of a number is $2 \times 5 \times 7$.
   What was his number?

10 Explore Can every number can be written as the product of prime numbers?
   Look back at the maths you have learned in this lesson.
   How can you use it to answer this question?

11 Reflect Write your own short definition for each mathematics word.
   • prime
   • factor
   • decomposition
   Now use your definitions to write the meaning of this phrase in your own words.
   • prime factor decompositionCircle the prime factors.

Explore

Reflect

Master
P143

CHECK

Strengthen
P155

Extend
P159

Test
P163

7 Check up

Log how you did on your
Student Progression Chart.

Squares, cubes and roots

1 Work out

  a 4^2

  b 5^3

2 Write

  a the 7th square number

  b $\sqrt{81}$

3 What is the area of a square tile with side length 25 mm?

4 Work these out.
Round decimal answers to 1 decimal place.

  a $\sqrt{484}$

  b 1.6^2

  c 11^3

  d $\sqrt[3]{216}$

5 What is the side length of this square?

Area =
36 cm²

6 What is the side length of this cube?

Volume =
27 m³

Brackets and indices

7 Work out

  a $3^2 + 4^2$

  b $\sqrt{81} - \sqrt{16}$

  c $6^2 + 2^3 - \sqrt{25}$

  d $\sqrt{36} \times \sqrt[3]{27}$

8 Evaluate

  a $3^2 \times 3^2$

  b $10^2 \div 5^2$

9 **a** $(4^2 + 2^3) + 6$
  b $(\sqrt{25} + 7) - 5$
  c $4(3^2 + 2)$

10 Write as ordinary numbers
  a 5×10^2
  b 7×10^3

11 Write these multiplications using powers.
  a 7×7
  b $10 \times 10 \times 10 \times 10$
  c $2 \times 4 \times 2 \times 5 \times 5 \times 2$

Multiples, factors and primes

12 What is the HCF of 12 and 36?

13 What is the LCM of 12 and 36?

14 Sasha and Alex have saved the same amount of money.
Sasha only saves 20p pieces and Alex only saves 50p pieces.
What is the least amount they could each have saved?

15 Write the prime factors of 21.

16 Write each number as the product of prime factors.
  a 35
  b 36

17 **How sure are you of your answers? Were you mostly**
  😟 **Just guessing**   😐 **Feeling doubtful**   🙂 **Confident**
  **What next? Use your results to decide whether to strengthen or
  extend your learning.**

Reflect

Challenge

18 **a** Explore multiplying a number by its square.
  $2 \times 2^2 =$
  $3 \times 3^2 =$
  $4 \times 4^2 =$
  $5 \times 5^2 =$
  $6 \times 6^2 =$
  $10 \times 10^2 =$

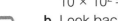

  b Look back or work out 2^3, 3^3, 4^3, 5^3, 6^3 and 10^3. Compare these
  with your answers to part **a**. What do you notice?
  c Write 8×8^2 and $11^2 \times 11$ as single numbers with a power and
  work out the answers.

Master
P143

Check
P153

STRENGTHEN

Extend
P159

Test
P163

7 Strengthen

You will:
- Strengthen your understanding with practice.

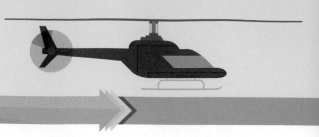

Squares, cubes and roots

1 Write the first 10 square numbers and their square roots.
The first two have been started for you.

$1 \times 1 = 1^2 = 1$ $\qquad \sqrt{1} = 1$

$2 \times 2 = 2^2 = \square$ $\qquad \sqrt{\square} = \square$

2 a What is the area of a square with side length 9 mm?
b A square has area 64 cm².
What is the length of each side?

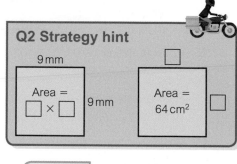

Q2 Strategy hint

3 Practise using the 'squared' and 'square root' keys on your calculator to work out

a 23^2 $\qquad$ **b** 2.3^2

c $\sqrt{324}$ $\qquad$ **d** $\sqrt{289}$

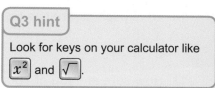

Q3 hint

Look for keys on your calculator like
x^2 and $\sqrt{}$.

4 a What is the area of a square with side length 16 cm?
b A square has area 361 cm².
What is the length of each side?
c Write the value of
i 16^2 $\qquad$ **ii** $\sqrt{361}$

5 Real

a A chessboard is a square with 8 smaller squares in each row.
How many small squares are on the board?

b 'Snakes and ladders' has 100 small squares on a square board.
How many squares are in each row?

6 Copy and complete these statements.

a A cube with side 2 cm has volume $2 \times 2 \times 2 = 2^3 = \square$ cm³

b A cube with side $\square$ cm has volume $\square \times \square \times \square = \square^3 = 27$ cm³

c A cube with side 4 cm has volume $\square \times \square \times \square = \square^3 = \square$ cm³

d A cube with side $\square$ cm has volume $\square \times \square \times \square = \square^3 = 125$ cm³

Q7 hint

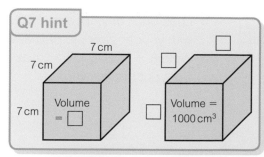

7 a What is the volume of a cube with side length 7 cm?
b A cube has volume 1000 cm³.
What is the length of each side?

8 Use your calculator to work out

a 12^3 $\qquad$ **b** 1.2^3

c 10.5^3 $\qquad$ **d** $\sqrt[3]{2197}$

e $\sqrt[3]{1000}$ $\qquad$ **f** $\sqrt[3]{4913}$

g $\sqrt[3]{8000}$

Q8 hint

Look for keys on your calculator like
x^3 and $\sqrt[3]{}$.

Topic links: Rounding to 1 decimal place, Area, Volume, Calculator skills, Calculating with decimals, Venn diagrams

9 Work out these powers and roots.
Write all the numbers on the calculator display, then round the answer to 1 decimal place.
The first one has been done for you.

Q9 hint

If the display on your calculator does not show a decimal, press the $S \Leftrightarrow D$ toggle key.

a $\sqrt{85} = 9.219544457 = 9.2$ to 1 d.p.   b 13.5^2
c 22.6^2 d $\sqrt{120}$
e 7.5^3 f $\sqrt[3]{800}$
g 3.8^3 h $\sqrt[3]{160}$

10 **Problem-solving**
a A number is squared and the answer is 121.
What is the number?
b The square root of a number is 14.
What is the number?
c A number is cubed and the answer is 216.
What is the number?
d The cube root of a number is 10.
What is the number?

Brackets and indices

1 Work out
a $24 \div (6 + 2) = 24 \div 8 = \square$ b $5 \times (4 - 1)$
c $(6 \times 8) - 14$ d $6^2 - 2 = \square - 2 = \square$
e $\sqrt{25} + 20 = \square + 20 = \square$ f $2^2 + 3^2$
g $\sqrt{36} - \sqrt{16}$

Q1, 2 hint

Work out
• brackets
• indices (or roots)
• × and ÷
• + and −

2 Work out
a $(3^2 - 1) + 2 = (\square - 1) + 2 = \square + 2$ b $(7^2 + 1) - 30$
c $(6 - \sqrt{16}) + 3 = (6 - \square) + 3$ d $(2^2 + 3^2) - 3 = (\square + \square) - 3$
e $5 \times (4^2 - 3^2) = 5 \times (\square - \square)$ f $6(3^3 - 5^2)$

3 Evaluate
a $2^2 \times 5^2 = \square \times \square = \square$ b $4^2 \div 2^2 = \square \div \square = \square$
c $3^2 \times 6$ d $10^2 \div 2^2$

4 Work out
a $10^2 = \square \times \square = \square$ b $10^4 = \square \times \square \times \square \times \square = \square$
c 10^5 d 10^3

Q4 hint

How many 10s are being multiplied together each time?

5 Write as ordinary numbers
a 5×10^2 b 3×10^4
c 5×10^3 d 8×10^5

Q5 hint

Use your answers to Q4.

6 Copy and complete
a $5 \times 5 \times 5 = 5^{\square}$ b $3 \times 3 \times 3 = \square^3$
c $4 \times 4 = \square^{\square}$ d $8 \times \square = 8^2$
e $4 \times \square \times \square = 4^3$ f $\square \times \square = 6^2$
g $\square \times \square \times \square = 7^3$ h $\square \times \square \times \square = 10^{\square}$

Q6a hint

There are $\square$ lots of 5 multiplied together.

7 Write these powers as multiplications.
The first one has been started for you.
a $5^2 \times 3^3 = 5 \times \square \times 3 \times \square \times \square$
b $6^3 \times 9^2$

8 Copy and complete these multiplications using index notation.
The first one has been started for you.
a $2 \times 2 \times 2 \times 3 \times 3 = 2^3 \times \square^2$
b $5 \times 5 \times 5 \times 4 \times 4$
c $10 \times 4 \times 10 \times 4 \times 10$
d $2 \times 2 \times 3 \times 3 \times 3 \times 3 \times 4 \times 4$
e $5 \times 2 \times 5 \times 5 \times 2 \times 3$
f $7 \times 2 \times 5 \times 7 \times 2$

Q8 hint

Rearrange the numbers into numerical order first.
When the index is 1, just write the number itself.

Multiples, factors and primes

1 a List the factors of 32 and the factors of 48.
  b Copy this Venn diagram.

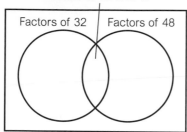

Factors of 32 and 48

Factors of 32 | Factors of 48

Q1c Literacy hint

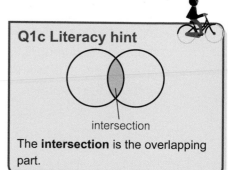

intersection

The **intersection** is the overlapping part.

  c Write the common factors of 32 and 48 in the **intersection**.
  d Write in the other factors of 32.
  e Write in the other factors of 48.
  f Which number is the highest of the common factors (the HCF) of 32 and 48?

Q1f hint

Look for the highest number in the intersection.

2 a Copy and complete this Venn diagram for the factors of 28 and 36.

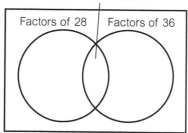

Factors of 28 and 36

Factors of 28 | Factors of 36

  b Find the HCF of 28 and 36.

3 a List the first 10 multiples of 3 and the first 5 multiples of 9.
  b Draw a Venn diagram for these multiples of 3 and 9.
  c Find the LCM of 3 and 9.

Q3b hint

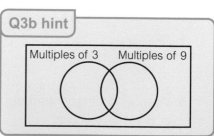

Multiples of 3 | Multiples of 9

4 **Problem-solving** Complete these multiplications using only prime numbers.
  a $\square \times \square = 21$ b $\square \times \square = 34$
  c $\square \times \square = 55$ d $\square \times \square \times \square = 30$

Q4 hint

First list the prime numbers from 1 to 20 to help.

5 a Copy and complete this factor tree for 40.
  b Circle the prime factors.
  c Write the product.
    Put the numbers in order: $\square \times \square \times \square \times \square$
  d Write the product using powers.

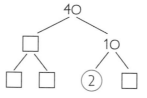

6 For each starting number in parts **a** and **b**
   i copy and complete the factor tree
   ii write the number as the product of prime factors
   iii rewrite the product using powers, for any repeated prime factors.

a
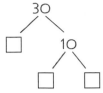

b

Q6 hint

Use the method in Q5 to identify the prime factors in your factor tree.

7 Write each number as the product of its prime factors.
   a 18   **b** 120   **c** 264

8 Match each number to its prime factor decomposition.

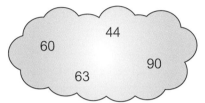
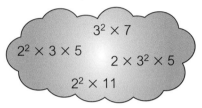

Enrichment

1 a Find the difference between **consecutive** cube numbers.

$2^3 - 1^3$

$3^3 - 2^3$

and so on.

   b What is special about the differences?

Q1 Literacy hint

Consecutive means following in order without a gap.
For example, 5, 6, 7 are consecutive numbers.

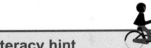

2 a Choose two prime numbers from the cloud.
   Work out their product: □ × □ = □

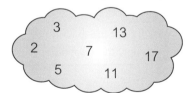

   b Write the factors of the answer.
   One pair has been done for you.

   7 × 11 = 77   Factors of 77: 1, 7, 11, 77

   c Repeat 5 more times with different pairs.
   What do you notice about the number of factors?

3 Reflect Harry says, 'I could have done better in these lessons if I'd practised multiplication and division more, but I'm pleased with how well I did on square numbers.'
Look back at your work in these strengthen lessons.
Write one maths skill you think you need to practise more, and one thing you are pleased with from these lessons.

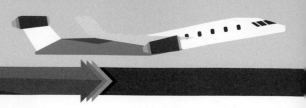

7 Extend

You will:

• Extend your understanding with problem-solving.

1 a Match the square numbers to their square root.

b For the two numbers without a pair, write their square or square root.

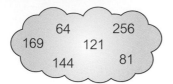

64   256
169   121
144   81

16   13
14   8
9   12

Investigation   **Problem-solving**

1 Work out the output when the input is 1.

Input   Output

square number → √ → ×2 → +1 → + the square number → ☐

2 Work out the output when the input is 100.

3 Choose another square number as the input and work out the output.

4 What do you notice about your answers?

5 Use the function machine to work out the next square number after 121.

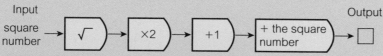

---

 2 Work out

a $\sqrt{4} \times \sqrt{4}$ **b** $\sqrt{100} \times \sqrt{100}$ **c** $\sqrt{9} \times \sqrt{9}$

d Predict the answers to $\sqrt{7} \times \sqrt{7}$ and $\sqrt{11} \times \sqrt{11}$.

Check using your calculator.

> **Q2 hint**
>
> Work out the two square roots then multiply them together.

3 Problem-solving Put the correct operations ($+$, $-$, $\times$, $\div$) between the numbers to make these calculations correct.

a $5 \,\square\, (3 \,\square\, 8) = 55$ **b** $25 \,\square\, 5 \,\square\, 2 = 10$ **c** $11 \,\square\, 9 \,\square\, 22 = 77$

d $36 \,\square\, (4 \,\square\, 2) = 6$ **e** $18 \,\square\, (3 \,\square\, 2) = 12$

4 Simplify these ratios fully using the HCF of both parts.

a $24 : 30$ **b** $21 : 42$ **c** $35 : 45$

d $36 : 27$ **e** $32 : 24$

5 Problem-solving Chris is organising a barbecue.

There are 24 bread rolls in a bag and 16 burgers in a box.

He needs exactly the same number of bread rolls as burgers.

a What is the smallest number of each he can buy?

b How many bags of rolls and boxes of burgers will he need?

6 Problem-solving / STEM Two electricians have the same length of cable. Graham cuts his into 5 m lengths. Sarah cuts hers into 8 m lengths. Both use all of their cable with none left over.

a What length of cable did they each start with?

b How many lengths of cable did they each cut?

> **Q6a hint**
>
> Find the shortest possible length.

Topic links: Rounding, Calculator skills, Calculating with decimals, Venn diagrams

7 Reasoning Use the square roots and square numbers you know to work out

a 40^2 b 60^2 c $\sqrt{400}$ d $\sqrt{2500}$

e 900^2 f 700^2 g $\sqrt{90\,000}$ h $\sqrt{640\,000}$

Q7a hint

$40^2 = 4 \times 4 \times 10 \times 10$

8 Write the answers to these multiplications as ordinary numbers.

a $10^2 \times 5 = 100 \times 5 = \square$ b 6×10^3 c 5.2×10^2

d $10^3 \times 21.4$ e 0.6×10^2 f $10^3 \times 0.75$

9 Work out the HCF of each set of numbers.

a 12,18 and 30   b 16,12 and 24

c 30, 15 and 75   d 50, 75 and 125

10 Work out the LCM of each set of numbers.

a 8, 10 and 12   b 12, 15 and 18

c 20, 15 and 10   d 15, 20 and 40

11 Reasoning / Problem-solving A bag contains all the numbers between 1 and 50. Raadiya chooses two numbers and works out their HCF.

a What could the two numbers be when the HCF is

    i 10   ii 15   iii 12?

b Find another pair of numbers for each HCF in part **a**.

12 Put these numbers in order, smallest to largest.

$2^4 \times 5^3$

$2 \times 3 \times 5^2 \times 11$

$2^3 \times 5 \times 11^2$

$2^2 \times 3^2 \times 5^3$

$2^3 \times 3^2 \times 7^2$

Q12 hint

Work out the products.

13 Reasoning For each squared decimal in parts **a** to **e**

    i estimate the value

    ii use a calculator to work out the exact answer

    iii round this answer to 1 d.p.

Show your working. The first one has been done for you.

a 5.6^2

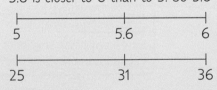

> i 5.6 is between 5 and 6. So 5.6^2 is between $5^2 = 25$ and $6^2 = 36$
> 5.6 is closer to 6 than to 5. So 5.6^2 is closer to 36 than to 25
>
> |———————|———————|
> 5   5.6   6
>
> |———————|———————|
> 25   31   36
>
> Estimate: 31
> ii $5.6^2 = 31.36$
> iii 31.4 (to 1 d.p.)

b 6.2^2 c 2.7^2 d 4.8^2 e 9.3^2

14 Write or work out these cube numbers.

a 1^3 b 2^3 c 3^3 d 4^3 e 5^3 f 10^3

15 Reasoning Use the symbols > or < to compare each pair of numbers.

a $\sqrt{110} \,\square\, 11$ b $\sqrt{99} \,\square\, 9$ c $12^2 \,\square\, 150$

d $\sqrt[3]{120} \,\square\, 5$ e $\sqrt[3]{1000} \,\square\, 9.9$ f $5.1^3 \,\square\, 125$

Q15a hint

Use inverses to compare each side. The inverse of taking the square root is squaring.

$11^2 = 121$

So you need to compare 110 and 121.

16 Use inverse operations to check which of these are correct. Write 'True' or 'False' for each one.

a $\sqrt{1024} = 32$ **b** $21.2 = \sqrt{451}$ **c** $\sqrt{6.25} = 3.5$

d $9.8^2 = 96.04$ **e** $\sqrt[3]{1331} = 21$ **f** $12^3 = 1728$

g $\sqrt[3]{512} = 8$ **h** $7.5^3 = 421.5$

Q16 hint

Use the method in Q15.

17 **Reasoning** Work out the mystery numbers.

a A number cubed is 125. What is the number?

b The cube root of a number is 4. What is the number?

c A number cubed is 1000. What is the number?

d The cube root of a number is 7. What is the number?

Key point

A square number has an integer (whole number) square root.
A cube number has an integer cube root.

18 Which of these are square or cube numbers?

     125   361   500   800   676   1728

19 Work out

a $(14 - 11)^2 + 3 \times 8$ **b** $\sqrt{75 - 11} - 30 \div 6$

c $7^2 - \sqrt{81}$ **d** $\sqrt{121} - \sqrt[3]{64}$

e $\sqrt{144} + (4 + 5)^2$ **f** $(16 - 8)^2 - \sqrt[3]{125}$

Q18 hint

Use the 'square root' and 'cube root' keys on your calculator.
Look for keys like $\sqrt{}$ and $\sqrt[3]{}$.

20 Work out these divisions.
Check your answers using a calculator.

a $\dfrac{12 + 30}{5 - 3}$ **b** $\dfrac{6^2 + 4}{2 \times 5}$ **c** $\dfrac{4^2 + 2}{3^2}$ **d** $\dfrac{\sqrt{25} + 4}{\sqrt{4} + 1}$

21 Write each number as the product of its prime factors.

a 75   **b** 120   **c** 250

Q21 hint

Draw a factor tree.
Start with any factor pair.

22 **Reasoning**

a Write 4, 8, 16 and 32 as products of their prime factors. Record them using index notation.

   i $4 = 2 \times 2 = 2^{\square}$ **ii** $8 = \square \times \square \times \square = \square^{\square}$

   iii 16   **iv** 32

b Explain the pattern in your answers.

c What is the value of 2^6?

d What is 128 as the product of its prime factors?

23 **Reasoning** $80 = 2^4 \times 5$

Use this fact to answer these questions.

a What is 40 as the product of its prime factors?

b What is 240 as the product of its prime factors?

c What number is $2^4 \times 5 \times 7$?

d What number is $2^4 \times 5^2$?

Q23 hint

How many times smaller or larger than 80 is the new number?

24 **Reasoning**

a Work out 150 as the product of its prime factors.

b Use your answer to part **a** to

   i write 300 as the product of its prime factors

   ii write 75 as the product of its prime factors

   iii write 450 as the product of its prime factors

   iv work out $2 \times 3 \times 5^3$

   v work out $2^3 \times 3 \times 5^2$

   vi work out $2 \times 3 \times 5^2 \times 7$

25 Leo finds that the prime factor decomposition of a number is $2^3 \times 5^2$.
What was his number?

26 Reasoning Alex says that 800 is $2^5 \times 5$ as the product of its
prime factors.
Is he right?

27 a Write the prime factor decomposition of 24 and of 36.
b Copy and complete the Venn diagram showing the
prime factors of 24 and 36.
c Multiply all the numbers in your Venn diagram together.
Have you found the LCM or the HCF?
d Multiply just the numbers in the intersection.
Is this the LCM or the HCF?

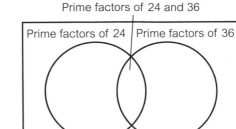

Prime factors of 24 and 36

28 Use a Venn diagram and prime factor decomposition to
work out the HCF of each pair of numbers.
a 12 and 30 **b** 30 and 40 **c** 50 and 75

29 Use a Venn diagram and prime factor decomposition to work out
the LCM of each pair of numbers.
a 30 and 40 **b** 36 and 40 **c** 21 and 35

30 Here are some cards showing the prime factor decomposition of
several numbers.

$60 = 2 \times 2 \times 3 \times 5$

$105 = 3 \times 5 \times 7$

$72 = 2 \times 2 \times 2 \times 3 \times 3$

$42 = 2 \times 3 \times 7$

$80 = 2 \times 2 \times 2 \times 2 \times 5$

$66 = 2 \times 3 \times 11$

Use the cards to work out the HCF and the LCM of each pair of
numbers.
a 60 and 80 **b** 72 and 80 **c** 42 and 105
d 66 and 42 **e** 60 and 105

Investigation   Reasoning / Problem-solving

1 Is $(a + b)^2$ the same as $a^2 + b^2$?
  a Roll dice to generate two numbers for a and b (for example, 4 and 5).
  b Use these numbers to work out $(a + b)^2$ and $a^2 + b^2$
  c Repeat this at least 5 times with different pairs of numbers.

2 Is $(a - b)^2$ the same as $a^2 - b^2$?
  a Roll dice to generate two numbers for a and b (for example, 4 and 5).
  b Use these numbers to work out $(a - b)^2$ and $a^2 - b^2$
  c Repeat this at least 5 times with different pairs of numbers.

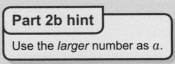

Part 2b hint

Use the *larger* number as a.

---

31 Reflect Which of the questions in these extend lessons made you
think the hardest?
Why?
What could you do so that questions like this are easier to do in
the future?

7 Unit test

Log how you did on your Student Progression Chart.

1 Work out
  a 6^2
  b 11^2
  c $\sqrt{49}$
  d $\sqrt{144}$
  e the 5th square number.

2 Work out the HCF of
  a 64 and 72
  b 30, 60 and 75

3 Work out the LCM of
  a 12 and 18
  b 5, 2 and 3

4 Work out
  a 2^3
  b 4^3
  c $\sqrt[3]{27}$
  d $\sqrt[3]{1000}$

5 Work out these powers and roots.
Round decimal answers to 1 decimal place.
  a $\sqrt{529}$
  b 4.3^2
  c 8^3
  d $\sqrt[3]{123}$

6 a What is the volume of a cube with side length 15 cm?
  b What is the area of one of the faces of a cube with side length 15 cm?

7 Work out
  a $12^2 - 7^2$
  b $8^2 \div \sqrt{16}$
  c $\sqrt{3} \times \sqrt{3}$

8 a A number squared is 196.
  What is the number?
  b The cube root of a number is 16.
  What is the number?

9 Evaluate
  a $2^2 \times 4^2$
  b 0.8×10^2

10 Which of these numbers are squares or cubes?

764   784
625 700 560
2197 3375

11 Work out

   a $5^2 + 2^3 - \sqrt{36}$ **b** $\sqrt{81} \times \sqrt[3]{8}$

   c $5(\sqrt{25} + 3)$ **d** $2(4^2 - \sqrt{9})$

12 Write 54 as the product of its prime factors.

13 Write these multiplications using powers.

   a 3×3 **b** $4 \times 4 \times 4 \times 4$

   c $10 \times 10 \times 10$ **d** $2 \times 3 \times 2 \times 3 \times 3 \times 2$

14 Use the fact that $100 = 2^2 \times 5^2$ to work out the prime factor decomposition for

   a 300

   b 50

15 Andy and Zoe are collecting World Cup cards. There is always the same number of cards in each packet.

Andy bought some packets and has 72 new cards.

Zoe bought some packets and has 108 new cards.

What is the highest number of cards that could come in each packet?

Challenge

16 How many different totals can you get by multiplying together any three of these prime numbers?

17 Reflect In this unit you have done calculations involving

- factors
- roots
- powers
- decimals
- measures.

Which type of calculation did you find easiest?

What made it easy?

Which type of calculation did you find hardest?

What made it hard?

Write a hint, in your own words, for the type of calculation you found hardest.

Q17 hint

You could ask your teacher or a classmate for help.

Reflect

8.1 Generating sequences

You will learn to:
- Recognise, describe and continue number sequences
- Find and use pattern and term-to-term rules.

CONFIDENCE

Why learn this?
Recognising patterns and sequences in population growth can help scientists make predictions about future needs.

Fluency
Count up from 7 in 5s.
Count down from 38 in 4s.

Explore
Leap years happen every 4 years.
The year 2000 was a leap year.
How many leap years are there this century?

Exercise 8.1

Warm up

1 Write the next two numbers in each **sequence**.
- **a** 2, 4, 6, 8, ☐, ☐
- **b** 12, 22, 32, 42, ☐, ☐
- **c** 8, 15, 22, 29, ☐, ☐
- **d** 19, 17, 15, 13, ☐, ☐
- **e** 49, 40, 31, 22, ☐, ☐
- **f** −12, −10, −8, −6, ☐, ☐

2 Write the **first term** and the **term-to-term rule** for each sequence.
- **a** 3, 6, 9, 12
- **b** 1, 4, 7, 10
- **c** 65, 60, 55, 50
- **d** 1, 2, 4, 8
- **e** 200, 100, 50, 25

3 Draw the next pattern in each sequence.

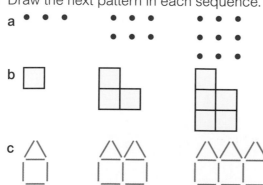

> **Key point**
>
> A **sequence** is a set of numbers that follow a rule.
> Each number in a sequence is called a **term**.
> A sequence can be described by giving a **first term** and a **term-to-term rule**. The term-to-term rule tells you how to get from one term to the next.

> **Q2a hint**
>
>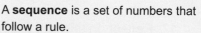
> term-to-term rule
> ☐ ☐ ☐
> 3 6 9 12
> first term

> **Q3a hint**
>
> You could write down the number of dots in each pattern.

Topic links: Adding and subtracting decimals, Negative numbers

Subject links: Science (Q9)

4 Write the 5th term of each sequence in Q2.

5 Write the first five terms in each sequence.
   a First term 5, term-to-term rule '+3'
   b First term 10 000, term-to-term rule '÷10'
   c First term 3, term-to-term rule '×2'
   d First term 20.5, term-to-term rule '−0.5'
   e First term 3.2, term-to-term rule '+0.4'
   f First term 10, term-to-term rule '−5'
   g First term −7, term-to-term rule '+2'

6 Is each sequence **ascending** or **descending**?
   a 3, 5, 7, 9, 11, …
   b 10, 12, 14, 16, 18, …
   c 20, 18, 16, 14, 12, …
   d 9, 8.5, 8, 7.5, 7, …
   e 1, 1.3, 1.6, 1.9, 2.2, …
   f −8, −10, −12, −14, −16, …
   g −9, −4, 1, 6, 11, …
   h −20, −17, −14, −11, …

7 Reasoning Decide whether each sequence is **finite** or **infinite**.
   a The odd numbers smaller than 10
   b The even numbers
   c The multiples of 3 between 10 and 20
   d The multiples of 10 larger than 100
   e The multiples of 10 between 0 and 100

8 Modelling Marie puts £100 in her bank. Each year, her bank gives her £5 interest. How much will she have in the bank after
   a 1 year   **b** 6 years?
   Discussion Is there another way to work out how much she has in the bank after 15 years?

9 Modelling / Problem-solving A plant is 3 cm tall.
   A botanist predicts it will grow 2 cm each week.
   How many weeks until it is likely to be 19 cm tall?
   Discussion Is this a sensible prediction? Will the plant continue to grow at this rate?

10 Real Ranjit has £450 in his bank account.
   a He spends £50 every month. How much will he have after 4 months?
   b How months years will it be before the account is empty?

11 Explore Leap years happen every 4 years. The year 2000 was a leap year. How many leap years are there this century?
   Look back at the maths you have learned in this lesson.
   How can you use it to answer this question?

12 Reflect Joanna says, 'A sequence is a list of numbers.'
   Hari says, 'A sequence is a pattern.'
   Think carefully about your work on sequences. How would you define a sequence in your own words? Write your definition.
   Compare your definition with a classmate's.

Q4 hint
Use your term-to-term rule.

Q5a hint
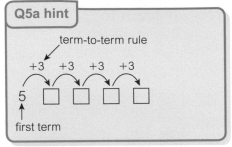
term-to-term rule
+3   +3   +3   +3
5
first term

Key point
Sequences where the numbers **increase** are **ascending** sequences. Sequences where the numbers **decrease** are **descending** sequences.

Key point
A sequence that carries on for ever is **infinite**.
A sequence with a fixed number of terms is **finite**.

Q7 hint
Can you write down all the terms in the sequence? If so, the sequence is finite.

Q8b hint
Write down the terms in the sequence.

Explore

Reflect

8.2 Extending sequences

You will learn to:

- Use the term-to-term rule to work out terms in a sequence
- Recognise an arithmetic sequence
- Describe sequences arising in real life.

CONFIDENCE

Why learn this?
High tide happens roughly every 12 hours and 24 minutes. Continuing the sequence enables sailors to know when there is enough water to leave port safely.

Fluency
What are the multiples of 12?
What is the term-to-term rule for this sequence?
- 6, 12, 18, 24, …

Explore
A fence has a post every 5 m. How many posts will you need for a fence 60 m long?

Exercise 8.2

Warm up

1 Write the next three terms in each sequence.
  a 23, 30, 37, 44   **b** 27, 22, 17, 12   **c** 0.5, 1, 2, 4

2 The first term of a sequence is 6. The term-to-term rule is 'add 10'.
Work out the first five terms.

3 Work out the missing terms in each sequence.
  a 3, 6, ☐, 12, 15, ☐
  b 66, 55, 44, ☐, ☐, 11
  c 3, 8, 13, 18, ☐, ☐
  d 4.2, ☐, 4.8, 5.1, 5.4, ☐
  e 9, 8.8, ☐, ☐, 8.2, 8

> **Q3 hint**
> Use the term-to-term rule.

4 This pattern sequence is made from beams.
  a Draw the next term.
  b Copy and complete the table.

Pattern number	1	2	3	4
Number of beams				

  c What is the 5th term of the sequence?

Worked example

A sequence has first term −4.
The term-to-term rule is 'add 5, then multiply by 2'.
Write the first three terms in the sequence.

1st term = −4

2nd term   −4 → [+5] →¹ [×2] → 2

3rd term   2 → [+5] →⁷ [×2] → 14

−4, 2, 14

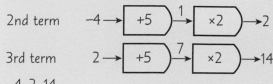

Topic links: Adding and subtracting decimals, Negative numbers   **Subject links:** Science (Q7)

5 Use the first term and the term-to-term rule to work out the first three terms of each sequence.

   a First term 1, term-to-term rule is 'add 1, then multiply by 2'

   b First term 30, term-to-term rule is 'subtract 5, then multiply by 3'

   c First term −10, term-to-term rule is 'add 10, then multiply by 5'

   d First term −6, term-to-term rule is 'add 10, then divide by 2'

6 Which of these sequences are **arithmetic**?

   a 3, 6, 9, 12, 15, …   **b** 30, 20, 0, −30, −70, …

   c The multiples of 12   **d** 1, 4, 9, 16, 25, …

   e 2, 3, 5, 7, 11, 13, …   **f** The odd numbers

   g −1, −4, −7, −10, −13, …   **h** 0.2, 0.5, 0.8, 1.1, 1.4, …

> **Key point**
>
> An **arithmetic sequence** goes up or down in equal steps.
> For example, 7, 11, 15, 19, … goes up in steps of 4.

7 **Modelling** Kolo reads on a website that his height should increase by 7 cm a year. His height is 129 cm when he is 9 years old.

   a Write his predicted heights for the next 6 years.

   b What would his height be after another 5 years?

   c Is this a good mathematical model? Explain your answer.

8 **Finance** Penny and Leonard are both saving up for a computer game that costs £42.

Penny starts with £20 and saves £3 per week.

Leonard starts with £10 and saves £6 per week.

Who will be the first to have enough money for the game?

Discussion How many ways are there to solve this?

9 Work out the first five terms of each arithmetic sequence.

   a First term 5, **common difference** +7

   b First term 80, common difference −9

   c First term 20, common difference −0.2

   d First term −10, common difference +11

   e First term −8, common difference −5

Discussion How can you tell if an arithmetic sequence is ascending or descending without working out any terms?

> **Key point**
>
> You can describe an arithmetic sequence using the first term and the **common difference** (the difference between terms).
> For the sequence 7, 11, 15, 19, …, the first term is 7 and the common difference is +4.

10 These sequences are arithmetic. Write the next two terms of each sequence.

   a 10, 9, …   **b** 0.7, 1.1, …   **c** −5, −3, …

11 **Explore** A fence has a post every 5 m. How many posts will you need for a 60 m fence?

Look back at the maths you have learned in this lesson.

How can you use it to answer this question?

12 **Reflect** Look back over this lesson. Sequences are shown in three different ways:

   • diagrams

   • tables

   • lists of numbers.

Which of these ways helped you the most to understand sequences and answer the questions?

Think of one other area of mathematics where you have found this way useful.

Explore

Reflect

8.3 Special sequences

You will learn to:
- Describe and continue special sequences
- Recognise a geometric sequence.

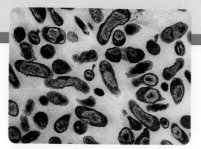

Why learn this?
Scientists use sequences to predict bacterial growth.

Fluency
What are the term-to-term rules for the sequences
- 6, 11, 16, 21, …
- 9, 7, 5, 3, …?

Explore
How do you generate a Fibonacci sequence like this?
1, 1, 2, 3, 5, 8, …

Exercise 8.3

1 Describe each arithmetic sequence by giving the first term and the common difference.

    a 3, 5, 7, 9, 11, …
    b 15, 25, 35, 45, …
    c 10, 7, 4, 1, −2, …
    d −3, −1, 1, 3, 5, …
    e −20, −16, −12, −8, …

2 Is each sequence in Q1 ascending or descending?

3 The diagram shows the first three terms in a pattern sequence.
    a Draw the next term in the sequence.
       Write the number of squares underneath.
    b What is the name for the numbers in the sequence?
    c Write the next four terms in the sequence.
    Hilary works out the differences between consecutive terms like this.
    d Copy and continue the pattern to work out the differences between the terms.

1   4   9

1   4   9   ☐   ☐   ☐
    +3   +5   +☐

4 The table shows the first four triangle numbers.

Pattern	•	• ••	• •• •••	• •• ••• ••••		
Number of dots	1	3	6			

    a Copy and complete the table.
    b Work out the differences between consecutive terms.
    c How many dots will there be in the 7th term?
       Draw the pattern to check your answer.
    Discussion Do the triangle numbers make an arithmetic sequence? What about the square numbers?

Topic links: Negative numbers, Multiples, Square numbers, Area, Perimeter   **Subject links:** Science (Q11)

5 Work out the next two terms in each sequence.

    a 10, 20, 40, 70, 110, ...   **b** −70, −20, 20, 50, ...

6 Work out the next two terms of each **geometric sequence**.

    a 1, 10, 100, 1000, 10 000, ...   **b** 1, 5, 25, 125, ...

Q6 hint

Look at the differences between terms in each sequence.

7 Use the first term and the term-to-term rule to work out the first four terms of each geometric sequence.

    a First term 3, term-to-term rule '×10'

    b First term 10, term-to-term rule '×2'

    c First term 500, term-to-term rule '÷5'

    d First term 800, term-to-term rule '×0.5'

Key point

In a **geometric sequence** the term-to-term rule is 'multiply or divide by a number'.

For example:

$$\times 2 \quad \times 2 \quad \times 2 \quad \times 2$$
$$1, \quad 2, \quad 4, \quad 8, \quad 16, \; ...$$

Each term is multiplied by 2.

8 Is each sequence geometric, arithmetic or neither?

    a 3, 6, 12, 24, 48, ...   **b** 2, 4, 6, 8, 10, ...

    c 2, 2, 4, 6, 10, 16, ...   **d** 1, 4, 9, 16, 25, 36, ...

    e 1, 3, 6, 10, 15, ...   **f** −10, −25, −40, −55, −60, ...

    g First term 4, term-to-term rule '+6'

    h First term −5, term-to-term rule '×2'

9 **Problem-solving** The second term of a geometric sequence is 6. The term-to-term rule is '×2'. What is the first term?

10 **Problem-solving** A sequence begins 1, 3, 9, 27, ...
How many terms smaller than 100 are there in the whole sequence?

11 **Modelling / Problem-solving** The population of rabbits in a field over 6 months is recorded.

Month	1	2	3	4	5	6
Number of rabbits	2	2	4	6	10	16

How long before there are more than 200 rabbits in the field?

12 **Explore** How do you generate a Fibonacci sequence like this?
1, 1, 2, 3, 5, 8, ...
Look back at the maths you have learned in this lesson.
How can you use it to answer this question?

13 **Reflect** Hassan says this riddle about a sequence:
'My first term is 3. My third term is 27. I am geometric.
What is in between?'

    a Write down every step you take to work out Hassan's sequence. You might begin, 'I write down all the numbers I know, leaving gaps for any missing numbers: 2, ___, 27, ...'

    b Look at the steps you have written. Underline any of them (or parts of them) that you think might help you when solving mathematics problems in the future.

Explore

Reflect

8.4 Position-to-term rules

You will learn to:
- Generate terms of a sequence using the position-to-term rule.

CONFIDENCE

Why learn this?
A position-to-term rule lets you work out any term in a sequence without working out all the previous terms.

Fluency
What are the 1st, 3rd and 5th terms in these sequences?
- 3, 5, 7, 9, 11
- 5, 10, 15, 20, 25
- 1, 6, 11, 16, 21

Explore
How many centimetres do you grow each year for the first 15 years of your life?

Exercise 8.4

Warm up

1 Work out the value of $n - 7$ when
   a $n = 1$ **b** $n = 2$ **c** $n = 3$ **d** $n = 10$

2 Work out the value of $3n$ when
   a $n = 1$ **b** $n = 2$ **c** $n = 3$ **d** $n = 8$

3 Work out the missing function for each machine.

a
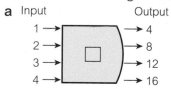
Input → Output
1 → 4
2 → 8
3 → 12
4 → 16

b
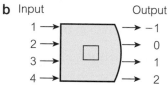
Input → Output
1 → −1
2 → 0
3 → 1
4 → 2

4 A sequence starts 10, 20, 30, 40. What is
   a the 5th term   **b** the 10th term?
   Discussion How did you find the 5th and 10th terms? Is there more than one way?

5 Work out the 10th term of each sequence.
   a 3, 6, 9, 12, …
   b 8, 16, 24, 32, …
   c 11, 22, 33, 44, 55, …

6 **a** Draw pattern 4 in this sequence.

Pattern 1   Pattern 2   Pattern 3

   b Copy and complete the table to show the number of dots in each pattern.

Pattern number	1	2	3	4	5
Number of dots	3	4			

   c How many dots will there be in pattern 8?

> **Key point**
> Each term in a sequence has a position.
> The 1st term is in position 1, the 2nd term is in position 2, the 3rd term is in position 3 and so on.
> The **position-to-term** rule tells you how to work out a term in a sequence when you know its position.

Topic links: Negative numbers, Multiples

7 Real A picture framer uses 4 pieces of wood for each frame.

a Copy and complete the table to show how many pieces of wood he needs for different numbers of frames.

Number of frames	1	2	3	4	5
Number of pieces of wood	4	8			

b How many pieces of wood will he need for 10 frames?

Discussion How did you work out your answers to Q6 part **c** and Q7 part **b**?

Worked example

The nth term of a sequence is $3n$.
Work out the first five terms.

Position (n)	1	2	3	4	5
Term ($3n$)	$3 \times 1 = 3$	$3 \times 2 = 6$	$3 \times 3 = 9$	$3 \times 4 = 12$	$3 \times 5 = 15$

> **Key point**
> You use algebra to write the position-to-term rule.
> It is called the n**th term** because it tells you how to work out the term at position n (any position).

> Substitute the position number into the expression $3n$.

8 Copy and complete the tables to work out the first five terms of each sequence.

a General term = $n + 2$

Position (n)	1	2	3	4	5
Term ($n + 2$)	$1 + 2 = 3$	$\square + 2 = \square$			

b General term = $2n$

Position (n)	1	2	3	4	5
Term ($2n$)	$2 \times 1 = \square$	$2 \times \square = \square$			

c General term = $n - 3$

Position (n)	1	2	3	4	5
Term ($n - 3$)					

d General term = $5n$

Position (n)	1	2	3	4	5
Term ($5n$)					

9 Work out the 10th term of the sequence with nth term

a $3n$ **b** $n + 12$ **c** $5n$ **d** $n - 8$

e $n - 15$ **f** $n + 0.5$ **g** $n - 0.7$ **h** $0.5n$

> **Q9 hint**
> For the 10th term, $n = 10$.

10 Problem-solving The nth term of a sequence is $4n$.
How many terms are less than 25?

11 Problem-solving The nth term of a sequence is $n - 5$.
How many negative terms are there in the sequence?

12 Explore How many centimetres do you grow each year in the first 15 years of your life?
Is it easier to explore this question now you have completed the lesson? What further information do you need to be able to answer this?

13 Reflect Think about the term-to-term rule and the position-to-term rule for the 4 times table.
Which rule is '×4' and which is '+4'?
Make sure you know the difference between the term-to-term rule and the position-to-term rule.
Write a hint, in your own words, to help you remember which is which.

8.5 Finding the nth term

You will learn to:
- Find the nth term of a simple sequence.

Why learn this?
Finding the nth term saves you making lots of repetitive calculations.

Fluency
What are the first five multiples of 7?
Which of these are arithmetic sequences?
- 1, 3, 5, 7
- 1, 2, 4, 8
- 4, 8, 12, 16

Explore
What is the quickest way to work out the 100th term in a sequence?

Exercise 8.5

1 Work out the 10th term of each sequence.
  a 1, 2, 3, 4, …
  b 2, 3, 4, 5, …
  c 3, 4, 5, 6, …

2 Work out the first three terms of the sequence with nth term
  a $6n$
  b $n + 4$
  c $n - 3$

Worked example

Work out the nth term of this sequence.
7, 14, 21, 28, …

Position: 1   2   3   4   … n
Term: 7 ×7 14 ×7 21 ×7 28 ×7 … $n × 7$ ×7

$7n$ $n × 7 = 7n$

> Write out the position numbers and terms. Work out what you do to the position number to get the term.

3 Work out the nth term of each sequence.
  a 8, 16, 24, 32, 40, ….
  b 11, 22, 33, 44, 55, …
  c 10, 20, 30, 40, 50, …
  d 9, 18, 27, 36, 45, …
  e 1, 2, 3, 4, 5, …

  Discussion What is the nth term of the multiples of 2?
  What about the multiples of 12?

4 Find the nth term of each sequence. The first one is started for you.
  a 11, 12, 13, 14, 15, …

  Position: 1 +☐ 2 +☐ 3 +☐ 4 +☐ 5 +☐ n +☐
  Term: 11   12   13   14   15   ☐

  term = position number + ☐ nth term = $n + ☐$

  b 5, 6, 7, 8, 9, …
  c 12, 13, 14, 15, 16, …
  d 21, 22, 23, 24, 25, …
  e 0, 1, 2, 3, 4, 5, …
  f −3, −2, −1, 0, 1, 2, …
  g −9, −8, −7, −6, −5, −4, …

Q4a hint
Compare each term to its position number.

Q4e hint
Position:) −☐
Term:

Topic links: Negative numbers, Multiples

Subject links: Science (Q8)

5 Problem-solving Match each sequence to the nth term.

i 101, 102, 103, 104, …	**A** $15n$
ii −8, −7, −6, −5, …	**B** $n - 9$
iii 15, 30, 45, 60, 75, …	**C** $4n$
iv 20, 40, 60, 80, 100, …	**D** $n + 100$
v 4, 5, 6, 7, 8, …	**E** $20n$
vi 4, 8, 12, 16, 20, …	**F** $n + 3$

6 Problem-solving Some of the terms of this sequence are missing.

☐, ☐, 18, 24, 30, ☐

a Work out the missing terms.

b Work out the nth term.

c Work out the 20th term.

7 Modelling Phoebe runs for 12 minutes on her first day of training, then 12 minutes more each day.

a Continue this sequence to the 6th term.   12, 24, …

b What is the nth term for this sequence?

c How many hours will Phoebe run for on the 10th day?

d Do you think Phoebe will be able to stick to the model for 50 days? Explain your answer.

8 Real / STEM A scientist records the number of dandelions in a 1 m square patch of ground each month.

Month	Number of dandelions
1	2
2	4
3	6
4	8

Predict the number of dandelions after 12 months.

9 For each pattern sequence, work out

   i the nth term for the number of counters

   ii the number of counters in the 10th pattern.

a b

10 Problem-solving a Work out the nth term of this arithmetic sequence.

☐, 18, ☐, 36, ☐, 54, ☐.

b Work out the 100th term.

Q10a hint

Work out the missing terms in the sequence first.

11 Explore What is the quickest way to work out the 100th term in a sequence?

Look back at the maths you have learned in this lesson.

How can you use it to answer this question?

12 Reflect Charley says, 'Finding the nth term is just like finding the position-to-term rule, but you write 'n' instead of the position number.'

Do you agree with Charley?

What else do you need to think about when writing the nth term?

Explore

Reflect

Master
P165

CHECK

Strengthen
P177

Extend
P181

Test
P185

8 Check up

Log how you did on your
Student Progression Chart.

Sequences

1 a Draw the next pattern in the sequence.

Pattern 1   Pattern 2   Pattern 3

b Copy and complete the table.

Pattern number	1	2	3	4
Number of dots				

c What is the first term?

d What is the term-to-term rule?

2 Work out the first four terms of each sequence.
a First term 10, term-to-term rule 'add 7'
b First term 18, term-to-term rule 'subtract 5'

3 Which sequence in Q2 is ascending?

4 Copy and complete the name of this sequence.

1, 4, 9, 16, 25, …

The _____ numbers

5 Decide if each sequence is finite or infinite.
a The whole numbers
b The odd numbers between 20 and 40

6 This pattern sequence is made from matchsticks.

a Copy and complete this table for the sequence.

Pattern number	1	2	3	4	5
Number of matchsticks					

b Work out the number of matchsticks in the 7th pattern.

7 Work out the first five terms in each sequence.
a First term −3, term-to-term rule 'add 2'
b First term 4, term-to-term rule 'subtract 0.4'
c First term −10, term-to-term rule 'add 10, then multiply by 2'

8 Decide if each sequence is arithmetic or geometric.
a 2, 4, 8, 16, 32, …
b 2, 4, 6, 8, 10, …
c First term 6, term-to-term rule '+4'
d First term −3, term-to-term rule '×5'

9 Describe each sequence by giving the first term and the term-to-term rule.

  a 9, 18, 27, 36, …

  b 10, 8, 6, 4, …

  c 1, 3, 9, 27, …

Sequences in real life

10 Mary has £200 in her bank account. She spends £25 each month. How many months will it be before the account is empty?

11 A fence is made from posts and fence panels.

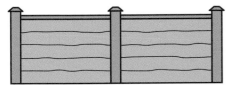

post   fence panel   post

  a Copy and complete the table.

Number of fence panels	1	2	3	4	5	6
Number of posts	2					

  b How many posts are needed for 10 fence panels?

The nth term

12 Work out the first five terms of the sequence with nth term

  a $n - 7$

  b $5n$

  c $n + 12$

13 Work out the nth term of each sequence.

  a 12, 24, 36, 48, …

  b 9, 10, 11, 12, …

14 a Work out the nth term of the sequence −7, −6, −5, −4, −3, …

  b What is the 100th term?

15 How sure are you of your answers? Were you mostly

  🙁 **Just guessing**   😐 **Feeling doubtful**   🙂 **Confident**

  What next? Use your results to decide whether to strengthen or extend your learning.

Challenge

16 A competition offers a choice of two prizes.

  • Prize A – £20 000 a year for 5 years, and after that the prize halves each year, or

  • Prize B – £10 000 a year for the next 20 years.

  Which is the better prize? Explain.

Reflect

Master
P165

Check
P175

STRENGTHEN

Extend
P181

Test
P185

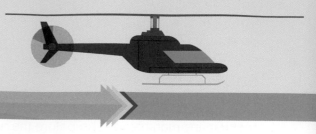

8 Strengthen

You will:
- Strengthen your understanding with practice.

Sequences

1 A sequence starts like this.
   a How many extra rectangles are added each time?
   b Draw the next term in the sequence.

2 These patterns are made from matchsticks.

a

b

c

For each sequence
   i draw the next term
   ii write the number of matchsticks added each time
   iii copy and complete the table.

Pattern number	1	2	3	4
Number of matchsticks				

3 Draw the next term in each sequence.

a | •• | ••• | •••• | ••••• |

b | •• | •••• | •••••• | •••••••• |

c | • | •••• | ••••••• | •••••••••• |

Q3 hint

How many dots are added each time?

4 The first term of a sequence is 5, and the term-to-term rule is 'add 3'.
   a Copy and complete the first five terms
      of the sequence.

   5   8   ☐   ☐   ☐
        +3   +3   +3   +3

   b Is the sequence ascending (going up)
      or descending (going down)?

Q4b hint

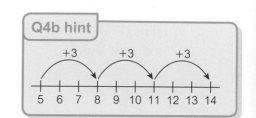

5 Write the first five terms of each sequence.
   a First term 10, term-to-term rule 'add 6'

   10   16   ☐   ☐   …
        +6   +6

   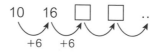

   b First term 20, term-to-term rule 'subtract 4'

   20   16   ☐   ☐   …
        −4   −4

   c First term 7, term-to-term rule 'add 10'
   d First term 18, term-to-term rule 'subtract 3'
   e Which two sequences are descending?

6 a Write
  i the even numbers between 30 and 50
  ii the multiples of 5 smaller than 20.

b Why can't you write every odd number?

c Decide if each sequence is finite or infinite.
  i The odd numbers between 10 and 50
  ii All the even numbers
  iii All the multiples of 10

Q6b hint

A sequence of numbers which goes on for ever is infinite.

7 The first term of a sequence is 9.
The term-to-term rule is 'add 1, then multiply by 2'.
  a To find the next term in the sequence, work out the output of this function machine.

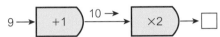

  b Put the output of the function machine from part **a** into the function machine again to work out the third term.

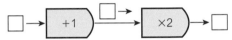

  c Work out the fourth term in the sequence.

Q8 hint

Use the method in Q7.

8 Work out the first three terms of each sequence.
  a First term 5, term-to-term rule 'add 1, then multiply by 2'
  b First term 4, term-to-term rule 'multiply by 3, then subtract 5'

9 a Write the term-to-term rule for each sequence.

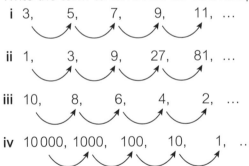

  i 3,   5,   7,   9,   11, …
  ii 1,   3,   9,   27,   81, …
  iii 10,   8,   6,   4,   2, …
  iv 10 000, 1000, 100,   10,   1, …

  b Which of the sequences in part **a** are arithmetic?
  Which are geometric?

  c Describe each sequence by giving the first term and the term-to-term rule.

Q9a hint

If the sequence is
- ascending, the term-to-term rule might be adding or multiplying
- descending, the term-to-term rule might be subtracting
- ascending very quickly, the term-to-term rule might be multiplying
- descending very quickly, the term-to-term rule might be dividing.

Q9b hint

If you are **A**dding or subtracting a common difference, the sequence is **A**rithmetic.
If you are multiplyin**G** or dividin**G**, the sequence is **G**eometric.

Q9c hint

First term
3   5

☐   term-to-term rule

Sequences in real life

1 A box contains 5 biscuits.
You eat 1 biscuit each day.
How many biscuits do you have to choose from on
  a day 1   **b** day 2   **c** day 5?

Q1 hint

Write a list.
Day 1 ☐
Day 2 ☐

2 On 1 car there are 4 tyres.
How many tyres are there on
  a 1 car   **b** 2 cars
  c 3 cars   **d** 10 cars?

3 A shop pays its employees more per hour for each year they stay with the company.

Year	1	2	3	4	5
Pay per hour	£6.50	£7	£7.50		

a What is the pay per hour in
   i year 4
   ii year 5?

Mr Andrews says, 'To work out the pay per hour in the 10th year, double the amount in the 5th year'.

b Work out the pay per hour in the 10th year.

c Is Mr Andrews correct?

Q3a hint

How much does the pay go up each year?

The nth term

1 The first five terms of a sequence are 4, 8, 12, 16, …
  a What is the 5th term?
  b Work out the 8th term.

Q1 hint

Is there a relationship between the term number and the term?

2 For each sequence find the position-to-term rule.

a

Position in sequence	1	2	3	4	5
Term	4	8	12	16	20

b

Position in sequence	1	2	3	4	5
Term	6	7	8	9	10

c

Position in sequence	1	2	3	4	5
Term	−3	−2	−1	0	1

Q2a hint

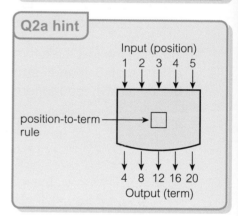

Input (position)
1 2 3 4 5

position-to-term rule

4 8 12 16 20
Output (term)

3 Copy and complete the function machines to find the first five terms of the sequences for these position-to-term rules.

  a $4n$
                        b $n + 15$

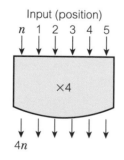
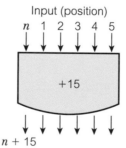

4 Copy and complete the tables to show the first five terms of the sequences for these position-to-term rules.
  a $n - 10$

Position number	1	2	3	4	5
Term					

  b $100n$

Position number	1	2	3	4	5
Term					

Q4 hint

Draw a function machine.

5 Work out the first five terms of each sequence.
  a $n + 5$ **b** $n - 20$ **c** $9n$ **d** $n + 2$

Q5 hint

You can draw a function machine or a table to help you.

6 a Work out the first five terms of the sequence with nth term

    i $2n$

    ii $3n$

    iii $4n$

    iv $9n$

  b Write the missing numbers.

    i nth term $2n$, sequence is multiples of ☐

    ii nth term $3n$, sequence is multiples of ☐

    iii nth term $4n$, sequence is multiples of ☐

    iv nth term $5n$, sequence is multiples of ☐

7 Find the nth term of each sequence.

  a 6, 12, 18, 24, 30, …

  b 10, 20, 30, 40, 50, 60, …

  c 11, 22, 33, 44, 55, …

  d 8, 16, 24, 32, 40, …

Q7 hint

Use your answers to Q6 to help.

8 A sequence starts

    4, 5, 6, 7, 8, …

Gill draws a function machine.

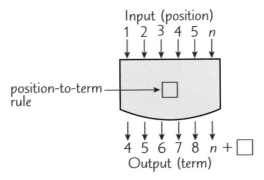

Input (position)
1 2 3 4 5 n

position-to-term rule

4 5 6 7 8 $n +$ ☐
Output (term)

  a Find the position-to-term rule.

  b Complete the general term of the sequence: $n +$ ☐

9 Find the nth term of each sequence.

  a 10, 11, 12, 13, 14, …

  b −2, −1, 0, 1, 2, …

  c 0, 1, 2, 3, 4, 5, …

  d 101, 102, 103, 104, …

Q9a hint

Use the method in Q8.

Q9b hint

nth term is $n -$ ☐

Enrichment

1 The first term of a sequence is 1. The term-to-term rule is '×1'.

  a What are the first five terms?

  b The first term of another sequence is 4.

    The term-to-term rule is 'add 12, then divide by 4.'

    What are the first five terms?

  c Design as many other sequences like this as you can.

2 Reflect Harriet says, 'The word 'term' is used a lot in this unit.

It must be important for understanding sequences.'

Write a definition, in your own words, for the word 'term' when it refers

to sequences.

Reflect

Master
P165

Check
P175

Strengthen
P177

EXTEND

Test
P185

8 Extend

You will:

• Extend your understanding with problem-solving.

1 Work out the first five terms in each sequence.

   a First term 1, term-to-term rule 'multiply by 0.5'
   b First term 1000, term-to-term rule 'multiply by 0.1'
   c First term 2, term-to-term rule 'divide by 2'
   d First term 1000, term-to-term rule 'divide by 10'
   e What do you notice about the sequences for parts **b** and **d**?
      Explain why.

2 **Problem-solving** An arithmetic sequence starts 4, 9, 14, …
   How many terms in the sequence are less than 50?

3 **Problem-solving** The 2nd term of an arithmetic sequence is 5.
   The 4th term is 9.
   □, 5, □, 9, □, ….
   What is the 12th term of the sequence?

Q3 Strategy hint

Find the missing terms, then the nth term.

4 Work out the next three terms in each sequence.

   a 2 kg, 1.75 kg, 1.5 kg, 1.25 kg, …
   b 4 cm, 3.4 cm, 2.8 cm, 2.2 cm, …
   c 20 cm, 60 cm, 1 m, 1.40 m, …
   d 200 ml, 400 ml, 800 ml, 1.6 l, …

5 **Reasoning** The **general term** of a sequence is $3n$.
   Could one of the terms in the sequence be 31? Explain your answer.

Q5 Literacy hint

The **general term** is the nth term.

6 An arithmetic sequence has first term 5 and common difference +7.
   In the first 10 terms how many are

   a prime
   b multiples of 5
   c factors of 20?

7 Work out the next term in each sequence.

   a x, $x + 1$, $x + 2$, $x + 3$, …   **b** x, $2x$, $3x$, $4x$, …
   c $x - 4$, $x - 6$, $x - 8$, …   **d** $x + 1$, $2x + 2$, $3x + 3$, …

8 An arithmetic sequence has first term 20 and common difference −3.
   How many positive terms are there in the sequence?

Q8 Strategy hint

Write down the first few terms of the sequence.

9 **Problem-solving** The first two terms in an arithmetic sequence
   are 10 and 20.
   What is the nth term of the sequence?

10 **Problem-solving** The 5th and 6th terms of an arithmetic sequence
   are 17 and 18.
   What is the nth term of the sequence?

Q10 hint

□, □, □, □, 17, 18, …

Topic links: Adding and subtracting decimals, Fractions, Negative numbers, Prime
numbers, Rules for divisibility, Area, perimeter and volume, Surface area of cuboids

11 Problem-solving a The first two terms in an arithmetic sequence are 1 and 5.
How many terms in the sequence are less than 100?
b The first two terms in a geometric sequence are 1 and 5.
How many terms in the sequence are less than 100?
c Which grows faster, the arithmetic or the geometric sequence?

12 These sequences are made of counters.

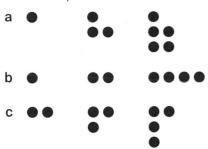

For each sequence, how many counters will be in
i the 5th term   **ii** the 10th term?

13 For two dots, the smallest number of lines
needed to join each dot to the other is 1.

For three dots, the smallest number of lines
needed to join each dot to the others is 3.

a For four dots, work out the smallest number
of lines needed to join each dot to the others.

b Copy and complete the table.

Number of dots	2	3	4	5	
Smallest number of lines	1				

c Predict the minimum number of lines for 10 dots.

> **Q13a hint**
>
> Includes diagonals.

> **Q13c hint**
>
> Work out the differences between terms. Follow the pattern.

14 The Fibonacci sequence starts
    1, 1, 2, 3, …
Each term is found by adding the previous two terms.
How many prime numbers are there in the first 15 terms of the Fibonacci
sequence?

15 a Draw the next two terms in this sequence.

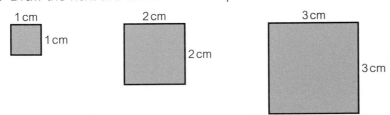

b Copy and complete the table.

Term	1	2	3	4	5
Side of square	1 cm	2 cm	3 cm		
Perimeter	4 cm				
Area	1 cm²				

c What is the perimeter of the 10th term in the sequence?
d What is the area of the 7th term in the sequence?
e What is the nth term for the perimeter of the squares in the sequence?

16 A sequence starts with 1.

The term-to-term rule is 'multiply by 2, then subtract 1'.

  a Work out the first five terms of the sequence.

  b What do you notice about the sequence?

  Discussion Could you describe this sequence as arithmetic?

  Could you describe this sequence as geometric?

17 **STEM** The number of bacteria in a sample doubles each day.

A student designs a spreadsheet to calculate the number of bacteria.

  a What formula should be entered into cells B6 to B9 to calculate the number of bacteria on days 5 to 8?

  b How many bacteria does the scientist start with on day 1?

  c Use a spreadsheet to work out how long before there are over 1 million bacteria.

  d Another scientist starts with 100 bacteria.

  Work out how long before there are over 1 million bacteria.

	A	B
1		Number of bacteria
2	Day 1	1
3	Day 2	= B2*2
4	Day 3	= B3*2
5	Day 4	= B4*2
6	Day 5	
7	Day 6	
8	Day 7	
9	Day 8	

18 **Reasoning** The general term of a sequence is $n + 7$.

Which of these are terms in the sequence?

  −4, 3, 6, 9, 11, 13

19 a Sketch the next two terms in this sequence.

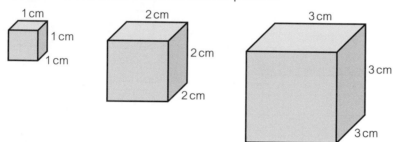

  b Copy and complete the table.

Term	1	2	3	4	5
Side of cube	1 cm	2 cm	3 cm		
Surface area	6 × 1 × 1 = 6 cm²				

  c Predict the surface area of a cube with sides of length 7 cm.

20 **Problem-solving / Real** In a restaurant the dessert is two scoops of ice cream.

Customers can choose from chocolate or vanilla and can choose to have one of each.

  a How many different options are there?

The restaurant decides to offer strawberry as well.

  b How many different options are there now?

  c Copy and compete the table.

Number of flavours	1	2	3	4	5
Number of different options	1				

  d How many options will there be if the restaurant has

  i 6 different flavours

  ii 10 different flavours?

> **Q20 hint**
>
> Write down the options
> (C for chocolate, V for vanilla).
> CV, CC, …
> CV and VC would be considered the same order.

21 Reasoning A Fibonacci-style sequence starts 10, 10, 20, 30, …
Will all the terms be multiples of 10? Explain your answer.

22 Work out the first five terms of each arithmetic sequence.
  a First term −3, common difference +0.3
  b First term −12, common difference −0.7
  c First term −4.5 common difference −0.2

23 Reasoning a Draw the next two terms in this sequence.

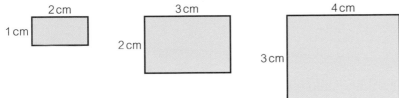

  b Copy and complete the table.

Rectangle	1 cm by 2 cm	2 cm by 3 cm	3 cm by 4 cm		
Perimeter	1 + 2 + 1 + 2 = 6 cm	2 + 3 + 2 + 3 = ☐			
Area	1 × 2 = 2 cm²	2 × 3 = 6 cm²			

  c For the 6th rectangle in the sequence, predict
    i the perimeter   **ii** the area.
  d Check your answers by drawing the rectangle.

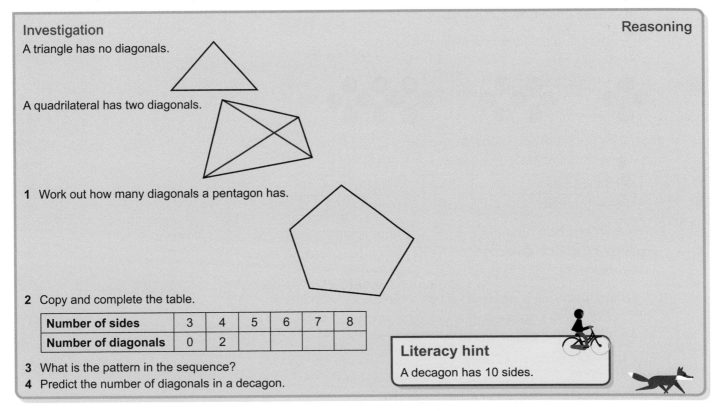

Investigation   **Reasoning**

A triangle has no diagonals.

A quadrilateral has two diagonals.

1 Work out how many diagonals a pentagon has.

2 Copy and complete the table.

Number of sides	3	4	5	6	7	8
Number of diagonals	0	2				

3 What is the pattern in the sequence?
4 Predict the number of diagonals in a decagon.

Literacy hint
A decagon has 10 sides.

24 Reflect Look back at Q9 and Q10.
What was the same and what was different about the methods you
used to work out the *n*th term for the two sequences?

8 Unit test

Log how you did on your Student Progression Chart.

1 Work out the next term for each sequence.
   a 0, 30, 60, 90, …
   b 20, 18, 16, 14, …
   c 3, 30, 300, 3000, …

2 Write the term-to-term rule and the next term for each sequence.
   a 80, 75, 70, 65, …
   b 4, 8, 16, 32, …

3 The first term of a sequence is 15. The term-to-term rule is '+6'.
   Work out the first five terms of the sequence.

4 Write the first four terms in the sequence of square numbers.

5 Jan is studying the sequence of even numbers starting at 0.
   a Is it ascending or descending?
   b Is it finite or infinite?

6 Brianne makes a flower bracelet from beads.
   It grows like this.

   a Draw the next term in the sequence.
   b Copy and complete this table.

Number of flowers	1	2	3	4	5
Number of beads	5	9			

7 The first term of a sequence is 12. The term-to-term rule is 'subtract 5 and multiply by 2'.
   Write down the first three terms of the sequence.

8 A recipe for biscuits states, 'Start with 100 g flour. Add an extra 25 g of flour for each egg used.'
   a How much extra flour would you need for
      i 1 egg
      ii 2 eggs
      iii 3 eggs?
   b Predict the extra flour added for 10 eggs.

9 Look back at the sequences in Q2.
   a Which is arithmetic?
   b Which is geometric?

10 The first term of a sequence is 20.
   The term-to-term rule is 'subtract 0.1'.
   Write the first five terms of the sequence.

11 Work out the first five terms of the sequence whose nth term is

   a $n + 8$

   b $3n$

   c $n - 6$

12 Look at this sequence.

      4, 8, 12, 16, …

   a Write the next three terms of the sequence.

   b Work out the nth term of the sequence.

   c Work out the 100th term.

13 The nth term of a sequence is $6n$. Which of the numbers in the cloud are terms of the sequence?

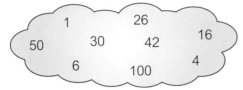

   1   26   16   50   30   42   6   100   4

14 A sequence starts:

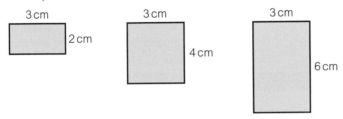

   a Draw the next term in the sequence.

   b Work out the area of each rectangle.

   c What will be the area of

      i the 5th rectangle

     ii the 7th rectangle in the sequence?

   d Check your answers to part **c** by drawing the rectangles.

Challenge

15 Count the total number of squares in each diagram.
Use the steps below to begin.

   a Write a sequence for the total number of squares in each diagram.

   b Use your sequence to predict the total number of squares in the 5th diagram.

   c Are there any other number patterns in these shapes?

> **Q15a hint**
>
> Don't forget to count squares made of smaller squares!

> **Q15b hint**
>
> Draw the 5th diagram to test your answer.

16 Reflect Write a heading 'Four important things about sequences'.
Now look back at the work you have done in this unit and list the four most important things you think you have learned.
For example, you might include

   • words (with their definitions)

   • methods for working things out

   • mistakes you made (with tips on how to avoid them in future).

9.1 Comparing fractions

You will learn to:
- Compare fractions
- Simplify fractions
- Identify equivalent fractions.

Why learn this?
Scientists use fractions when investigating how bacteria reproduce and survive.

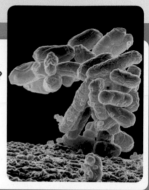

Fluency
What fraction is shaded?

Explore
How can you tell whether a fraction is bigger than, smaller than or equal to another fraction?

Exercise 9.1

1 Write > or < between each pair of fractions.

   a $\frac{4}{7} \,\square\, \frac{2}{7}$ **b** $\frac{1}{2} \,\square\, \frac{1}{4}$ **c** $\frac{1}{8} \,\square\, \frac{1}{5}$ **d** $\frac{1}{10} \,\square\, \frac{1}{9}$

2 Match pairs of equivalent fractions.

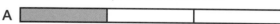

A
B
C
D
E
F

3 Copy and complete. Simplify each fraction.

  a $\overset{\div 5}{\frac{15}{20}} = \frac{\square}{\square}$ **b** $\overset{\div 4}{\frac{16}{20}} = \frac{\square}{\square}$ **c** $\overset{\div 3}{\frac{18}{21}} = \frac{\square}{\square}$ **d** $\overset{\div 6}{\frac{30}{36}} = \frac{\square}{\square}$
     $\div 5$ $\div 4$ $\div 3$ $\div 6$

4 List the common factors of
  a 18 and 24   **b** 10 and 30.

5 Write these fractions under the headings 'more than $\frac{1}{2}$' and 'less than $\frac{1}{2}$'.
  $\frac{7}{10}$ $\frac{5}{9}$ $\frac{2}{7}$ $\frac{2}{5}$ $\frac{11}{20}$ $\frac{9}{20}$ $\frac{4}{11}$ $\frac{6}{11}$

Q5 hint

Is the numerator more or less than half of the denominator?

Topic links: Multiplication, Division, HCF, Equivalent fractions

6 Draw two bars of the same length to work out which is the larger fraction in each pair. The first one has been done for you.

a $\frac{5}{6}$ and $\frac{7}{12}$ **b** $\frac{3}{10}$ and $\frac{2}{5}$ **c** $\frac{3}{4}$ and $\frac{5}{8}$

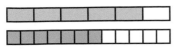

7 Write > or < between each pair of fractions.
Use the fraction wall to help you.

a $\frac{4}{5}$ and $\frac{7}{10}$ **b** $\frac{2}{3}$ and $\frac{5}{6}$ **c** $\frac{3}{4}$ and $\frac{5}{8}$ **d** $\frac{2}{3}$ and $\frac{3}{4}$

e $\frac{1}{3}$ and $\frac{2}{5}$ **f** $\frac{4}{5}$ and $\frac{3}{4}$ **g** $\frac{7}{12}$ and $\frac{5}{8}$

8 Reasoning Order these fractions, smallest to largest.
Use the fraction wall to help you.

a $\frac{1}{2}$ $\frac{5}{8}$ $\frac{1}{4}$ **b** $\frac{1}{2}$ $\frac{2}{5}$ $\frac{7}{10}$ **c** $\frac{7}{10}$ $\frac{1}{2}$ $\frac{3}{8}$ **d** $\frac{3}{4}$ $\frac{3}{12}$ $\frac{3}{5}$

9 Copy and complete to simplify.

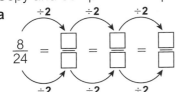

a

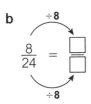

b

Discussion Which way is easier? Which way is quicker?

10 Reasoning Lucy has simplified $\frac{12}{18}$ to $\frac{6}{9}$. Is $\frac{6}{9}$ in its **simplest form**?

> **Key point**
> A fraction is in its **simplest form** when you cannot cancel it any further.

> **Key point**
> You can divide by the **HCF** of the numerator and denominator to write a fraction in its simplest form.

Worked example

Write $\frac{24}{30}$ in its simplest form.

The HCF of 24 and 30 is 6.

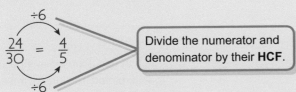

Divide the numerator and denominator by their **HCF**.

11 Use the HCF to simplify these fractions.

a $\frac{16}{32}$ **b** $\frac{15}{35}$ **c** $\frac{10}{40}$ **d** $\frac{24}{42}$ **e** $\frac{12}{30}$ **f** $\frac{18}{27}$

12 Problem-solving Find the matching pairs of equivalent fractions by simplifying each one.

$\frac{16}{20}$ $\frac{25}{35}$ $\frac{14}{21}$ $\frac{6}{8}$ $\frac{10}{14}$ $\frac{20}{30}$ $\frac{12}{16}$ $\frac{12}{15}$

13 Explore How can you tell whether a fraction is bigger than, smaller than or equal to another fraction? Look back at the maths you have learned in this lesson. How can you use it to answer this question?

14 Reflect After this lesson, Adam says, 'Fractions are not really like whole numbers.' Naringa says, 'Yes! Fractions can be written in many different ways.'
Look back at your work on fractions.
What do you think Adam means?
What do you think Naringa means?

Explore

Reflect

9.2 Fractions of amounts

You will learn to:
- Calculate with fractions mentally
- Calculate fractions of quantities
- Multiply a fraction by a whole number.

CONFIDENCE

Why learn this?
Model makers use fractions to work out the dimensions of their scale models.

Fluency
Work out
- $24 \div 6$
- $50 \div 5$
- $120 \div 2$
- $350 \div 7$
- $480 \div 8$
- $200 \div 4$

Explore
How long is a model aeroplane?

Exercise 9.2

Warm up

1 Write each fraction in its simplest form.

a $\frac{15}{20}$ 　　　　**b** $\frac{6}{8}$ 　　　　**c** $\frac{7}{14}$

2 Write each improper fraction as a mixed number.

a $\frac{9}{7}$ 　　　　**b** $\frac{6}{5}$

c $\frac{14}{4}$ 　　　　**d** $\frac{17}{6}$

3 Work out

a $\frac{1}{4}$ of 24 　　　　**b** $\frac{1}{10}$ of 80

c $\frac{1}{5}$ of 45 　　　　**d** $\frac{1}{6}$ of 300

e $\frac{1}{7}$ of 420 　　　　**f** $\frac{1}{8}$ of 320

> **Key point**
>
> You can use doubling and halving to find related fractions of the same amount.

4 Use halving to find $\frac{1}{2}$, $\frac{1}{4}$ and $\frac{1}{8}$ of these amounts.

a £24

$\frac{1}{2}$ of 24 = 24 ÷ 2 = 12

$\frac{1}{4}$ of 24 = 24 ÷ 2 ÷ 2 = □

$\frac{1}{8}$ of 24 = 24 ÷ 2 ÷ 2 ÷ □ = □

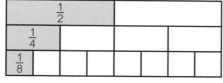

b £40 　　　　**c** £200

d £320 　　　　**e** £480

Discussion Is dividing by 4 the same as dividing by 2 twice?

> **Q4 hint**
>
> Find $\frac{1}{2}$ then halve the answer to find $\frac{1}{4}$. Halve *that* answer to find $\frac{1}{8}$.

5 Work out $\frac{1}{10}$ of each measurement, then double it to find $\frac{1}{5}$.

a 400 g

$\frac{1}{10}$ of 400 = □

$\frac{1}{5}$ of 400 = □ × 2 = □

b 600 ml 　　**c** 350 g 　　**d** 720 ml

e 2340 m 　　**f** 1450 g

> **Q5 hint**
>
>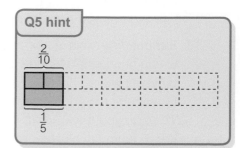

Topic links: Division, Multiplication, Measures

6 Use doubling or halving to find $\frac{1}{3}$, $\frac{1}{6}$ and $\frac{1}{12}$ of each amount.

   a 12   **b** 24

   c 480   **d** 720

Q6 hint

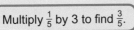

Worked example

Work out $\frac{3}{5}$ of £250.

$\frac{1}{5}$ is £250 ÷ 5 = £50

> Divide by 5 to find $\frac{1}{5}$.

$\frac{3}{5}$ is 3 × £50 = £150

> Multiply $\frac{1}{5}$ by 3 to find $\frac{3}{5}$.

Key point

To find a fraction of a number, divide by the denominator then multiply by the numerator.

7 Work out

   a **i** $\frac{1}{4}$ of £40   **ii** $\frac{3}{4}$ of £40

   b **i** $\frac{1}{5}$ of £500   **ii** $\frac{4}{5}$ of £500

   c **i** $\frac{1}{6}$ of £240   **ii** $\frac{5}{6}$ of £240

   d $\frac{5}{9}$ of £360

   e $\frac{3}{7}$ of 280 cm

   f $\frac{5}{8}$ of 400 cm

8 **Problem-solving** Put these amounts in order, smallest first.

   $\frac{3}{4}$ of 28 $\frac{2}{9}$ of 81 $\frac{3}{7}$ of 35 $\frac{2}{3}$ of 30

9 **Problem-solving** Simon says that $\frac{1}{3}$ of his class of 32 pupils wear glasses. Can this be true? Explain.

10 **Real / Reasoning** The Bradleys have completed $\frac{3}{5}$ of their 350 km journey. How far do they still have to travel?

11 **Real / Reasoning** Tom is $\frac{2}{3}$ the age of his 15-year-old sister. How old is Tom?

   Discussion Will Tom always be $\frac{2}{3}$ the age of his sister?

12 **Real** The wingspan of a Cessna 172 light aircraft is 11 m. Jake builds a model $\frac{1}{10}$ of its actual size. How long is the wingspan of the model?

Worked example

Work out

   a $\frac{1}{5} \times 4$

   b $\frac{3}{4} \times 5$

> Multiply the numerator 1 by the number 4.

   a $\frac{1}{5} \times 4 = \frac{1 \times 4}{5} = \frac{4}{5}$

> Multiply the numerator 3 by the number 5.

   b $\frac{3}{4} \times 5 = \frac{3 \times 5}{4} = \frac{15}{4}$

            $= 3\frac{3}{4}$

> Write the improper fraction as a mixed number.

Key point

To multiply a fraction by a whole number, multiply just the numerator, then simplify the fraction, if possible.

13 Multiply each fraction, simplifying where possible.

a $2 \times \frac{1}{3}$

b $\frac{1}{9} \times 6$

c $8 \times \frac{1}{5}$

d $\frac{1}{8} \times 10$

e $6 \times \frac{1}{6}$

f $14 \times \frac{1}{7}$

Q13b hint

$\frac{1}{9} \times 6 = 6 \times \frac{1}{9}$

14 Multiply each fraction, simplifying where possible.

a $4 \times \frac{2}{5}$

b $\frac{2}{3} \times 5$

c $5 \times \frac{3}{5}$

d $\frac{2}{7} \times 5$

e $6 \times \frac{3}{5}$

f $5 \times \frac{4}{5}$

Investigation   Problem-solving

1 Work out

a $\frac{3}{5}$ of 20 (use the method in the first worked example)

b $20 \times \frac{3}{5}$ (use the method in the second worked example).

What do you notice?

2 Does this work for

a $\frac{3}{4}$ of 16 and $\frac{3}{4} \times 16$

b $\frac{2}{3}$ of 9 and $9 \times \frac{2}{3}$?

---

15 **Problem-solving** Finn has read $\frac{2}{9}$ of his book.
Reuben has read 3 times as much of his.
What fraction of his book has Reuben read?

16 **Problem-solving** Renee is giving a pizza party for 8 people.
She wants $\frac{5}{8}$ of a pizza for each person.
How many pizzas does she need?

17 **Real** A model car is $\frac{1}{20}$th actual size. The real car is 4 metres long.
How long is the model, in cm?

18 **Problem-solving** The Empire State Building is 443 metres high.
Dale plans to build a scale model.
His shed doorway is 2 m high.
What scale should he use, to make sure the model will fit through his
shed door?

Q18 hint

Try different fractions of 443 m.

19 **Explore** How long is a model aeroplane?
What have you learned in this lesson to help you answer this
question? What other information do you need?

20 **Reflect** Write down an easy fraction calculation.
Write down a difficult fraction calculation.
What makes one fraction calculation easier or harder than the other?

Reflect Explore

9.3 Adding and subtracting fractions

You will learn to:
- Add and subtract fractions.

Why learn this?
Gardening experts use fractions to plan the layout of flower beds.

Fluency
Work out
- $\frac{1}{5} + \frac{3}{5}$
- $\frac{9}{11} - \frac{3}{11}$
- $\frac{2}{7} + \frac{3}{7}$
- $\frac{7}{9} - \frac{5}{9}$

Explore
How could you use fractions to plan how you spend your allowance?

Exercise 9.3

1 Find the LCM of
  a 4 and 5   **b** 3 and 5   **c** 10 and 15   **d** 4 and 8.

2 Copy and complete these equivalent fractions.

a
$\frac{2}{5} = \frac{\square}{\square}$

b
$\frac{5}{7} = \frac{\square}{\square}$

c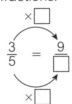
$\frac{3}{5} = \frac{9}{\square}$

d
$\frac{2}{3} = \frac{\square}{6}$

3 Match up the pairs of equivalent fractions.
$\frac{2}{3} \quad \frac{4}{5} \quad \frac{20}{36} \quad \frac{20}{25} \quad \frac{5}{9} \quad \frac{4}{6}$

Worked example

Work out $\frac{1}{3} + \frac{1}{6}$

$\frac{1}{3} + \frac{1}{6} = \frac{2}{6} + \frac{1}{6}$

$= \frac{3}{6}$

$= \frac{1}{2}$

$\frac{1}{3} = \frac{2}{6} \qquad \frac{1}{6}$

The LCM of 3 and 6 is 6.

Simplify the answer, if possible.

Key point
To add or subtract fractions write them as equivalent fractions with a **common denominator**.
Use the LCM as the common denominator.

Q4a hint
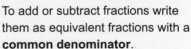
$\frac{1}{5} \qquad \frac{3}{10}$

4 Work out
  a $\frac{3}{10} + \frac{1}{5}$ **b** $\frac{1}{4} + \frac{3}{8}$ **c** $\frac{5}{12} + \frac{1}{3}$ **d** $\frac{6}{15} + \frac{2}{5}$

Discussion When you add two fractions, is your answer larger or smaller than each fraction?

Q5a hint
$\frac{2}{3} = \frac{\square}{9}$

5 Work out
  a $\frac{8}{9} - \frac{2}{3}$ **b** $\frac{7}{12} - \frac{1}{2}$ **c** $\frac{9}{10} - \frac{3}{5}$ **d** $\frac{4}{5} - \frac{1}{10}$

Warm up

6 Problem-solving / Reasoning

   a Ahmed has eaten $\frac{5}{12}$ of his pizza. Dom has eaten $\frac{5}{6}$ of his.
     How much more has Dom eaten?

   b Which of the boys has eaten more than half of his pizza?

7 Problem-solving The twins are saving to buy a computer game to
   share. Grace has saved $\frac{2}{5}$ of the amount and Anna has saved $\frac{3}{10}$.
   What fraction of the cost do they still need to save?

Worked example

Work out $\frac{1}{3} + \frac{1}{4}$

LCM of 3 and 4 is 12 ———— Find the LCM of the denominators.

$\frac{1}{3} = \frac{4}{12}$ $\frac{1}{4} = \frac{3}{12}$

$\frac{4}{12} + \frac{3}{12} = \frac{7}{12}$ Rewrite each fraction as an equivalent fraction with the LCM as the denominator.

---

8 Work out

  a $\frac{1}{3} + \frac{2}{5}$ **b** $\frac{2}{5} + \frac{1}{4}$ **c** $\frac{2}{9} + \frac{1}{6}$ **d** $\frac{1}{2} + \frac{1}{7}$

> **Q8a hint**
>
> LCM of 3 and 5 is 15.
> $\frac{1}{3} = \frac{\square}{15}$ $\frac{2}{5} = \frac{\square}{15}$

9 Work out

  a $\frac{2}{3} - \frac{2}{5}$ **b** $\frac{3}{4} - \frac{1}{3}$ **c** $\frac{4}{5} - \frac{1}{4}$ **d** $\frac{8}{9} - \frac{5}{6}$ **e** $\frac{9}{10} - \frac{1}{4}$

10 Reasoning Andy says that $\frac{1}{3} + \frac{4}{7} = \frac{5}{10}$.
   Explain why he is wrong.

11 Problem-solving

  a How much more than $\frac{11}{15}$ is $\frac{5}{6}$?

  b How much less than $\frac{7}{8}$ is $\frac{3}{5}$?

  c What is the sum of $\frac{2}{5}$ and $\frac{3}{8}$?

| $\frac{1}{3}$ | $\frac{1}{3}$ | $\frac{1}{3}$ |

| $\frac{1}{7}$ | $\frac{1}{7}$ | $\frac{1}{7}$ | $\frac{1}{7}$ | $\frac{1}{7}$ | $\frac{1}{7}$ | $\frac{1}{7}$ |

| $\frac{1}{10}$ | $\frac{1}{10}$ | $\frac{1}{10}$ | $\frac{1}{10}$ | $\frac{1}{10}$ | $\frac{1}{10}$ | $\frac{1}{10}$ | $\frac{1}{10}$ | $\frac{1}{10}$ | $\frac{1}{10}$ |

Investigation
Reasoning

1 Find the difference between fractions where the numerator and denominator are **consecutive** numbers.

$\frac{2}{3} - \frac{1}{2} = \frac{\square}{6} - \frac{\square}{6} =$ $\frac{3}{4} - \frac{2}{3} =$

$\frac{4}{5} - \frac{3}{4} =$ $\frac{5}{6} - \frac{4}{5} =$

Discussion Predict the answer to $\frac{9}{10} - \frac{8}{9}$. Work out the answer to check your prediction.

2 Find these differences.

$\frac{3}{4} - \frac{1}{2} =$ $\frac{5}{6} - \frac{3}{4} =$ $\frac{6}{7} - \frac{4}{5} =$

Discussion Is the answer getting smaller or larger? Predict the answer to $\frac{9}{10} - \frac{7}{8}$.

---

12 Explore How could you use fractions to plan how you spend your
   allowance? Look back at the maths you have learned in this lesson.
   How can you use it to answer this question?

13 Reflect Look back at Q4 and Q5. What steps did you take to work out
   these calculations?
   You might begin with, 'Step 1: I looked at the denominators and noticed …'
   Do your steps work for Q8 and Q9? If not, rewrite your steps.
   You might amend Step 1 to 'I looked at the denominators of both fractions
   and worked out …'

Topic links: Multiplication, Division, LCM   ActiveLearn   Pi 2, Section 9.3

Explore   *Reflect*

9.4 Fractions and percentages

You will learn to:
- Write a number as a fraction of another number
- Change between fractions and percentages.

Why learn this?
Examiners convert all scores to percentages to compare results.

Fluency
Which of these fractions are equivalent to $\frac{1}{2}$?

- $\frac{10}{20}$
- $\frac{6}{12}$
- $\frac{4}{9}$
- $\frac{10}{15}$
- $\frac{4}{8}$
- $\frac{15}{30}$

Explore
Why do we use percentages instead of fractions to compare test results?

Exercise 9.4

1 Write each fraction in its simplest form.

a $\frac{14}{20}$ b $\frac{15}{25}$ c $\frac{24}{40}$ d $\frac{40}{50}$ e $\frac{75}{100}$

2 Write each percentage as a fraction in its simplest form.

a 45% b 99% c 60% d 8%

3 Write each fraction as a percentage.

a $\frac{35}{100}$ b $\frac{56}{100}$ c $\frac{92}{100}$ d $\frac{7}{100}$

4 Aziz has 2 pets. One of them is a gerbil.
What fraction of his pets are gerbils?

5 Adrianna works a 4-hour shift at a restaurant.
She spends 1 hour waiting at tables.
What fraction of her shift does she spend waiting at tables?

6 Susan has 3 cousins. 2 of them are girls.
What fraction of Susan's cousins are girls?

7 The school rugby team wins 15 out of 20 matches. What fraction of their matches do they win? Write the fraction in its simplest form.

8 In a class of 32, 8 pupils have their birthday between September and December. What fraction of the class is this?
Write the fraction in its simplest form.

9 A survey of 100 people found that 20 people walk to work.
What fraction walk to work? Write the fraction in its simplest form.
Discussion What percentage walk to work?

10 What fraction of £1 is 10p?
Write the fraction in its simplest form.

Key point
You can write one number as a fraction of another.
3 out of 4 means $\frac{3}{4}$.

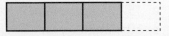

Q7 hint
Write the fraction
$$\frac{\text{number of games won}}{\text{total number of games}}$$
Write the fraction in its simplest form.

Q10 hint
£1 = 100 pence

11 Write these fractions as percentages.

a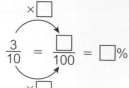
$$\frac{3}{10} = \frac{\square}{100} = \square\%$$

b
$$\frac{9}{50} = \frac{\square}{100}$$

c
$$\frac{4}{25} = \frac{\square}{100}$$

d
$$\frac{600}{1000} = \frac{\square}{100}$$

12 a What fraction of 1 litre is 500 m*l*?
Write the fraction in its simplest form.
b What percentage of 1 litre is 500 m*l*?

Q12a hint

1 litre = 1000 m*l*

$$\frac{500}{1000} = \frac{50}{100} = \frac{\square}{\square}$$

13 a Milly cut 30 cm off a 1 metre length of wood.
What percentage of the wood did she cut off?
b What percentage of the wood is left?

Q12b hint

Change the fraction into a percentage.

14 a A 400 m*l* mug of coffee contains 40 m*l* of milk. What fraction of the drink is milk? Write the fraction in its simplest form.
b What percentage of the drink is milk?

Q13a hint

Convert 1 m to centimetres first.

15 Real Write each of these test scores as a percentage.

Art   50 out of 100 = $\frac{50}{100}$ = $\square$%

DT   22 out of 50 = $\frac{\square}{50}$ = $\frac{\square}{100}$ = $\square$%

Maths   18 out of 25 = $\frac{\square}{25}$ = $\frac{\square}{100}$ = $\square$%

English 16 out of 20

RE   7 out of 10

16 Write these numbers of minutes as a fraction of 1 hour, in their simplest form.
a 5 minutes   **b** 10 minutes
c 15 minutes   **d** 20 minutes
e 30 minutes   **f** 40 minutes
g 45 minutes   **h** 50 minutes

Discussion Why do we give times as 'half past', 'quarter past' and 'quarter to'?

Q16 hint

1 hour = 60 minutes

17 Explore Why do we use percentages instead of fractions to compare test results?
Look back at the maths you have learned in this lesson.
How can you use it to answer this question?

18 Reflect Adrianna says, 'Percentages are just another way of writing fractions.'
Do you agree with Adrianna? Why?

Explore

Reflect

Topic links: Multiplication, Division, Measures, Pie charts   *Active*Learn   Pi 2, Section 9.4

9.5 Calculating percentages

You will learn to:
- Calculate percentages.

Why learn this?
Shops use percentages to work out the VAT on certain items.

Fluency
Work out
- 550 ÷ 10
- 75 ÷ 10
- 8 ÷ 10
- 600 ÷ 100
- 340 ÷ 100
- 72 ÷ 100

Explore
Jemima has read 30% of her e-book and Kaj has read 15% of hers. Who has read more?

Exercise 9.5

1 Work out
  a 10% of £60
  c 1% of 650
  e 50% of 842

  b 50% of 280
  d 10% of 25
  f 1% of 98

2 Write each percentage as a fraction, with denominator 100.
  a 12%
  b 35%
  c 3%

Worked example

Work out
a 20% of £120
b 30% of £120

> First work out 10% of £120.

10% of £120 is £120 ÷ 10 = £12

a 20% is 2 × £12 = £24 ← 20% = 2 × 10%

b 30% is 3 × £12 = £36 ← 30% = 3 × 10%

Key point
- 20% is double 10%.
- You can find 10% and use this to find other percentages.

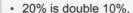

100%

| 10% | 10% | 10% | 10% | 10% | 10% | 10% | 10% | 10% | 10% |

20%

3 Work out 20% of
  a 50
  c 48
  e 750 ml
  g 540

  b 130
  d 300 cm
  f 96
  h 450

> **Q3 hint**
> Work out 10% then double it.

4 Work out these percentages by first finding 10%.
  a 30% of 60
  c 40% of 250

  b 30% of 220
  d 60% of 110

5 Work out 5% of

a 60   b 180
c 240   d 620
e 1000 ml   f 4000 g
g 124   h 844

Q5 hint

Work out 10% then halve it.

6 Al saves 20% of his £75 allowance.
How much does he save?

7 a There is a special offer of 5% extra free in a 500 g box of cereal.
How many grams extra is that?
  b How many grams are in the special offer box?

8 Work out 25% of these amounts by adding 20% + 5%.
The first one has been started for you.
  a 600

$$10\% \text{ of } 600 = 60$$

$$20\% = 120 \qquad 5\% = 30$$

25% of 600 = ☐ + ☐ = ☐
  b 480
  c 2000
  d 3600 ml
  e 840 m
  f 1500 g
  g Check your answers to parts **a** to **f** by finding 50% and
halving it to find 25%.

Key point
- 25% = 20% + 5%
- 25% = half of 50%

9 Finance A holiday company adds 25% to their prices in July and
August. What does each price increase by in July and August?
  a £500   **b** £880   **c** £1200

10 Work out 75% of each amount.
  a 120   **b** 360
  c 4000 ml   **d** 2800 km

Key point

75% = 50% + 25%

11 Finance Natalia paid a 30% deposit on a new bike.
The bike cost £550.
How much was the deposit?

Q11 hint

Use a mental or a written
multiplication method.

Investigation   **Reasoning**

1 Partition these percentages into ones you know how to work out.
Find at least 2 different ways for each.
  a 15%   10% + 5% or 25% − 10%
  b 35%
  c 45%
  d 95%
2 What is the best way to work out these percentages?
  a 11%
  b 24%
  c 49%
  d 99%
3 Work out 11%, 35% and 99% of 4000.

Topic links: Addition, Subtraction, Multiplication, Division,
Dividing by 10 and 100, Measures

12 **Finance** Here are the yearly wages of three employees.
They are all given a 15% pay rise.
a How much extra will each employee be paid each year?

> **Ali: £15 000**
> **John: £22 000**
> **Chrissy: £28 000**

b How much extra will they be paid each month?

13 **Reasoning**
a 10% of a number is 50. What is the number?
b 20% of a number is 15. What is the number?
c 25% of a number is 12. What is the number?

14 A sofa costs £420 plus 20% **VAT**.
How much is the VAT?

15 Work out these percentages.
a 12% of 480
b 45% of 1240
c 99% of 3500
d 3% of 180 cm

16 **Real** Work out the 20% VAT that will be added to the price of each item.
a A calculator that costs £9.99
b A games console that costs £114.90
c A climbing frame that costs £234

17 **Real** A train line advertises:
New engines cut journey times by 8%!
Work out how much shorter these journey times will be with the new engines.
a 45 minutes
b 90 minutes
c 3 hours 10 minutes
Round your answers to the nearest minute.

18 **Problem-solving** Eric earns £7.40 per hour, and works a 35-hour week.
He gets a 4% pay rise.
How much more does he earn for a year after the pay rise?

19 **Explore** Jemima has read 30% of her e-book and Kaj has read 15% of hers. Who has read more?
Look back at the maths you have learned in this lesson.
How can you use it to answer this question?

20 **Reflect** Nawaz says, 'To work out 12% of an amount I first work out 10%, then divide it by 5 to find 2%, then add 2% and 10%.'
Joy says, 'I work out 12% of an amount by multiplying it by $\frac{12}{100}$.'
Whose method do you prefer?
Which method would you use if you had a calculator?

Key point

To work out any percentage using a calculator, write the percentage as a fraction with denominator 100.
12% of 360 = $\frac{12}{100}$ × 360
Use the fraction button on your calculator to enter a fraction.

Q13a hint

How many lots of 10% make 100%?

Q14 Literacy hint

VAT stands for 'value added tax'. It is a tax you pay on most purchases.

Q16 hint

Round your answers to the nearest penny.

Q17c hint

Convert to minutes first.

Explore

Reflect

9.6 STEM: Percentages and proportion

You will learn to:
- Compare proportions using percentages
- Write one number as a percentage of another number.

CONFIDENCE

Why learn this?
Industrial chemists make alloys using different percentages of metals.

Fluency
Work out 10% and 50% of
- £68
- £340
- £5600
- £4500

Explore
How does a bank or building society use percentages?

Exercise 9.6: Proportions in science

Warm up

1 Change each percentage into a fraction, simplifying where possible.
  a 15%   **b** 60%   **c** 4%   **d** 55%

2 Write these as equivalent fractions of hundredths.
  a $8\% = \dfrac{\square}{100}$ **b** $\dfrac{32}{50} = \dfrac{\square}{100}$ **c** $\dfrac{20}{25} = \dfrac{\square}{100}$ **d** $72\% = \dfrac{\square}{100}$

3 Copy and complete these equivalences.
Show fractions in their simplest forms.
  a $10\% = \dfrac{\square}{\square}$ **b** $\dfrac{25}{100} = \square\%$ **c** $\dfrac{1}{2} = \square\%$ **d** $75\% = \dfrac{\square}{\square}$

4 This bar chart shows the percentage of the world's population in each continent.

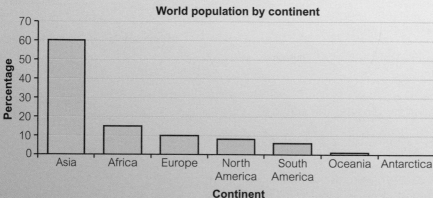

World population by continent

a What percentage of the world's population lives in Europe?
b Do more people live in North America or South America?
c Which continent has the largest population?
Discussion How does the graph show that more people live in Africa than in Oceania? Why is there no bar for Antarctica?

    Topic links: Graphs, Measures, Pie charts   **Subject links:** Science (Q5, 6, 7, 10), Geography (Q4)

Worked example

Write 126 out of 200 as a percentage.

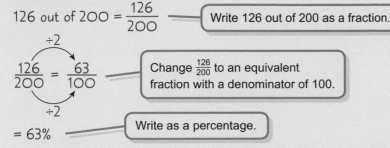

126 out of 200 = $\frac{126}{200}$ ——— Write 126 out of 200 as a fraction.

$\div 2$

$\frac{126}{200} = \frac{63}{100}$ ——— Change $\frac{126}{200}$ to an equivalent fraction with a denominator of 100.

$\div 2$

= 63% ——— Write as a percentage.

Key point

To write one number as a percentage of another number, write the numbers as a fraction, then convert to a percentage.

Q6 hint

First work out how many times the sample does not dissolve.

Q7 hint

1 kg = ☐ grams

Key point

Proportion compares a part to a whole.
You can write a proportion as a percentage.

5 **STEM / Problem-solving** 120 out of 200 insect specimens are female. What percentage of these insects are **male**?

6 **STEM / Problem-solving** In an experiment, a sample dissolves in 35 out of 50 trials. In what percentage of trials does the sample not dissolve?

7 **STEM** Bronze is an alloy of copper and tin. A bronze statue weighs 1 kg, of which 900 g is copper. What is the percentage of copper in the statue?

8 **Problem-solving** In a bag there are 11 blue cubes, 8 red cubes and 6 yellow cubes. Write the proportion of each colour as a percentage.
   a blue   **b** red   **c** yellow

Q8a hint

First write the fraction
$\frac{\text{blue cubes}}{\text{total number of cubes}}$
then convert to a percentage.

9 **Problem-solving** Robin scored a goal in 21 out of 25 matches and Fiona scored in 17 out of 20 matches. Who was the better scorer?

Q9 hint

Work out each score as a percentage and compare.

10 **STEM** The pie chart shows the proportions of **humus**, roots and organisms in the organic matter found in soil on Earth.
   a Use a protractor to measure the angle represented by roots.
   b Write down the fraction of the organic matter that is roots. Write this fraction in its simplest form.
   c Using the same method as in part **b**, find
     i the fraction of organisms in the organic matter
     ii the fraction of humus in the organic matter.
   d Write all three fractions as percentages.

Composition of organic matter in soil

organisms

roots

humus

Q10 Literacy hint

Humus is decayed plant material.

Q10b hint

How many degrees are there in the whole circle?
The fraction of the organic matter
that is roots is $\frac{\square}{360}$

11 **Explore** How does a bank or building society use percentages? Is it easier to explore this question now you have completed the lesson? What further information do you need to be able to answer this?

12 **Reflect** Melinda is working on Q9. She says, 'Robin is the better scorer because he scored more goals.' Explain how proportions show that she is incorrect.

Explore

Reflect

9 Check up

Log how you did on your Student Progression Chart.

Percentages

1 Work out each percentage.
    a 20% of 40
    b 5% of 80
    c 25% of 160
    d 75% of 320
    e 30% of 420

2 Sara's daily wage of £80 is increased by 15%.
    How much more will she earn?

3 Work out each percentage.
    a 24% of 50 m
    b 8% of £27

Working with fractions

4 Which is larger, $\frac{7}{8}$ or $\frac{5}{6}$?

5 Order these fractions, smallest to largest.
    $\frac{1}{2}$ $\frac{5}{8}$ $\frac{3}{10}$

6 Work out
    a $\frac{1}{2}$ of 32 g
    b $\frac{1}{4}$ of 32 g
    c $\frac{1}{8}$ of 32 g

7 Work out
    a $\frac{1}{8} + \frac{1}{2}$
    b $\frac{3}{5} - \frac{4}{15}$

8 Simplify each fraction.
    a $\frac{14}{28}$
    b $\frac{15}{60}$

9 Work out
    a $\frac{2}{5}$ of 200
    b $\frac{2}{3}$ of 300

10 There are 120 students in Year 8. $\frac{3}{5}$ of them are girls.
    a How many girls are in Year 8?
    b How many boys are in Year 8?

11 Work out
    a $\frac{3}{4} - \frac{2}{5}$
    b $\frac{1}{9} + \frac{5}{6}$

12 Multiply each fraction.

   a $3 \times \frac{1}{5}$

   b $\frac{1}{7} \times 5$

13 Multiply each fraction, simplifying where possible.

   a $3 \times \frac{2}{3}$

   b $\frac{2}{9} \times 6$

14 What is $\frac{5}{6}$ of 3 litres?

15 Each model aeroplane needs $\frac{4}{5}$ of a tin of paint.
How many tins are needed for 8 planes?

Proportion

16 Karim has 27 balloons. 9 of them are red.
What fraction of his balloons is red?

17 Izzy has 16 hats. 12 of them are woolly.
What fraction of her hats are woolly?

18 What fraction of £1 is 25p? Write the fraction in its simplest form.

19 What fraction of 1 km is 800 m? Write the fraction in its simplest form.

20 A survey of 120 people found that 40 people cycled to work.
What fraction cycle to work? Write the fraction in its simplest form.

21 Write each score as a percentage.

   a 9 out of 10

   b 34 out of 50

   c 19 out of 25

22 In a car park there are 5 black cars, 2 silver, 10 red and 3 blue.
What percentage of cars is black?

23 The hockey team won 12 out of 20 matches.
The cricket team won 16 out of 25 matches.
Which team won the greater proportion of their matches?

24 How sure are you of your answers? Were you mostly

   ☹ **Just guessing**   😐 **Feeling doubtful**   ☺ **Confident**

What next? Use your results to decide whether to strengthen or extend your learning.

Challenge

25 Copy this rectangle onto squared paper four times.

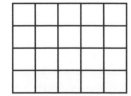

   a Show three different ways of shading 75% of the rectangle.

   b Design a pattern on squared paper that has 10% blue, 30% red and 60% yellow.

9 Strengthen

You will:
- Strengthen your understanding with practice.

Percentages

1 For each amount, work out
    i 10%   **ii** 1%

  a 560   **b** 745
  c 821   **d** 1234

Q1 hint
To find 10%, ÷ 10
To find 1%, ÷ 100

2 Simon's bank pays 1% interest if he has over £2000 in his account. How much interest will Simon get on £2500?

3 For each amount, work out
    i 10%   **ii** 20%   **iii** 5%

  a 40   **b** 200
  c 260   **d** 580

Q3 hint

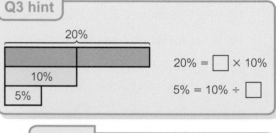

$20\% = \boxed{} \times 10\%$
$5\% = 10\% \div \boxed{}$

4 Sophie gets 20% off a holiday that costs £850. How much does she save?

5 For each amount, work out
    i 50%   **ii** 25%   **iii** 75%

  a £44   **b** £400
  c £840   **d** £720

Q5 hint

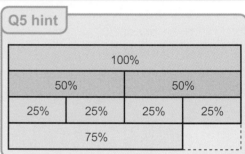

6 Work out 75% of £4800, showing all your working out.

7 Work out 30% of 400.

 8 Check your answers to Q6 and Q7 with a calculator.

Q7 hint
30% = 3 × 10%

 9 Work out each percentage.
  a 32% of 250   **b** 49% of 420
  c 78% of 3200   **d** 99% of 7800

Working with fractions

1 Draw a bar like this:

Divide it into parts and shade it to show $\frac{3}{8}$.

Q1 hint
$\frac{3}{8}$ means 3 shaded parts out of 8.

2 Write < or > between each pair of fractions.

  a $\frac{2}{3} \square \frac{1}{2}$

  b $\frac{1}{5} \square \frac{1}{6}$

  c $\frac{3}{4} \square \frac{4}{5}$

  d $\frac{2}{3} \square \frac{3}{5}$

Q2 Literacy hint
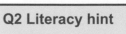
< means 'is less than'
> means 'is greater than'

Topic links: Multiplication, Division, HCF, Measures, LCM

3 Write these fractions in order of size, smallest first.

$\frac{3}{5}$ $\frac{7}{10}$ $\frac{2}{3}$

Q3 hint

Draw bars to help compare them.

4 Simplify each fraction.

a

b

c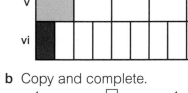

d $\frac{15}{25}$

5 Add these fractions by writing them with the same denominator.

a $\frac{3}{10} + \frac{2}{5}$ **b** $\frac{1}{2} + \frac{3}{8}$ **c** $\frac{2}{3} + \frac{5}{18}$

Q5a hint

$\frac{1}{5} = \frac{2}{10}$

$\frac{1}{5}$		$\frac{1}{5}$		$\frac{1}{5}$		$\frac{1}{5}$		$\frac{1}{5}$	
$\frac{1}{10}$	$\frac{1}{10}$	$\frac{1}{10}$	$\frac{1}{10}$	$\frac{1}{10}$	$\frac{1}{10}$	$\frac{1}{10}$	$\frac{1}{10}$	$\frac{1}{10}$	$\frac{1}{10}$

6 Subtract these fractions by writing them with the same denominator.

a $\frac{9}{10} - \frac{3}{5}$ **b** $\frac{5}{6} - \frac{5}{12}$ **c** $\frac{5}{7} - \frac{1}{14}$

7 a Write down the fraction shaded.

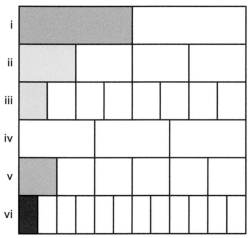

i
ii
iii
iv
v
vi

Q8a hint

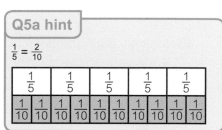

b Copy and complete.

i $\frac{1}{4}$ is half of $\frac{\square}{\square}$ **ii** $\frac{1}{8}$ is half of $\frac{\square}{\square}$ **iii** $\frac{1}{12}$ is half of $\frac{\square}{\square}$

8 Work out

a $\frac{1}{2}$ of 48   **b** $\frac{1}{4}$ of 48   **c** $\frac{1}{8}$ of 48

d $\frac{1}{3}$ of 60   **e** $\frac{1}{6}$ of 60   **f** $\frac{1}{5}$ of 35

Q9 hint

You can draw bars to help.

9 Work out

a $\frac{2}{3}$ of 30   **b** $\frac{3}{5}$ of 35

c $\frac{7}{10}$ of 40   **d** $\frac{5}{6}$ of 30

e $\frac{3}{4}$ of 24   **f** $\frac{2}{9}$ of 72

g $\frac{3}{8}$ of 24   **h** $\frac{3}{10}$ of 50

Q9a hint

First work out $\frac{1}{3}$ of 30.

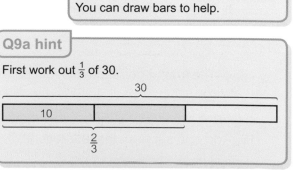

10 At sports day 140 ice creams were sold.
Work out how many of each flavour were sold.

a $\frac{1}{7}$ chocolate   **b** $\frac{2}{7}$ strawberry   **c** $\frac{4}{7}$ vanilla

Q10b, c hint

Use your answer to part **a**.

11 Write out the $\frac{1}{4}$ times table, simplifying where you can.
Some have been started for you.

$1 \times \frac{1}{4} = \frac{1}{4}$ 　　　　　　 $2 \times \frac{1}{4} = \frac{2}{4} = \frac{\square}{2}$

$3 \times \frac{1}{4} =$ 　　　　　　 $4 \times \frac{1}{4} = \frac{\square}{4} = 1$

$5 \times \frac{1}{4} = \frac{\square}{4} = 1\frac{\square}{4}$ 　　　 $6 \times \frac{1}{4} =$

$7 \times \frac{1}{4} =$ 　　　　　　 $8 \times \frac{1}{4} =$

$9 \times \frac{1}{4} =$ 　　　　　　 $10 \times \frac{1}{4} =$

Q11 hint

$2 \times \frac{1}{4} = 2$ quarters $= \frac{2}{4}$

$3 \times \frac{1}{4} = 3$ quarters $= \frac{3}{4}$

12 Work out, simplifying where you can.

a $7 \times \frac{1}{5}$ 　　　　 **b** $8 \times \frac{1}{6}$ 　　　　 **c** $9 \times \frac{1}{2}$

Q12a hint

$7 \times \frac{1}{5} = 7$ fifths

13 Multiply each fraction.
Write your answers in their simplest form.

a $2 \times \frac{4}{5}$ 　　　　 **b** $7 \times \frac{2}{3}$

c $\frac{3}{4} \times 5$ 　　　　 **d** $\frac{5}{6} \times 4$

Q13a hint

2×4 fifths $= 8$ fifths

14 An electrician uses $\frac{7}{10}$ of a metre of cable to wire up each socket.
How much cable will he need for 5 sockets?

15 Copy and complete.
The first two parts have been started for you.

a The lowest common multiple of 3 and 5 is 15.

$\frac{1}{3} + \frac{1}{5} = \frac{\square}{15} + \frac{\square}{15} = \frac{\square}{15}$

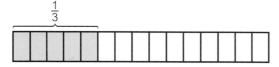

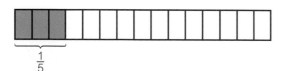

b The lowest common multiple of 2 and 7 is $\square$.

$\frac{1}{2} + \frac{3}{7} = \frac{\square}{\square} + \frac{\square}{\square} = \frac{\square}{\square}$

c The lowest common multiple of 10 and 3 is $\square$.

$\frac{3}{10} + \frac{1}{3} =$

16 Add and subtract these fractions.

a $\frac{1}{4} + \frac{1}{3}$ 　　　　 **b** $\frac{3}{4} - \frac{1}{3}$

c $\frac{2}{5} + \frac{1}{4}$ 　　　　 **d** $\frac{4}{5} - \frac{1}{4}$

e $\frac{2}{9} + \frac{1}{6}$ 　　　　 **f** $\frac{7}{9} - \frac{1}{6}$

Q16a hint

$4 \times 3 = 12$

Q16c, d hint

The LCM of 4 and 5 is 20.

Proportion

1 Write these as fractions.

  a 3 out of 4   **b** 2 out of 3   **c** 5 out of 8

2 Annie scored 7 out of 10 in a quiz. What proportion of the quiz did she get right? Write this as a fraction.

3 8 out of 12 meals in a restaurant are vegetarian. Write the proportion of vegetarian meals as a fraction in its simplest form.

4 40 out of the 120 pupils in Year 8 live less than 5 miles away from school. What fraction is that? Write the fraction in its simplest form.

5 David's train is late 3 out of 10 times. Lina's train is late 8 out of 20 times. Whose train is late the greater proportion of times?

6 Convert these fractions to percentages.

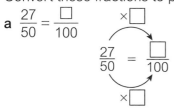

  a $\dfrac{27}{50} = \dfrac{\square}{100}$

  b $\dfrac{9}{10}$ **c** $\dfrac{15}{20}$ **d** $\dfrac{12}{25}$

7 Write each score as a fraction. Convert it to a percentage.

  a 6 out of 10   **b** 19 out of 50

  c 13 out of 25   **d** 11 out of 20

Enrichment

1 This graph shows how much of the cost of a pineapple goes to each group of workers.

  a Write the percentage that each group gets.

  b Copy and complete: 'The shop gets □ times more than the picker.'

  c When you pay £1 for a pineapple, how much of that does each group of workers receive?

  d How fair do you think this is?

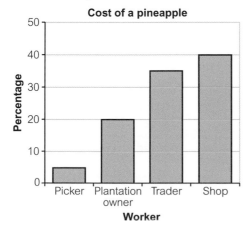

2 **Reflect** Theo says, 'In this lesson I have done lots of division and multiplication.' Look back at your work in these strengthen lessons.

  a Where did you use division? How did you use it?

  b Where did you use multiplication? How did you use it?

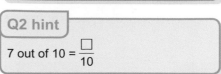

Q1a hint

Q2 hint

7 out of 10 = $\dfrac{\square}{10}$

Q5 Strategy hint

Write each proportion as a fraction in its simplest terms. Which fraction is larger?

Q6 hint

Change to fractions with denominator 100.

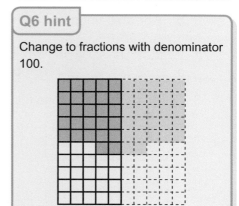

Reflect

Master
P187

Check
P2010

Strengthen
P203

EXTEND

Test
P211

9 Extend

You will:
- Extend your understanding with problem-solving.

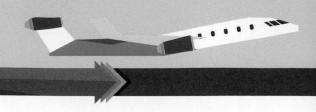

1 **Reasoning** **a** $\frac{1}{5}$ of an amount of money is £50.
   What is $\frac{1}{10}$ of that same amount?

   b $\frac{1}{6}$ of an amount is £24. What is $\frac{1}{3}$ of that same amount?

   c $\frac{1}{4}$ of an amount is £40. What is $\frac{1}{16}$ of that same amount?

   d $\frac{1}{10}$ of an amount is £45. What is $\frac{1}{5}$ of that same amount?

2 **Reasoning** What is the connection in each set of fractions?

   a $\frac{2}{2}, \frac{10}{10}, \frac{3}{3}, \frac{7}{7}, \frac{15}{15}$ **b** $\frac{2}{4}, \frac{5}{10}, \frac{10}{20}, \frac{16}{32}, \frac{11}{22}$ **c** $\frac{2}{8}, \frac{3}{12}, \frac{4}{16}, \frac{5}{20}, \frac{6}{24}$

> **Q2 hint**
> What is each fraction equivalent to?

3 Simplify these fractions fully to find three sets of 3 equivalent fractions.

   $\frac{100}{300}$ $\frac{40}{60}$ $\frac{120}{160}$

   $\frac{150}{200}$ $\frac{20}{30}$ $\frac{24}{72}$

   $\frac{24}{32}$ $\frac{50}{150}$ $\frac{120}{180}$

> **Q3 hint**
> Use the HCF of the numerator and denominator.

4 Work out

   a $\frac{3}{5}$ of 2500   **b** $\frac{4}{9}$ of 3600   **c** $\frac{3}{7}$ of 2800   **d** $\frac{5}{6}$ of 4200

5 **Problem-solving** A competition prize is £2400. The first place winner gets $\frac{5}{8}$ of the money, second place gets $\frac{1}{4}$ and the rest goes to third place. How much money does each get?

> **Q5 hint**
> You do not need to know the fraction of the 3rd place amount.

6 **Problem-solving** A selection of 36 sandwiches contains 9 ham, 6 egg, 12 cheese, 4 tuna and the rest are chicken. What proportion of the selection is

   a ham   **b** egg   **c** cheese   **d** tuna   **e** chicken?

7 **Problem-solving** For each statement
   i what proportion of the ingredient is used
   ii what proportion of the ingredient is left?
   Write your answers as fractions in their simplest form.

   a 250 g of flour from a 1 kg bag

   b 200 ml milk from a 1 litre container

   c 600 g of sugar from a 1 kg bag

   d 200 g margarine from a 500 g pot

> **Q7 hint**
> 1 kg = 1000 g
> 1 litre = 1000 ml

8 Put these amounts in order, largest to smallest.

   $\frac{4}{5}$ of £300 $\frac{1}{8}$ of £2000 $\frac{5}{6}$ of £270

Topic links: Multiplication, Division, HCF, Measures, Perimeter

9 **Finance** For each amount

   i multiply the amount by $\frac{2}{3}$ and simplify

   ii work out $\frac{2}{3}$ of the amount (divide by 3 then multiply by 2).

   The first one has been started for you.

   a $150

       i $150 \times \frac{2}{3} = \frac{300}{3} = \$\square$

       ii $150 \div 3 \times 2 = \$\square$

   b $210   **c** $450

   d $360   **e** $600

   Discussion Did you get the same answer with both methods?
   Which method did you find easier?

10 **Finance** The wage for different jobs at a company is a proportion of
   the boss's wage of £24 an hour. What is the hourly rate for each job?

   Job A: $\frac{3}{4}$ of the boss's wage

   Job B: $\frac{2}{3}$

   Job C: $\frac{5}{8}$

   Job D: $\frac{7}{12}$

11 **Reasoning** Work out the original amount from the fraction given.

   a $\frac{3}{5}$ of an amount of money is £60. What is the amount?

   b $\frac{5}{6}$ of an amount is £10. What is the amount?

   c $\frac{3}{4}$ of an amount is £90. What is the amount?

   d $\frac{4}{9}$ of an amount is £80. What is the amount?

Q11a hint

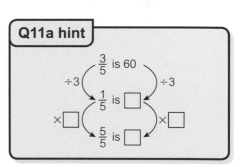

12 **Reasoning**

   a Add these fractions. Simplify your answers where possible.

      i $\frac{1}{2} + \frac{1}{3} + \frac{1}{6} = \frac{\square}{6} + \frac{\square}{6} + \frac{\square}{6} =$

      ii $\frac{1}{2} + \frac{1}{4} + \frac{1}{8} = \frac{\square}{8} + \frac{\square}{8} + \frac{\square}{8} =$

      iii $\frac{1}{2} + \frac{1}{5} + \frac{1}{10}$

      iv $\frac{1}{2} + \frac{1}{6} + \frac{1}{12}$

      v $\frac{1}{2} + \frac{1}{7} + \frac{1}{14}$

      vi $\frac{1}{2} + \frac{1}{8} + \frac{1}{16}$

   b Will the answer to $\frac{1}{2} + \frac{1}{10} + \frac{1}{20}$ be smaller or larger than $\frac{1}{2} + \frac{1}{8} + \frac{1}{16}$?

Q12 hint

Change to equivalent fractions using
the HCF of the 3 denominators.

13 Work out 50%, 25%, 10%, 5%, 15%, 20% and 1% of 1800.

14 **Reasoning** Use your answers to Q13 to work out these percentages.

   a 35% of 1800   **b** 21% of 1800

   c 49% of 1800   **d** 99% of 1800

   e 74% of 1800   **f** 3% of 1800

   g 25% of 900   **h** 15% of 3600

Q13 hint

Use the 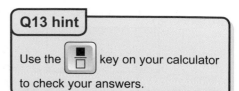 key on your calculator
to check your answers.

15 Here are some fabric labels. Work out the weight of each material in 500 g of each fabric.

a Jeans
60% cotton
40% polyester

b Top
95% acrylic
5% elastane

c Sweatshirt
80% cotton
20% polyester

d Tights
88% nylon
10% polyester
2% elastane

16 Work out
  a $\frac{3}{4}$ of 3764
  b $\frac{4}{9}$ of 3753
  c $\frac{7}{12}$ of 1476
  d $\frac{5}{6}$ of 9264
  e $\frac{4}{5}$ of 9265
  f $\frac{4}{7}$ of 1715

Q16a hint

$\frac{3}{4} \times 3764$

17 Fiona's calculator does not have a fraction key.
Explain how she can work out $\frac{3}{4}$ of 3764.

Q17 hint

Work out $\frac{1}{4}$ of 3764 first.

18 Use written division and multiplication to work out
  a $\frac{1}{3}$ of 9375
  b $\frac{3}{4}$ of 8324
  c $\frac{3}{5}$ of 2945
  d $\frac{4}{9}$ of 8262

19 Multiply these fractions, writing the answers as whole or mixed numbers.
  a $5 \times \frac{3}{4}$
  b $\frac{3}{5} \times 5$
  c $7 \times \frac{2}{3}$
  d $\frac{2}{9} \times 7$
  e $8 \times \frac{3}{7}$
  f $8 \times \frac{5}{8}$

20 **Problem-solving** Use the symbols <, = or > to compare
  a $\frac{3}{4} \times 8$ and $\frac{2}{3} \times 9$
  b $\frac{4}{5} \times 10$ and $\frac{7}{8} \times 8$
  c $\frac{4}{11} \times 9$ and $\frac{5}{9} \times 8$
  d $\frac{5}{7} \times 9$ and $\frac{5}{8} \times 7$
  e $\frac{2}{9} \times 6$ and $4 \times \frac{2}{3}$
  f $\frac{3}{10} \times 8$ and $\frac{3}{5} \times 4$

21 a Work out
  i $\frac{1}{2} - \frac{1}{3}$
  ii $\frac{1}{3} - \frac{1}{4}$
  iii $\frac{1}{4} - \frac{1}{5}$

  b **Reasoning** Write down, without working out
  i $\frac{1}{5} - \frac{1}{6}$
  ii $\frac{1}{9} - \frac{1}{10}$

22 **Problem-solving** What is the perimeter of each of these shapes?

  a

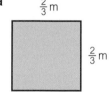

$\frac{2}{3}$ m

$\frac{2}{3}$ m

  b

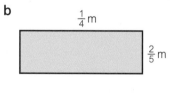

$\frac{1}{4}$ m

$\frac{2}{5}$ m

Q22 hint

You can use addition or multiplication of fractions.

23 **Problem-solving** What is the perimeter of these regular shapes?

  a

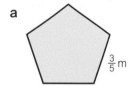

$\frac{3}{5}$ m

  b

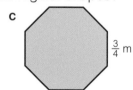

$\frac{5}{8}$ m

  c

$\frac{3}{4}$ m

Q23 hint

In a regular shape, all the sides are equal.

24 Work out the area of this rectangle.

2 m

$\frac{7}{8}$ m

25 **Real** In Luxembourg 17 out of 20 people are fluent French speakers. In Belgium 1 in 4 people is fluent in French. Which country has the larger proportion of French speakers?

26 Real In 2014 the proportion of young people in England who were not in education, employment or training was 3 out of 20. What percentage of young people is that?

27 Real / Problem-solving In 3 out of 4 countries people drive on the right-hand side of the road. There are 196 countries in the world. In how many countries must you drive on the left?

28 Work out
  a 10% of $2400
  b 5% of $2400
  c 2.5% of $2400
  d 17.5% of $2400

Q28 hint
What percentage is half of 5%? Use parts **a**, **b** and **c** to work out part **d**.

29 Work out 12.5% of £1600.

Q29 hint
What percentages can you use to make up 12.5%?

30 Problem-solving / Finance Marc gives 5% of his weekly wage to a children's charity. He earns £360 a week. How much does he give the charity in 8 weeks?

31 Draw a spider diagram with £3600 in the middle. Work out 8 percentages that are **not** multiples of 10%.

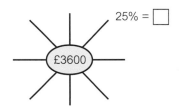

25% = ☐

£3600

Investigation

Problem-solving / Reasoning / Finance

Paul is working out the costs of a holiday for his family.
He is comparing the offers on two internet sites.
Which site should he choose for each destination?

Turkey £1200

Site A	Site B
$\frac{1}{3}$ off for early booking	Save 30%

USA £2400

Site A	Site B
Save $\frac{1}{4}$ off the cost when you travel in May	May discount: 20% reduction

UK £900

Site A	Site B
25% off	Save $\frac{2}{5}$ off the cost

---

32 Put these amounts in order, smallest to largest.
  a $\frac{3}{5}$ 59%   0.61   14 out of 25
  b 52% $\frac{9}{20}$ 0.49   20 out of 40
  c 0.72 $\frac{3}{4}$ 73%   35 out of 50

Q32 hint
Change all the values to percentages.

33 Reflect Look back at the questions you answered in these extend lessons.
  • Which question(s) did you find easiest?
  • What made them easy?
  • Which question(s) did you find most difficult?
  • What made them difficult?
  • Are there particular kinds of questions you need more practice on? If so, what kinds?

Reflect

Master
P187

Check
P201

Strengthen
P203

Extend
P207

TEST

9 Unit test

Log how you did on your
Student Progression Chart.

1 Work out each percentage.
  a 20% of 1200
  b 5% of 320
  c 25% of 848
  d 75% of 3200
  e 15% of 1600

2 Work out each percentage.
  a 72% of 600
  b 9% of 1400

3 A £180 dress has gone up by 5%.
  How much more will it cost?

4 Write < or > between each pair of fractions.
  a $\frac{2}{3} \square \frac{4}{5}$
  b $\frac{11}{20} \square \frac{8}{15}$

5 Order these fractions, smallest to largest.
  $\frac{1}{2}$ $\frac{4}{5}$ $\frac{3}{10}$

6 Work out
  a $\frac{9}{10} - \frac{3}{5}$
  b $\frac{3}{8} + \frac{1}{2}$
  c $\frac{4}{5} - \frac{7}{15}$

7 Simplify each fraction.
  a $\frac{50}{60}$
  b $\frac{10}{35}$

8 Work out
  a $\frac{1}{3}$ of 270
  b $\frac{3}{7}$ of 280

9 There are 180 students in Year 8. $\frac{8}{9}$ are of them right-handed.
  How many are right-handed and how many are left-handed?

10 A survey of 150 people found that 50 people work out at a gym.
  What proportion of them work out at a gym?
  Write the fraction in its simplest form.

11 What fraction of 1 litre is 250 ml?
  Write the fraction in its simplest form.

12 Work out
  a 35% of 220
  b 99% of 500
  c 3% of 550
  d 2.5% of 480

13 Multiply each fraction, simplifying where possible.
  a $3 \times \frac{2}{7}$
  b $\frac{5}{9} \times 6$
  c $5 \times \frac{4}{5}$

14 What is $\frac{9}{10}$ of 4 km?

15 Work out
  a $\frac{2}{7} + \frac{2}{3}$
  b $\frac{8}{9} - \frac{1}{4}$

16 Write each score as a percentage.
  a 22 out of 25
  b 19 out of 20

17 In a kitchen cupboard there are 10 cans of tomato soup, 4 cans of chicken soup, 5 cans of vegetable soup and 1 can of mushroom soup. What percentage of the cans of soup are vegetable?

18 Reasoning

    a For each number word, write the proportion of

| three | four | eleven |

      i vowels   **ii** consonants.

    b Which words have the same proportion of vowels?

19 The pie charts show the proportion of netball games won by two teams.

    Team A played 20 games and Team B played 36 games.

    Who won more games?

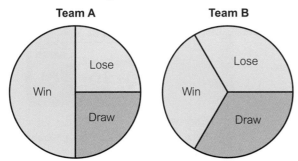

Team A   **Team B**

20 Put these in order, smallest to largest.

    a 0.42 $\frac{2}{5}$ 41%   22 out of 50

    b 36%   0.34 $\frac{3}{10}$ 70 out of 200

Challenge

21 Roll a 1–6 dice 3 times.

    Use the numbers to make three unit fractions.

    Add them together.

    For example, $\frac{1}{3} + \frac{1}{5} + \frac{1}{6}$

22 Roll a 1–9 dice 4 times. Use the numbers to make two fractions.

    Add and subtract them.

    Put the larger fraction first in the subtraction. Change the fraction into a decimal with a calculator if you are not sure which is larger.

    For example, $\frac{2}{3} + \frac{4}{5}$ and $\frac{4}{5} - \frac{2}{3}$

    Simplify the fractions, where possible, before working out the calculations.

23 Reflect Alix and Steffan begin to answer this question:

    Find

    a 12.5% of £40

    b 17.5% of £40

Alix	Steffan
a 25% of £40 is £10	**a** 10% of £40 is £4
12.5% = $\frac{1}{2}$ of 25% = £5	5% is $\frac{1}{2}$ of 10% = £2
	2.5% is $\frac{1}{2}$ of 5% = £1
	£4 + £1 = £5

Which way do you think is easier? Why?

What could Alix do next to work out 17.5%?

Q23 hint

Could Alix use the percentages she has already worked out?

What could Steffan do next to work out 17.5%?

Would they both work out 17.5% the same way?

Reflect

10 Probability

MASTER | Check P227 | Strengthen P229 | Extend P233 | Test P237

10.1 The language of probability

You will learn to:

• Use the language of probability
• Use a probability scale with words
• Understand that probabilities can be written as fractions, decimals and percentages.

Why learn this?
In elections, news broadcasters use probabilities to say which party is more likely to win.

Fluency
What do these words mean?

• possible
• impossible
• certain
• likely
• unlikely

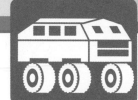

Explore
How can you describe the probability that it will be sunny tomorrow?

Exercise 10.1

1 What are the missing values on these scales?

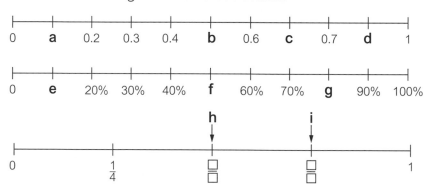

| 0 | **a** | 0.2 | 0.3 | 0.4 | **b** | 0.6 | **c** | 0.7 | **d** | 1 |

| 0 | **e** | 20% | 30% | 40% | **f** | 60% | 70% | **g** | 90% | 100% |

0   ¼   h   i   1

2 Choose a **probability** from a box to match each statement.

likely   unlikely   impossible

certain   **even chance**

a You will win a jackpot prize on the lottery.
b It will rain sometime in the next 2 weeks.
c When you flip a coin it will land heads up.
d The day after Saturday will be Sunday.
e You can run a mile in 60 seconds.
f There are more girls than boys in your Year group at school.

> **Key point**
> **Probability** is the chance that something will happen. **Even chance** means that something is as likely to happen as not.

> **Q2 Literacy hint**
> Here are some other ways of describing an even chance: fifty-fifty, equally likely.

Topic links: Fractions, decimals and percentages

3 Describe the probability of each **event** using the words from Q2.

   a Tossing a coin and it landing tails up

   b Rolling a double 1 on two **fair** dice

   c Picking a picture card from a normal pack of playing cards

   d More than five cars in the school car park being red

   Discussion What do you think is the probability that the UK will be affected by a hurricane next year?

4 Copy this **probability scale**.

impossible   unlikely   even chance   likely   certain

   Mark each event in Q3 on your probability scale.

5 **Reasoning** This spinner is spun. Amir says that it is very likely the spinner will land on a blue segment.

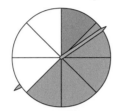

   a Is Amir correct? Explain your reasoning.

   b Describe the probability that the spinner will land on

     i a red segment

     ii a blue or white segment.

6 Rory takes a ball from this bag. Describe the probability of taking

   a a red ball

   b a yellow ball

   c a green ball

   d a ball that is not blue

   e a ball that is red or black or yellow.

7 Copy this probability scale.

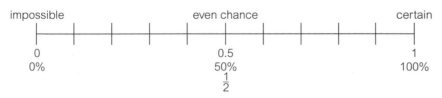

impossible   even chance   certain

0   0.5   1

0%   50%   100%

          $\frac{1}{2}$

   Mark the probability of each event on your probability scale.

   a The probability that a newborn baby will be a girl is 50%.

   b The probability that a person is right-handed is 0.9.

   c The probability that a boy will be colour-blind is about 8%.

   d The probability that a train will be delayed is $\frac{1}{10}$.

   Discussion Can you describe probabilities more accurately using numbers? What are the advantages and disadvantages of using numbers to describe probabilities?

Key point

In probability, an **event** is something that might happen.

Q3 Literacy hint

A **fair** dice is equally likely to land on 1, 2, 3, 4, 5 or 6.

Key point

You can show probabilities on a **probability scale**.

Key point

All probabilities have a value between 0 and 1.

You can use fractions, decimals or percentages to describe probabilities.

An impossible event has probability of 0 or 0%.

A certain event has probability of 1 or 100%.

Q7 Strategy hint

This probability scale is divided into 10 equal parts, so each part represents $\frac{1}{10}$, 10% or 0.1.

8 Reasoning Write down an event for the events **a–d** on this probability scale.

impossible   unlikely   even chance   likely   certain

9 Problem-solving The probabilities of four spinners landing on red are shown on the scale.

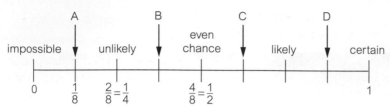

a Write the probabilities represented by A, B, C and D.

b Match each probability in part **a** to the probability of these spinners landing on red.

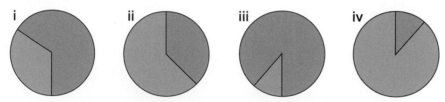

i   ii   iii   iv

10 Real / Reasoning A manufacturer calculates the probability that one of its dishwashers will develop a fault in the first 3 years is 0.07. It writes this statement in an advert:

> *Highly unlikely to need repairing in the first three years.*

Do you think this is a reasonable statement? Explain your answer.

11 The weather forecast says the probability of rain tomorrow is 45%. Do you think you should cancel an outdoor party planned for tomorrow? Explain your answer.

12 Explore How can you describe the probability that it will be sunny tomorrow?
What have you learned in this lesson to help you answer this question? What other information do you need?

13 Reflect This lesson used probability scales labelled with words, decimals, fractions and percentages.
a Did the scale help you to understand probability?
b What other areas of maths use scales?

10.2 Outcomes

You will learn to:
- Find all the possible outcomes of an event
- Use equally likely outcomes to calculate probabilities.

Why learn this?
Board game designers need to understand probabilities to make sure their games are fair.

Fluency
What are
- the first five square numbers
- the first five prime numbers?

Explore
How likely are you to pick your favourite flavour at random from a bag of sweets?

Exercise 10.2

1 Simplify each fraction.

a $\frac{2}{4} = \frac{\square}{\square}$

b $\frac{2}{10} = \frac{\square}{\square}$

c $\frac{3}{12} = \frac{\square}{\square}$

d $\frac{5}{15} = \frac{\square}{\square}$

2 Write each fraction as a percentage.

a $\frac{50}{100}$

b $\frac{20}{100}$

c $\frac{40}{100}$

d $\frac{5}{100}$

3 What fraction of each shape is shaded?

a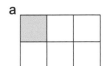

b

c

d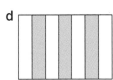

4 In a batch of 12 brownies, 3 contain chocolate chips.
Write this proportion as a fraction.

5 For each event, write all the possible **outcomes**.
   a A normal six-sided dice is rolled.
   b A letter from this set of cards is picked **at random**.

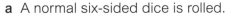

   c A ball is taken from this bag.
   d A day of the week is picked at random.

Key point

Outcomes are all the possible results of an event. The possible outcomes of flipping a coin are 'heads' and 'tails'.

Q5 Literacy hint

At random means every outcome has an equal chance of occurring.

Warm up

6 This spinner has 6 possible outcomes.
Write them down.

Q6 hint

Some of the outcomes might be the same. Two outcomes are:
green, green, …

Worked example

Work out the probability that this spinner will land on purple.

Probability of landing on purple = $\frac{2}{5}$

There are five possible outcomes: purple, purple, green, green, green

There are two **successful outcomes**: purple, purple

Key point

Successful outcomes are the outcomes you want.

7 Work out the probability that this spinner will land on
   a red
   b blue
   c white.

Q7b, c hint

Write your fractions in their simplest forms.

8 Jamie picks one of these number cards at random.

   a How many possible outcomes are there?
   b He wants to pick a square number.
   Write down the successful outcomes.
   c Work out the probability that Jamie picks a square number.

Q8b hint

The successful outcomes are the cards that have square numbers written on them.

9 Sara picks one of the cards from Q8 at random. What is the probability she picks
   a a prime number   **b** a number less than 5?

10 a List the possible outcomes when this spinner is spun.
   b Find the probability that the spinner lands on 4.
   c Find the probability that the spinner lands on an odd number.

11 A fair coin is flipped. What is the probability that it lands tails up?

12 A letter is picked at random from the letters in the word OUTCOMES.
Work out the probability the letter is a vowel.

Q12 Literacy hint

The vowels in the alphabet are A, E, I, O and U.

13 A pack of cards contains 13 clubs, 13 spades, 13 hearts and 13 diamonds. Dhevan picks a card at random.
   a Find the probability that he picks a heart. Write your answer as a fraction in its simplest form.
   b What is the probability that he picks a black card?

Q13 hint

♦   ♥   ♠   ♣

14 Problem-solving There are 6 balls in a bag. All the balls are black or white. The ratio of back to white is 2 : 1.
A ball is taken from the bag at random. Work out the probability of
   a taking a white ball from the bag
   b taking a black ball from the bag.

15 Problem-solving A drawer contains 7 red socks and some black socks. The probability of picking a red sock is $\frac{1}{4}$.

  a How many socks are there altogether in the drawer?

  b How many black socks are in the drawer?

Q15 Strategy hint

Start by working out the total number of socks in the drawer.

16 Reasoning Which of these spinners is most likely to land on red? Write the probabilities of each spinner landing on red as percentages to explain.

  a   **b**   **c**

17 Problem-solving **a** What is the probability of picking an odd number from this set of cards?

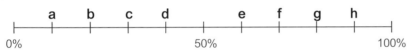

  b Design a set of 8 number cards where the probability of picking an even number is $\frac{3}{4}$.

  c Design another set where the probability of picking an odd number is $\frac{5}{8}$.

18 Real 100 raffle tickets are sold. One ticket is picked at random to win the prize. Frederique has 20 tickets.

Which letter on this scale shows the probability that Frederique wins the prize?

    a   b   c   d   e   f   g   h

0%   50%   100%

Q18 hint

What is the probability that Frederique wins the prize?

19 Design spinners with these probabilities:

  a red: $\frac{1}{6}$ blue: $\frac{5}{6}$ **b** white: $\frac{1}{4}$ red: $\frac{3}{4}$

20 Explore How likely are you to pick your favourite flavour at random from a bag of sweets?

Look back at the maths you have learned in this lesson.

How can you use it to answer this question?

21 Reflect In this lesson you have used some new vocabulary. Write a list of all the words you have learned this lesson. Write your own definition for each of the words.

Q21 hint

You could use an example to help with your definition.

Explore

Reflect

10.3 Probability calculations

You will learn to:
- Use probability notation
- Calculate the probability of an event not happening
- Find all the possible outcomes of two simple events.

CONFIDENCE

Why learn this?
Manufacturers calculate the probability of products failing. Then they advertise how likely it is the product will not fail.

Fluency
- Which of these numbers is prime?
  4, 5, 6, 7, 8
- What are the possible outcomes when a coin is flipped?

Explore
A student is picked at random from your school. What is the probability he or she likes the same television programmes as you?

Exercise 10.3

1 Work out

   a $1 - \frac{3}{4}$ **b** $1 - 0.8$

   c $100\% - 20\%$ **d** $1 - \frac{2}{5}$

   e $1 - 0.36$

2 Paolo picks one of these number cards at random.

| 1 | 2 | 3 | 4 | 5 | 6 | 7 | 8 | 9 | 10 |

What is the probability he picks
   a the number 7
   b an odd number
   c a number less than 4?

3 A normal six-sided dice is rolled. Calculate
   a P(5)
   b P(even number).

4 **Reasoning** **a** Work out the probability that this spinner will land on blue or red.

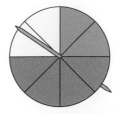

   b Louis says, 'P(blue or red) is the same as P(not yellow).'
     Is Louis correct? Explain.

Key point

P(X) means 'the probability of X happening'.
P(green or blue) means 'The probability of landing on green or blue'.

Q3a hint

P(5) means 'The probability of rolling a 5'.

Q4a hint

The successful outcomes are the spinner landing on the blue segments and the red segments.

Topic links: Fractions, decimals and percentages

Warm up

5 This dice has 10 sides, numbered from 1 to 10.
The dice is rolled.
Find
   a P(7 or 8)
   b P(a number greater than 7 or less than 3)
   c P(square number or prime number)
   d P(not prime number).

Investigation   **Problem-solving / Reasoning**

Write your answers as tenths.
A letter is chosen at random from these letter cards.

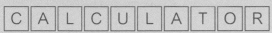

1 Work out
   a P(A)
   b P(not A)
   c P(vowel)
   d P(not vowel).
2 What do you notice about your answers to parts **a** and **b**, and your answers to parts **c** and **d**?
   Write a general rule and test it on P(L) and P(not L).

Worked example

The probability that Alastair wins his tennis match is $\frac{5}{8}$.
What is the probability that Alastair does not win his tennis match?

P(*does not win*) = 1 − P(*wins*)

$$1 - \frac{5}{8} = \frac{3}{8}$$ ———— $\boxed{1 - \frac{5}{8} = \frac{8}{8} - \frac{5}{8}}$

Key point

P(event not happening)
= 1 − P(event happening)

---

6 The probability that Kalinda makes a basketball shot is $\frac{7}{12}$. Work out the probability that she does not make the basketball shot.

7 In a river, P(catching a fish) = 0.27.
   Calculate P(not catching a fish).

8 **Real** A software company calculates the probability its software will crash is 2%. Copy and complete this statement for an advert for the company:
   'The probability our software will not crash is ____ %'

Q8 hint

P(event not happening)
= 100% − P(event happening)

9 **Problem-solving** Copy this blank spinner. Shade it so that P(shaded) = P(not shaded).

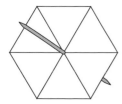

Discussion Have all your classmates shaded the spinner in the same way?

10 Jamal spins both of these spinners at the same time.

Spinner 1 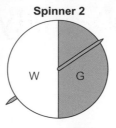 **Spinner 2**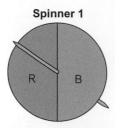

a Copy and complete this list of possible spinner outcomes.

Spinner 1	Spinner 2
R	W
R	G
B	☐
☐	☐

Q10a hint

Row 1 of the table means Spinner 1 lands on red and Spinner 2 lands on white.

b How many possible outcomes are there?

c Work out the probability that Spinner 1 lands on blue and Spinner 2 lands on grey.

11 Problem-solving A coin is flipped and this spinner is spun at the same time.

 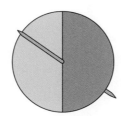

a List all of the possible outcomes.

b Work out the probability of getting heads on the coin and green on the spinner.

Q11a hint

There are four possible outcomes.

12 Explore A student is picked at random from your school. What is the probability that he or she likes the same television programmes as you?
What have you learned in this lesson to help you answer this question? What other information do you need?

13 Reflect In this lesson, you found probabilities using a normal six-sided dice, a ten-sided dice, and a coin.

Would you find it easier to use a fraction, decimal or percentage to write the probability of:
• rolling 1 on the six-sided dice
• rolling 1 on the ten-sided dice
• flipping the coin and getting heads?
Explain your answers.

Explore

Reflect

10.4 Experimental probability

You will learn to:
- Use data from an experiment to estimate probabilities
- Collect data from an experiment, and make calculations based on results.

Why learn this?
Scientists use probability experiments to build super-fast quantum computers.

Fluency
How many people were surveyed in total?

Men   ~~IIII~~ ~~IIII~~ ~~IIII~~ I

Women   ~~IIII~~ III

Explore
What is the probability that a piece of toast will land butter side down when it's dropped?

Warm up

Exercise 10.4

1 Paula recorded her friends' favourite types of film.

Type of film	Frequency
action	2
comedy	4
thriller	1
romcom	7

What is the total frequency?

2 In a group of 20 students, 5 are left-handed.
Write this as
a a fraction
b a percentage.

Worked example

Raul and Charlie played noughts and crosses lots of times.
They recorded who won in a frequency table.
Calculate the **experimental probability** of each player winning.

Winner	Frequency	Experimental probability
Raul	61	$\frac{61}{100}$
Charlie	39	$\frac{39}{100}$
Total frequency	100	

You can write this as 0.61 or 61%.

Work out the total frequency first.

> **Key point**
>
> You can use the results of an **experiment** to estimate probabilities. This is called **experimental probability**.
> Experimental probability
> $= \dfrac{\text{frequency of event}}{\text{total frequency}}$

3 Chandak spins this spinner 100 times. He records his results in a frequency table.

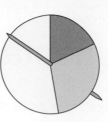

Colour	Frequency	Experimental probability
red	17	$\frac{17}{\square}$
green	28	
yellow	55	
Total frequency	$\square$	

Calculate the experimental probability of landing on each colour.

 4 **STEM / Reasoning** A biologist records the number of leaves on some clover plants. He recorded his results in a frequency table.

Number of leaves	Frequency
3	156
4	26
5	18
Total frequency	

a Work out the experimental probability of each number of leaves.
b The biologist concludes that it is very unlikely that a clover plant will have more than four leaves. Do you agree with this statement? Explain.

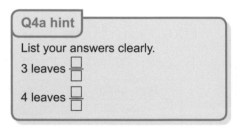

Q4a hint

List your answers clearly.

3 leaves $\frac{\square}{\square}$

4 leaves $\frac{\square}{\square}$

5 A manufacturer of chocolate biscuit bars tests 500 bars.
17 of these bars have no biscuit inside.
Estimate the probability that a chocolate biscuit bar has no biscuit.
Discussion Why is experimental probability only an estimate of the probability?

Q5 hint

To estimate the probability, calculate the experimental probability.

6 Bella asked 50 students in her school how they travel to school. Here are her results.

Method of transport	Frequency
walk	19
bike	5
bus	16
car	10

Estimate the probability that a student chosen at random travels to school by
a bike
b bus or car.

7 **Problem-solving / Reasoning** Ali is playing computer solitaire. He tallies the number of times he wins and loses.
a Use Ali's results to estimate the probability of him winning the next solitaire game.
b How could Ali improve the accuracy of his estimate?

Win	II
Lose	IIII I

Key point

The more times you repeat an experiment, the more accurate the experimental probability.

Topic links: Collecting data, Frequency tables

Subject links: Science (Q4)

8 Real A driving test centre recorded the number of minor faults for each candidate in one day. Here are the results.

Number of minor faults	0–5	6–10	11–15	16–20	21 or more
Frequency	16	30	13	17	4

  a How many candidates took their driving test at this test centre on that day?

  b In order to pass the driving test, you need 15 or fewer minor faults. Estimate the probability that a candidate has 15 or fewer minor faults.

9 Problem-solving Paul, Surinda and Amy are investigating how likely it is that a drawing pin will land point up or point down when you drop it. Here are the results of each of their experiments.

	Paul	Surinda	Amy
Point up	8	41	17
Point down	2	9	3

  a Calculate the experimental probability of the drawing pin landing point up for each person.

  b Which result do you think is the most accurate? Give a reason for your answer.

  c Combine the data from all three experiments to work out

    i how many times the pin was dropped

    ii how many times the pin landed point up

    iii a more accurate estimate for the probability that the drawing pin will land point up.

Investigation   **Problem-solving / Reasoning**

You will need a coin and a piece of lined paper. Work in pairs or small groups. You will be investigating the number of lines that a coin flipped onto lined paper will cross.

  a Design a suitable **data collection sheet** for your experiment.

  b Flip your coin onto the lined paper 20 times and record your results in your data collection sheet. (You will need to decide what to do if the coin just touches a line. Whatever you decide, make sure you use the same rule for every trial.)

  c Calculate the experimental probabilities from your results and write a conclusion.

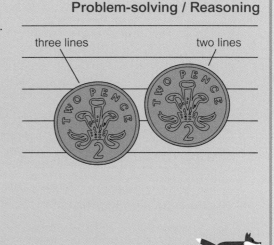

three lines   two lines

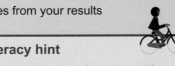

Literacy hint

A **data collection sheet** is a table for recording results.

---

10 Explore What is the probability that a piece of toast will land butter side down when it's dropped?

  What have you learned in this lesson to help you answer this question? What other information do you need?

11 Reflect In this lesson, you collected your own data for the investigation and worked out the experimental probability. Other questions gave you the data to use. Which was easier? Explain.

Explore

Reflect

10.5 FINANCE: Comparing probabilities

You will learn to:
* Compare and interpret probabilities.

Why learn this?
Insurance brokers use probabilities to compare and calculate risks.

Fluency
Which do you think is more likely?
* A coin landing heads up
* Picking a spade from a deck of cards

Explore
How can you design a profitable game for a school fête?

Exercise 10.5: Comparing probabilities

1 Simon records the coins he has collected in a jar.
a How many coins are in the jar?
b How much money is in the jar?

Coin	Frequency
1p	25
2p	30
5p	3
10p	15

2 Write > or < between each pair of fractions.

a $\frac{3}{8} \square \frac{5}{8}$ 　　　b $\frac{30}{100} \square \frac{28}{100}$ 　　　c $\frac{2}{5} \square \frac{1}{5}$ 　　　d $\frac{11}{50} \square \frac{9}{50}$

3 A number card is picked at random from this selection.

| 9 | 13 | 3 | 2 | 18 | 7 | 10 | 5 |

a Calculate the probability of picking an even number.
b Calculate the probability of picking a prime number.

4 **Finance** At a charity fête there are two spinner games. Both games cost £1 to enter and have the same prize.

Key point
You can compare probabilities written as fractions, decimals or percentages to work out which event is most likely to occur.

Game 1　　　　Game 2

a Calculate the probability of winning the prize in game 1.
b Calculate the probability of winning the prize in game 2.
c Which game would you play? Give a reason for your answer.
Discussion Would your decision be the same if game 1 had a much bigger prize than game 2?

225

5 Finance / Reasoning A tombola has paper tickets numbered from 1 to 100. The tickets are folded and players pick one at random. If you pick a ticket that ends in 5 or 0 you win 20p.
Emma says that the probability of not winning is far greater than the probability of winning.
Do you agree with Emma? Give a reason for your answer.

> **Q5 hint**
>
> Calculate P(win) and P(not win).

6 Finance / Problem-solving Draw a spinner with 8 equal segments.
Use the labels

| No prize | win £2 | win £5 |

> **Q6 hint**
>
> You can use the same label more than once.

to label segments so that:
- P(win £2) > P(win £5)
- P(winning a prize) > P(not winning a prize)

Discussion Have all of your class designed the same spinner?

7 Finance A hoops game at a funfair has cash prizes. The table shows the prizes won one evening.
  a How many people played the game?
  b Calculate the experimental probability of winning £10.
  c Estimate the probability of winning a prize.
  d The stallholder says most people win a prize. Do you agree? Explain.
The hoops game costs £1 to play.
  e Calculate the total amount of money paid to the stallholder.
  f Calculate the total amount of money paid out in prizes.

Prize	Frequency
no prize	64
£1	25
£5	8
£10	3

> **Q7c hint**
>
> What is P(win £1, £5 or £10)?

Discussion How could you alter the game to make it more profitable for the stallholder?

Investigation   *Problem-solving / Reasoning*

> **Dice game: £1 per roll**
> Roll 1, 2 or 3: No prize
> Roll 4 or 5: Win £2
> Roll 6: Win £5

  a Play this dice game with a partner using plastic money.
   Choose one person to be the stallholder and one person to be the player. Start with £10 each.
   Who runs out of money first?
  b Design your own dice game. Choose an amount to charge.
   Choose the numbers that win and the numbers that lose, and how much the prizes are.
   Play the game 10 times and see if you make a profit.
   Try to design your game so it is attractive to customers but which still makes a profit.

---

8 Explore How can you design a profitable game for a school fête?
Choose some sensible numbers to help you explore this situation. Then use what you've learned in this lesson to help you answer the question.

9 Reflect Lucie wants to design a fundraising game that raises money for charity.
She makes a list of all the mathematics she needs to use:

Probability

Experimental probability

What other mathematics skills can you add to Lucie's list?

Explore

Reflect

10 Check up

Log how you did on your Student Progression Chart.

The language of probability

1 Choose the correct box to complete each sentence.

a It is [likely / unlikely] that you will roll a 6 on a normal dice.

b It is [likely / certain] that the sun will rise in the east tomorrow.

c It is [unlikely / impossible] that you will get hit by lightning.

2 Here are eight number cards. One card is picked at random.
Describe, in words, the probability of picking an even number.

| 1 | 2 | 3 | 4 | 5 | 6 | 7 | 8 |

3 The probabilities of four different spinners landing on red are shown on this probability scale. Match each probability with the correct spinner.

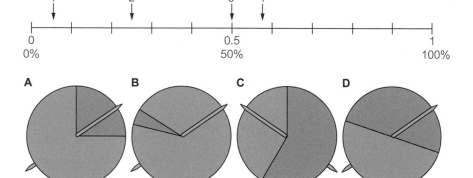

Calculating probability

4 Joanne picks a counter at random from this bag.
  a List the four possible outcomes.
  b Work out the probability that Joanne picks a red counter.
    Write your answer as a fraction.

5 This dice has 12 sides numbered from 1 to 12.
The dice is rolled. Work out the probability of rolling
  a 7   b 5 or 9
  c an odd number   d a prime number.

6 A person at a concert is picked at random.
The probability that they drove to the concert is 80%.
Work out the probability that the person did not drive to the concert.

7 Tasha and Ingrid are playing a game with a normal six-sided dice. Tasha wins if she rolls an even number. Ingrid wins if she rolls a 1 or a 3. Who is more likely to win? Explain.

8 These two spinners are spun at the same time.

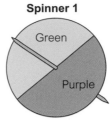
Spinner 1

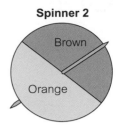
Spinner 2

  a Copy and complete this list of possible outcomes:

    Green, orange ...

  b Work out the probability of getting green on Spinner 1 and brown on Spinner 2.

Experimental probability

9 On a journey, Soujit and Jamie recorded the colour of each traffic light as they reached it.
Here are their results.

  a Calculate the experimental probability for each colour.

  b Soujit says that it is unlikely that a traffic light will be on amber when he reaches it. Do you agree with Soujit's statement?

Colour	Frequency
red	19
amber	7
green	24
Total frequency	

10 A computer chip manufacturer tested 2000 chips made at one factory. It discovered that 45 had faults.
Estimate the probability that a chip from this factory is faulty.

11 Here is a spinner for a game.
Isabella spins the spinner 10 times. Tim spins the spinner 50 times.

Result	Isabella	Tim
win	6	24
lose	4	26

  a Calculate the experimental probability of winning for each person.

  b Whose results give a more accurate estimate of the probability of winning? Explain.

12 How sure are you of your answers? Were you mostly
  😟 **Just guessing**   😐 **Feeling doubtful**   🙂 **Confident**
What next? Use your results to decide whether to strengthen or extend your learning.

Challenge

13 A bag contains lemon, strawberry and orange flavour sweets.
One sweet is chosen at random.

  $P(\text{lemon}) = \frac{1}{4}$ $P(\text{strawberry}) = \frac{1}{3}$

  a What is the smallest number of sweets that could be in the bag?

  b What is the smallest number of lemon sweets?

14 Write the letters in your name. Write three probability facts about the probability of choosing different letters or combinations of letters.

10 Strengthen

You will:
• Strengthen your understanding with practice.

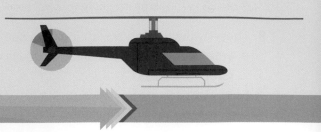

The language of probability

1 Match each description to a probability.

An event

| A cannot happen |
| B often happens |
| C rarely happens |
| D happens and doesn't happen the same amount |
| E always happens |

The probability is

| 1 unlikely |
| 2 likely |
| 3 certain |
| 4 impossible |
| 5 even chance |

2 Choose a word to describe each event.
  a Winning the lottery
  b April having 35 days next year
  c Rain in Birmingham sometime in October
  d A coin landing heads up when it is flipped

> **Q2 hint**
> Look back at your answers to Q1.

3 Copy this probability scale. Mark on it the letter of each event below.

impossible   unlikely   even chance   likely   certain

  A It will be dark outside at midnight tonight.
  B When you drop a piece of buttered toast it will land with the buttered side facing up.
  C It will snow in England sometime in the next year.
  D When a normal dice is rolled it lands on 6.
  E You will see a zebra on your way home from school.

4 Which colour is this spinner more likely to land on?

5 Draw three copies of this spinner.
Shade a spinner so that the probability of landing on a shaded segment is
  a even chance   **b** unlikely   **c** certain.

> **Q5 hint**
> Use different spinners for parts **a**, **b** and **c**.

6 Here are three spinners. The probability of them landing on white is shown on the probability scale.
Match each spinner to the probability of it landing on white.

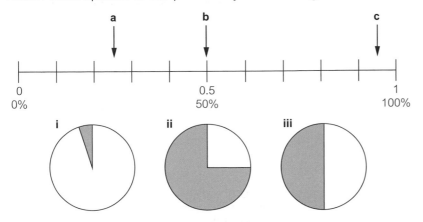

Q6 hint

Which spinner has an even chance of landing on white or green?

7 Which one of these could not represent a probability? Explain why.

0.7   30%   2.5 $\frac{3}{5}$

Q7 hint

Which value is not on the probability scale in Q6?

Calculating probability

1 This spinner is spun.

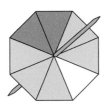

a How many possible outcomes are there?
b How many successful outcomes are there for each event?
  i Landing on red   **ii** Landing on green   **iii** Landing on white
c Write the probability of each event in part **b**.

Q1a hint

There are 8 equal segments so there are ☐ equally likely outcomes.

Q1b hint

There are ☐ red sections, so landing on red can happen in ☐ ways.

Q1c hint

Probability of an event happening
= $\frac{\text{number of successful outcomes}}{\text{total number of possible outcomes}}$

2 Near the end of a word game, these tiles are left in a bag.

a A letter is picked at random. Calculate
  i P(E)   **ii** P(A or S)   **iii** P(vowel)
  iv P(not a vowel)   **v** P(Z).
b Mark your answers to part **a** on a copy of this probability scale.

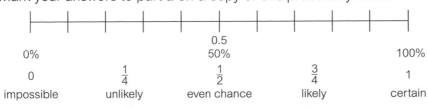

c Describe the probability of each event from part **a** in words.

Q2a i hint

P(E) means the probability of picking an E.

3 A letter is picked at random from these letter cards.

| P | A | R | A | L | L | E | L | O | G | R | A | M |

Work out the probability of picking

a a vowel   **b** L   **c** P   **d** R or G   **e** Q.

Q3 hint

How many possible outcomes are there?

4 The probability that the school rugby team wins a match is $\frac{5}{8}$.
Work out the probability that the team does not win the match.

5 For a computer game, P(win) is 18%.
Work out P(not win).

Q4 hint

Probability of *not* winning = 1 − probability of winning

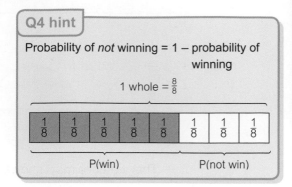

6 **Problem-solving** These two spinners are spun at the same time.

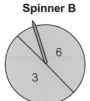

Spinner A   Spinner B

a Copy and complete this table showing the possible outcomes.

Spinner A	Spinner B
2	3
2	
7	

Q5 hint

1 whole = 100%

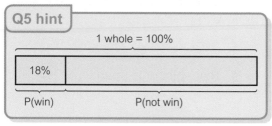

Q6a hint

When A lands on 2, what could B land on?

b Work out the probability that both spinners land on an odd number.

7 Benjamin puts these counters in a bag and picks one at random.
a Work out P(red).
b Work out P(blue).
c Is Benjamin more likely to pick red or blue?

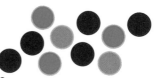

Q7c hint

Which has the greater probability?

Experimental probability

1 A bag contains 20 red, white or purple beads.
Lou takes one out and writes its colour in this table, then puts it back.

Colour	Frequency	Experimental probability
red	12	$\frac{12}{40}$
white	24	
purple	4	
Total frequency		

a Calculate the total frequency.
b Calculate the experimental probability of picking each colour.
c Which colour bead is most likely to be picked?

Q1b hint

Frequency of red = 12
Total frequency = 40
Experimental probability of red = $\frac{12}{40}$

2 Reasoning During Euro 2008, Paul the Octopus predicted the results of Germany's matches. This table shows his results for each match.

Match	Paul's prediction
Germany v Poland	correct
Germany v Croatia	incorrect
Germany v Austria	correct
Germany v Portugal	correct
Germany v Turkey	correct
Germany v Spain	incorrect

   a How many matches did Germany play in total?

   b How many results did Paul correctly predict?

   c Calculate the experimental probability that Paul will correctly predict the result of the match.

   d Give a reason why your answer to part **c** might not be very accurate.

> **Q2d hint**
>
> More repeats of experiments give more accurate estimates of probability.

Enrichment

1 Reasoning This weather map shows the percentage probabilities of rain, snow and sunshine in different parts of the UK on one day. Write a short weather forecast using the language of probability.

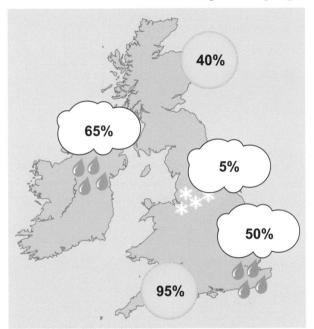

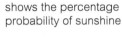 shows the percentage probability of sunshine

 shows the percentage probability of snow

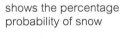 shows the percentage probability of rain

2 Problem-solving Here is a blank net of a dice.
Copy the net and label each face with a number so that when the dice is folded up and rolled all three of these conditions are true:
P(prime number) = $\frac{1}{2}$ P(even number) = 0 P(square number) = $\frac{1}{6}$

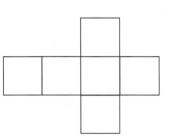

3 Reflect For these strengthen lessons: choose at least four sentences to copy and complete from:
- I showed I am good at ____
- I found ____ hard
- I got better at _____ by ____
- I was surprised by ____
- I was happy that ____
- I still need help with ____

Reflect

10 Extend

You will:
• Extend your understanding with problem-solving.

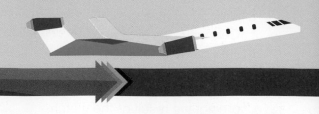

1 Write a set of 10 number cards so that
 • P(square number) is very unlikely
 • P(6, 8 or 10) is even chance
 • P(multiple of 4) is very likely
 • P(even number) is certain

Q1 Strategy hint
You can use the same number on more than one card.

2 **Problem-solving** Here is a blank net of a dice.
 Copy the net and label each face with a number so that when the dice is folded up and rolled all three of these conditions are true:

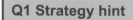

$P(\text{prime number}) = \frac{1}{3}$ $P(\text{odd number}) = \frac{1}{6}$ $P(\text{square number}) = \frac{1}{3}$

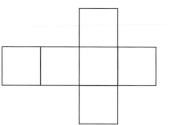

3 **Problem-solving** A single coin is placed on a table.
 A spinner is spun to decide where to place the next coin.

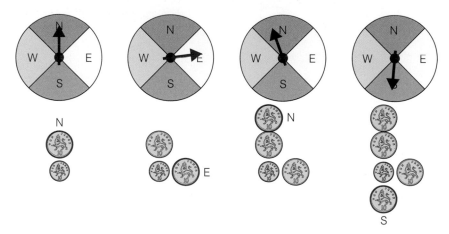

Match each spinner to the coin pattern that it will produce.

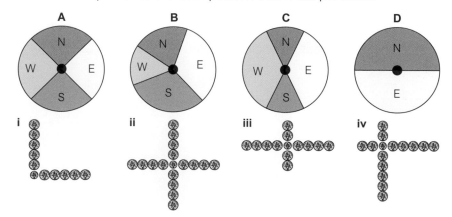

4 Reasoning An event is certain to happen. What is the probability of it not happening? Explain your answer.

5 STEM A biologist measured the acidity levels (pH) of a group of soil samples from a field. The median of her data was 7.9.
Estimate the probability that a soil sample taken from this field has a pH greater than 7.9.

Q5 hint

The median is the middle value.

7.9

| Data lower than 7.9 | Data higher than 7.9 |

6 Josie records the rolls of a dice in this table.

Number	1	2	3	4	5	6
Frequency	16	20	11	14	20	15

  a How many times did she roll the dice altogether?
  b Display the information from the table in a bar chart.
  c Which numbers did she roll the most?
  d Write an estimate for the probability of rolling each number.
  e Write an estimate for the probability of rolling
    i a number less than 3
    ii an even number
    iii a 10
    iv not a 1.

7 Reasoning In a battleship game you choose a square on a grid at random. If the square contains a battleship you win a prize.

Q7 hint

What is the probability of a hit on each grid?
Work out the probabilities as percentages.

Grid A   **Grid B**

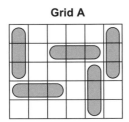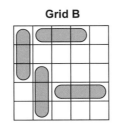

Ali says that there are 5 battleships on Grid A and only 4 on Grid B, so he is more likely to win if he plays on Grid A.
Do you agree with Ali's statement? Give a reason for your answer.

8 One of these shape cards is picked at random.

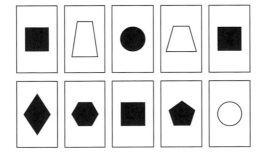

Calculate the probability of picking
  a a white shape
  b a pentagon
  c a quadrilateral
  d a circle or a square
  e a black trapezium.

9 **Problem-solving** Each of these cards has a different number between 1 and 20 written on it. A card is picked at random. The probability of picking a prime number is $\frac{3}{4}$.
Write the three possible numbers that could be written on the hidden card.

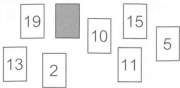

10 **Problem-solving** In a raffle, 500 tickets have been sold. The winning ticket is picked at random. Calculate the number of tickets you would need to have bought to have a probability of winning of 15%.

11 **Problem-solving** Mohamed needs to fill a bag with counters.
He has four different colours. How many of each colour could he use so that:
P(green) = $\frac{1}{20}$ P(blue) = $\frac{1}{4}$ P(red) = $\frac{1}{5}$ P(orange) = $\frac{1}{2}$

12 **Problem-solving** A fair coin is tossed and this spinner is spun.
Calculate the probability of getting blue on the spinner and tails on the coin.

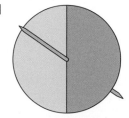

13 **Real / Reasoning** A road-safety organisation investigated how the speed of the car affects the likelihood that a pedestrian will be killed in an accident. They recorded this data.

Q13 hint

Be careful – the total frequency is different for each speed.

Speed of car (mph)	25	30	35
Number of accidents in which a pedestrian was killed	350	182	450
Total number of accidents	1000	350	500

Calculate the experimental probability of a pedestrian being killed for each speed.

14 **Finance / Real** Lottery scratchcards have the probability of winning a prize printed on them.
A shop records the number of this type of scratch card sold and the number of prizes won each day for 3 days.

	Saturday	Sunday	Monday
Number of scratch cards sold	100	25	20
Number of prizes	28	9	8

a Calculate the experimental probabilities for each of the three days. Give your answers as percentages.

b Maggie says that you should buy scratch cards on Mondays because you're more likely to win. Do you agree? Explain.

c Combine the data from all three days to estimate the probability of winning a prize. Give your answer as a percentage to the nearest whole number. Do you think the probability claimed on the card is accurate?

15 Problem-solving These two spinners are spun at the same time.

a Work out the probability that the sum of the two numbers is a prime number.

b Work out the probability that the product of the two numbers is greater than 20.

16 A coin is flipped 100 times. The results are shown in the table below.

Outcome	Frequency	Experimental probability
heads	24	
tails	76	

a What is the experimental probability, as a percentage, of flipping
  i heads
  ii tails?

b Do you think this coin is **biased**? Give a reason for your answer.

17 A biased coin can land on heads or tails. P(heads) = 0.65. Calculate P(tails).

18 This is a four-sided dice. Its four faces are shown below.

Face 1   Face 2   Face 3   Face 4

a Calculate the **theoretical probability** of the dice landing on the square.

Kaylin rolls the dice 100 times. This table shows her results.

b Copy and complete the table to show the experimental probabilities. Give your answers as percentages.

Outcome	Frequency	Experimental probability
square	42	
circle	31	
rhombus	11	
triangle	16	

c Do you think this dice is fair or biased? Give a reason for your answer.

19 Reflect Probability is used in:
• sport
• medicine
• insurance
• crime detection
• weather forecasting.

For each one, write down one way it uses probability.

What career are you interested in? Do you think you will need to use probability in your job? How?

Q15a hint

List all the possible outcomes.

A	B	Sum
7	5	12

Key point

Biased means not fair. If a coin or dice is biased, the outcomes are not necessarily equally likely. You can tell whether a coin is biased by comparing the **theoretical probability** that P(heads) = 50% with the experimental probability.

Q16b hint

A fair coin has an even chance of getting heads or tails.

Q18c hint

Compare the experimental probabilities with the theoretical probabilities.

Reflect

10 Unit test

Log how you did on your Student Progression Chart.

1 Choose a word from a box to describe the probability of each event.

| impossible | unlikely | even chance | likely | certain |

  a Flipping a coin and it lands tails up
  b Rolling a normal dice and getting a 7
  c A power cut happening tonight
  d Picking a number card from a normal pack of playing cards

2 Here are four spinners.

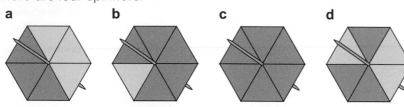

   a   **b**   **c**   **d**

Choose words from this probability scale to describe the probability of each spinner landing on green.

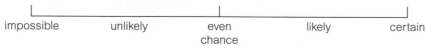

impossible   unlikely   even chance   likely   certain

3 Match each probability to a description.

  100%   50%   20%   0%

  a impossible   **b** unlikely   **c** certain   **d** an even chance

4 In a survey of 200 trees in a forest, 79 were taller than 15 m.
Estimate the probability that a tree picked at random in the forest will be taller than 15 m.

5 One of these letter cards is picked at random.

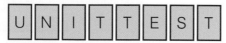

  U   N   I   T   T   E   S   T

  a Calculate the probability of
    i picking the letter T
    ii picking the letter L
    iii picking a letter that is not a vowel
    iv picking the letter S or the letter N.
  b Mark your answers to part **a** on a copy of this probability scale.

0             $\frac{1}{2}$ 1

  c Which event in part **a** is most likely to happen?

6 A counter is pulled from the bag at random.
This bag contains red, blue and black counters.
Calculate

  a P(red)

  b P(blue)

  c P(blue or black)

  d P(not black).

7 The probability that Milly wins a table tennis match is 0.4. What is the probability that she does not win the table tennis match?

8 The probability that a match will light first time is $\frac{9}{10}$. Calculate the probability that the match will not light first time.

9 Alina records the colours of 40 cars that pass the school gates.

  a Work out the experimental probability of each colour.

  b Alina says that it is unlikely that the next car to pass the school gates will be red. Do you agree? Explain.

  c How could Alina get more accurate estimates of these probabilities?

Colour	Frequency
black	18
red	7
blue	3
silver	9
other	3

10 Kyle spins this spinner 30 times to see if it is fair.
Here are his results. Do you think the spinner is fair? Explain.

Colour	Frequency
green	24
yellow	6

Challenge

11 Both of these spinners are spun at the same time.

  a Copy and complete this table showing all the possible outcomes for the sum of the two numbers.

Spinner 1   **Spinner 2**

Spinner 1	Spinner 2	Sum
4	5	4 + 5 = 9

  b Work out the probability that the sum of the numbers on the two spinners is even.

12 **Reflect** Think carefully about the work you have done in this unit.
Write down, in your own words, a short definition for:

- probability
- probability scale
- possible outcomes
- successful outcomes.

The word 'event' is used a lot in probability. How is it used differently in probability to everyday life?

INDEX

A

addition
- decimals 97–9, 107, 109–10, 113–18
- fractions 192–3, 201, 204, 205, 208, 211
- large numbers 1–3, 15, 17, 21, 25–6
- negative numbers 6–7, 15, 16, 18, 21–3, 25–6

angles
- calculating 131, 134–5, 137–40
- drawing 119–21, 131, 132, 133–4, 135–6, 139, 140, 141–2
- measuring 119–21, 131, 133–4, 137–40, 141
- nets of 3D solids 129–30, 132, 136, 140, 142
- triangles 124–8, 132
- vertically opposite 122–3

area 38, 43–4, 45–8

arithmetic sequences 165–6, 175, 178, 181–6

B

bar charts 54–9, 63–4, 66–7, 69–71, 73–4

brackets 4, 18, 25, 83–4, 86, 90, 146–7, 153–4, 156–7, 159

C

centimetres 38, 40, 43–4, 45–8

cube roots 145, 153, 155–6, 160–61, 163–4

cubes and cuboids
- nets of 30–2, 40, 45, 46, 49, 50
- surface area of 33–4, 39–40, 42–3, 45–8
- volume of 35–6, 38, 43

D

3D solids
- 2D representation of 27–9
- edges 27–9, 39, 41–2, 44, 45, 49
- faces 27–9, 39, 41–2, 44, 45, 49
- names of 41, 44, 49
- nets of 30–2, 39, 40, 41–3, 45, 46, 49, 50, 129–30, 132, 136, 140, 142
- surface area of 33–4, 39–40, 42–3, 45–8, 49–50
- vertices 27–9, 39, 41–2, 44, 45, 49
- volume of 35–6, 40, 43, 49–50

data collection sheets 51–3, 63, 65, 73

decimals
- addition 97–9, 107, 109–10, 113–18
- multiplication 100–2, 107–8, 110–11, 113–18
- ordering 103–4, 108, 111–12, 115–16
- probability as 213–15
- problem-solving with 105–6
- rounding 103–4, 108, 111–12, 117
- subtraction 97–9, 107, 109–10, 113–18

division
- large numbers 25–6
- negative numbers 8, 15, 16, 18, 21–3, 25–6

E

edges of 3D solids 27–9, 39, 41–2, 44, 45, 49

equations, solving 81–2, 85, 89, 91–4

experimental probability 222–4, 228, 231–2, 236

expressions and equations
- brackets 83–4, 86, 90
- functions 78–80, 85, 87–8, 92, 95, 96
- simplifying 75–7, 85, 88–9, 91, 95
- solving equations 81–2, 85, 89, 91–4, 95–6

extending sequences 167–8

F

faces of 3D solids 27–9, 39, 41–2, 44, 45, 49

fractions
- addition 192–3, 201, 204, 205, 208, 211
- of amounts 189–91, 201, 207–8, 211
- comparing 187–8, 201, 203–4, 207, 211
- multiplying by whole number 190–1, 202, 205, 209
- and percentages 194–5
- probability as 213–15
- subtraction 192–3, 201, 204, 205, 209, 211

functions 78–80, 85, 87–8, 92, 95, 96

G

generating sequences 165–6, 175–6, 177–9, 181–6

geometric sequences 169–70, 175, 178, 185

H

highest common factors (HCF) 148–50, 154, 157–8, 159, 160

I

index notation 146–7, 153–4, 159–61, 163–4

L

large numbers 25–6
- addition 1–3, 15, 17, 21
- multiplication 4–5, 17
- subtraction 1–3, 15, 17

length 37–8, 43–4, 46–8

litres 37–8, 40, 43–4, 45

lowest common multiples (LCM) 148–50, 154, 157–8

M

measurement 37–8, 39, 40, 43–4, 45–8